Inspiring Leadership

Inspiring
Leadership

Staying afloat in turbulent times

Jane Cranwell-Ward, Andrea Bacon and Rosie Mackie

THOMSON
™

Australia • Canada • Mexico • Singapore • Spain • United Kingdom • United States

THOMSON ™

Inspiring Leadership: Staying afloat in turbulent times

Copyright © Jane Cranwell-Ward, Andrea Bacon and Rosie Mackie 2002

The Thomson logo is a registered trademark used herein under licence.

For more information, contact Thomson, High Holborn House, 50/51 Bedford Row, London WC1R 4LR or visit us on the World Wide Web at: http://www.thomsonlearning.co.uk

British Library Cataloguing-in-Publication Data
A catalogue record for this book is available from the British Library

ISBN 1-86152-982-1

Typeset by Saxon Graphics Ltd, Derby

Printed in Great Britain by TJ International, Padstow, Cornwall

Dedicated to the skippers and crew of the
BT Global Challenge 2000/1
in recognition of
their time and assistance with this research project
and to
Erica Paterson for her enthusiastic and
unstinting support throughout

Inspiring Performance
Maritime House
Maritime Way
Southampton
Hampshire
SO14 3AE

Tel:+44 (0) 23 8063 9333
Fax:+44 (0) 23 8063 9334

http://www.inspiringperformance.com
Email: info@inspiringperformance.com

Henley Management College
Greenlands
Henley-on-Thames
Oxfordshire
RG9 3AU

Tel:+ 44 (0) 1491 418855
Fax:+ 44 (0) 1491 418846

http://www.henleymc.ac.uk
Email: janecw@henleymc.ac.uk

BT
BT Centre
81 Newgate Street
London
EC1A 7AJ

Tel:+44 (0) 207 356 5000

http://www.bt.com

CONTENTS

IV A GREAT PLACE TO BE

V SUMMARY

LIST OF PLATES

 **A S E**

 **BG Group**

 **BRITISH AIRWAYS**

 **CAP GEMINI ERNST & YOUNG**

 **CHALLENGE Business**

 **Microsoft**®

 **Nationwide**

 **the nec group**
birmingham

Rank Group
Gaming Division

 **Nuffield Hospitals**

 **TENON**
www.tenongroup.com

Telelogic

TESCO
Every little helps.

 **Thomson Travel Group plc**

UCB Home Loans

 **VAIL WILLIAMS**

THE DOCUMENT COMPANY
XEROX

INSPIRATIONAL INTELLIGENCE RESEARCH FORUM

The Inspirational Intelligence Research Forum (IIRF) was established in January 2000 through a partnership between Inspiring Performance and Henley Management College. Sponsored by BT and supported by organisations from a diverse range of business sectors, the Forum research focused on human performance during the BT Global Challenge 2000/1 Round the World Yacht Race.

This leading-edge research project set out to identify the components of success for individuals and teams during the race. It studied the skippers' key attributes, skills and behaviours before and during the race and set out to establish the impact of emotional intelligence on individual and team performance. The BT Global Challenge provided a level playing field for this study.

Data was collected through a series of interviews conducted with skippers, crew members, leggers, sponsors and race organisers before and during the race. Forum members played an important role in assisting the research team in the collection of this data at each of the six ports of call.

During the course of the project twelve Forum meetings were held where interim findings were discussed and business parallels drawn. Project groups were set up to look at business issues and Forum members researched and collated data for contribution to each of the chapters within this book.

Forum members

ASE (a division of NFER-NELSON) http://www.ase-solutions.com
BG Group plc http://www.bg-group.com
British Airways plc http://www.britishairways.com
BT http://www.bt.com

Cap Gemini Ernst & Young http://www.cgey.com
The Challenge Business International Ltd
   http://www.challengebusiness.com
The Document Company Xerox http://www.xeroxmodicorp.com
Henley Management College http://www.henleymc.ac.uk
Inspiring Performance Ltd http://www.inspiringperformance.com
Microsoft Ltd http://www.microsoft.com
Nationwide Building Society http://www.nationwide.co.uk
The NEC Group (Birmingham) http://www.necgroup.co.uk
Nuffield Hospitals http://www.nuffieldhospitals.org.uk
Rank Group plc http://www.rank.com
Telelogic UK Ltd http://www.telelogic.com
TENON Ltd http://www.tenon.com
Tesco Stores Ltd http://www.tesco.com
Thomson Travel Group http://www.thomson-holidays.com
UCB Home Loans Ltd http://www.ucbhomeloans.co.uk
Vail Williams http://www.vailwilliams.com

For further information on any of the Forum members please visit
their web pages.

BOOK PARTNERS

Inspiring Performance Ltd is an international research-based performance development consultancy with offices in the UK, USA and the Middle East. Consultants work globally across a number of key business sectors providing personal, management, leadership and team development programmes.

Inspiring Performance's philosophy is to provide pragmatic, relevant performance development for individuals and teams from first promotion to board level.

Henley Management College is one of the world's leading business schools, operating in 32 countries. Henley adopts a partnership approach when working with its corporate clients. A flexible and innovative approach is developed based on understanding business needs and challenges. The college has a strong faculty keeping ahead with leading-edge thinking and with an emphasis on being pragmatic. Henley employs the latest technology for flexible learning.

Henley is a broad-based business school with activities in three major areas: executive development, graduate business studies and research and doctoral programmes.

BT is one of the world's leading communication companies. Its principal activities include local, long distance and international telecommunications services, Internet services and IT solutions. They believe that better communications lead to better relationships and a better world. They have operations worldwide where their focus is to meet the European needs of global multi-site corporates and the international needs of European-based corporate customers.

Their technology helped to bring the BT Global Challenge race participants home safely and enabled different countries to experience a flavour of the world's toughest yacht race when the crews arrived at the ports. Their connections brought together 200 sponsors and suppliers in one of the world's largest relationship marketing programmes.

ABOUT THE AUTHORS

Andrea Bacon is Research Director for Inspiring Performance. After working in corporate communications in the City for seven years, Andrea competed in the BT Global Challenge 1996/7, on board the winning yacht Group 4. The lessons Andrea learned in leadership and team work were so immense that she decided to combine them with her knowledge of business and went on to co-author the book *Global Challenge, Leadership Lessons from the World's Toughest Yacht Race.*

Andrea regularly presented these lessons to international business audiences but realised there was room to develop these findings. She was instrumental in the formation of the Inspirational Intelligence Research Forum. She went back to the BT Global Challenge and used the 2000/1 race as a live case study, in order to study the key elements of sustained human performance and the impact of emotional intelligence on human performance. This took research on high-performing teams and leadership to a new level.

Rosie Mackie, a Director and Senior Performance Consultant for Inspiring Performance, is a key member of the Inspirational Intelligence Research Team. Rosie started her consultancy career with the Leadership Development Team of MaST International plc, which subsequently merged with members of the research unit of The London Business School to form the Centre for High Performance Development. Working globally, Rosie used the research on high-performance behaviours to help teams and individuals globally to attain high performance.

Rosie's work led her to become involved in the selection and training of the skippers in the BT Global Challenge 1996/7, through which she found a further opportunity to continue her research into successful teams. The findings led her to co-author *Global Challenge, Leadership Lessons from the World's Toughest Yacht Race.*

She subsequently joined the Inspirational Intelligence Research Project as part of Inspiring Performance. She researched the key elements of sustained human performance and the impact of emotional intelligence on human performance.

Jane Cranwell-Ward is Director of the Henley Learning Partnership at Henley Management College, is a key member of the Inspirational Intelligence Research Team and represents Henley in the Inspirational Intelligence Research Forum. At Henley, Jane runs the Henley Learning Partnership, which provides development opportunities for managers addressing the latest business issues.

Jane helps managers achieve high performance, focusing on the development of appropriate skills and attributes. She regularly speaks at conferences and has written two books on stress. Jane was previously at Kingston University and began her career at Harrods. Jane welcomed the opportunity to study the impact of leadership and emotional intelligence on high performance during the BT Global Challenge Round The World Yacht Race.

FORUM ACKNOWLEDGEMENTS

Special thanks and acknowledgements to Forum members who supported the Inspiring Peformance Research Team

LEG 1 – Boston
British Airways plc: Cleone Dolan, Peter Mulcahy;
Nuffield Hospitals: Jacqui Land; UCB Home Loans Ltd: Charles Reed;
Vail Williams: Ian Rudland.

LEG 2 – Buenos Aires
British Airways plc: Peter Mulcahy; BT: Pauline Blaney;
Nuffield Hospitals: Jacqui Land; The NEC Group: Carol Whitaker;
Vail Williams: Ian Rudland.

LEG 3 – Wellington
Nuffield Hospitals: Jacqui Land.

LEG 4 – Sydney
British Airways plc: Peter Mulcahy, Liz Straker, Carrie Tennant;
BT: Jo Brook; Henley Management College: Jane Cranwell-Ward;
The NEC Group: Carol Whitaker.

LEG 5 – Cape Town
British Airways plc: Liz Straker;
Cap Gemini Ernst & Young: Karen Gervais, Nicole Girard;
Henley Management College: Jane Cranwell-Ward;
Nuffield Hospitals: Jacqui Land; UCB Home Loans Ltd: Charles Reed;
Vail Williams: Ian Rudland.

LEG 6 – La Rochelle
British Airways plc: Sarah Bailey;
Nationwide Building Society: Paul Beesley;
Nuffield Hospitals: Jacqui Land; TENON Ltd: Mike Shreeve;
The NEC Group: Mary Coles, Carol Whitaker, Sue Gover.

Forum meeting attendees

ASE – a division of NFER-NELSON: Ian Florence;
BG Group plc: Nicola Dunn, Caroline Godefroy;
British Airways plc: Davina Bannister, Cleone Dolan, Jane Hulmston,
Peter Mulcahy, Liz Straker;
BT: Pauline Blaney, Alan Brough, Monica Cadrecha, Colin Dunn,
Phil Hayward, Julia Lloyd-Evans, Steve Munn, Stacy Wood;
Cap Gemini Ernst & Young: Pam Evans, Karen Gervais, Nicole Girard,
Norma James, Lisa Murch;
The Challenge Business International Ltd: Vicky Hill;
The Document Company Xerox: Sue Gover;
Henley Management College: Jane Cranwell-Ward, Pam Calvert,
Margaret Locke, Suzanne Pollack;
Inspiring Performance Ltd: Andrea Bacon, Nick Coombe, Sara Elliott,
Margaret Gordon, Rosie Mackie, Erica Paterson, Humphrey Walters;
Microsoft Ltd: Helen Duguid, Julia Hennessy, Kate Winsper;
Nationwide Building Society: Paul Beesley;
The NEC Group: Mary Coles, Martin Dyer, Terry Hodgetts,
Carol Whitaker;
Nuffield Hospitals: Venetia Harper, Jacqui Land, Julie Williams;
Rank Group plc: Chris Mace;
Telelogic UK Ltd: Alison Milton;
Tesco Stores Ltd: John Metherell, Stephanie Storell;
Thomson Travel Group: Louise Palmer;
TENON Ltd: Jeannie Brown, Paul Johnson, Mike Shreeve,
Ross Wilson;
UCB Home Loans Ltd: Mark Allan, Charles Reed;
Vail Williams: Ian Rudland.

GENERAL ACKNOWLEDGEMENTS

Skippers

Will Carnegie, Richard Chenery, Andy Dare, Mark Denton, Nick Fenton, Manley Hopkinson, Conrad Humphreys, Neil Murray, Will Oxley, Lin Parker, Alex Phillips, John Read, Jeremy Troughton, Stephen Wilkins.

The Challenge Business International Limited

Sir Chay Blyth CBE, BEM, Simon Walker, Andrew Roberts, Rachel Anning, Lizzie Brown, Sarah Bullock, Ann Carvey, Alistair Hackett, Jane Hall, Kate Hall, Vicky Hill, Tony Humphreys, Sally Kiff, Mandy Lauchlan, Elle Littlejohn, Lisa Mari, Ian McCabe, Matthew Ratsey, Virginia Read, Linda Rogers, Louise Schofield, Claire Smyly, Paul Thompson, training skippers and mates.

BT Global Challenge project team

John Luff, Phil London, Alan Brough, Lisa Davis, Colin Dunn, Chris Eames, Harriet Fowles, Phil Hayward, John Keating, Ian Keith, Steve Munn, Beverley Robinson, Steve Sargent, Grant Thompson, Janette Ward, Stacy Wood.

Yacht sponsor project managers

BP: Joe Murphy, Rosie Gardner; CGNU: Mabel Derry-Collins; Compaq: Berni Miles-Taylor; Invest HK: Martin Kay; Isle of Man: Bransom Bean; LG FLATRON: Grace Harding; Logica: Penny Green; Olympic Group: John Mitchell; Quadstone: Vanessa Jones; Serco for Save the Children: Gail Johnson; TeamSpirIT: Edward Scott; VERITAS: Nuala Fadden.

Crew representatives

Will Brammer, Tony Botterill, Christian Bowerman, Glyn Billinghurst, Ashley Carpenter, Ned Caswell, Jonathan Cutts, Jasmine Georgiou,

Bart Hallmark, Richard Keeling, Beverley Lufkin, Chris McLaren, Laura Parish, Ian Sinclair, Tina Williamson.

Henley Management College

Professor Colin Carnall, Katherine Diggins, Tereena Hartin, Lyndsey Mann, June Sebley, John Symons.

ASE – a division of NFER-NELSON

Ian Florence, Helen Bradley, Christina Merchant, Gloria Pitt.

Inspiring Performance Ltd

Peter Mackie, Paul Bennett, Nick Coombe, Lin Elder, Margaret Gordon, Erica Paterson, Nicky Richards, Nicola Thomas.

General research and book support

Jeff Allen, Steve Anscell, Lady Felicity Blyth, Robin Britton, Rona Cant, Sarah Carnegie, Vikki Cheung, Stuart Cole, Dale Crofts, Sue Devine, Emily Elliot-Square, Marcel and Patrice Escandell, Rachel Fellows, Nicky Fenton, Ali Foord, Melanie Fyans, Di Gilpin, Mike Golding, Sandra Goodchild, Alison Hamilton, Mike Hewson, Kate Hopkinson, Mike Iles, Dick Johnson, Paul Kelly, Kate Laven, Sas Lockwood, Jane London, Amanda Macdonald, Ali McKichan, Heather Murray, Denise Norman, Mark Pepper, Michael Redford, Peter Sharp, Christian Spencer, John Steele, Mandy Troughton, Calshot Activities Centre, Kuties Brasserie, New Place Management Centre.

FOREWORD

As a leader in today's uncertain and turbulent world, my biggest challenge is to inspire others and build their confidence. I recognise the importance of creating an environment where people want to be, and where performance is driven through loyalty and commitment. There is absolutely no doubt in my mind that developing inspiring leadership is the most powerful source of competitive advantage for companies that aspire to success in the 21st century. Leaders need not only to create an environment within which teams can achieve their full potential, but also to do so in a way that is sensitive to the needs of others.

I was privileged to undertake a leg of the BT Global Challenge 2000/1 Round the World Yacht Race on board our yacht BP Explorer. I met with many of the participants and I have no doubt that, through their involvement, each and every one of these men and women has obtained deep insights into who they are, and what they can achieve in life. I find reflecting on my own experience a source of great inspiration, at work and at home.

Inspiring Leadership is a powerful book with simple and transparent lessons. It provides a lively, stimulating and pragmatic approach to knowing yourself and to leading and managing others, illustrated through a vivid and dramatic case study – the BT Global Challenge. Analysis of the leadership attributes of the skippers in this race confirms that many of the skills required to compete successfully are essential for business leaders competing in today's uncertain and turbulent world.

Like me, I am sure many of you would not wish to go to such extreme lengths to develop these attributes. We should therefore be grateful to the authors of this book who offer us a blueprint for inspiring leadership. By using our emotional intelligence to understand ourselves better and get the most out of others, we will be able to inspire those around us to realise their true potential and ultimately achieve success.

Richard L. Olver
Managing Director
BP

INTRODUCTION

Tracking the leadership and performance of the skippers and teams competing in the BT Global Challenge 2000/1 Round the World Yacht Race provided us with some powerful and pragmatic lessons for leaders working in today's business environment. Reflecting on current leadership theory and focusing on some of the common issues facing leaders today, we have set out to synthesise this thinking and bring together the theory with our own research findings. Relevant theory has been included to help those who are engaged in a related course of study.

Acknowledging that we are living and working in an extremely complex and turbulent world, the Global Challenge provided a perfect metaphor for our study. The intensity of the environment accelerated the development of the skippers and through close tracking we have been able to identify the changes in behaviour and the impact of this on their ability to lead successfully. We have identified key attributes, skills and behaviours essential for leading today.

The lessons are transparent, easy to relate to and highlight the importance of leadership for everyone. While we make no claims that our findings are all original, we believe that the lessons we have drawn from the research are portrayed in a way that will help the practising manager apply them in business. We have used the term 'leader' in its broadest sense to embrace anyone who has the responsibility for achieving goals through and with others.

Leadership is not a position or a place in an organisation but a sense of responsibility. In these turbulent times the responsibility is onerous and the question of how to lead has become increasingly urgent. This book is a pragmatic leadership textbook for those who are ready to take on the responsibility of leadership. With *Inspiring Leadership* we hope that you will create an environment at work that makes it 'A Great Place To Be'.

Full details of the teams, results, etc. can be found in Appendix 1.

HOW TO READ THIS BOOK

This book is designed to be read from the perspective of transferring the lessons from the race into the working environment. For those of you wishing to study leadership, it offers some of the relevant theories together with simple practical lessons that will enable you to deal with these challenging issues. It has been written as a reference book with stand-alone chapters.

The book is written in five parts.

Part I – Background

In this part you will gain a fuller understanding of today's environment and leadership requirements. It sets out the context of the research by explaining the background to the BT Global Challenge Round the World Yacht Race and the reasons behind the research team's choice of the race as a case study. It looks at the environment in which we must operate today and the leadership that we are likely to need in the turbulent times ahead.

Part II – Research findings

This section discusses the rationale and methodology for the research and summarises the key findings from the research project. From these findings you will gain a clear understanding of what made the difference in the performance of the skippers. The findings show the personal, managerial and leadership skills and attributes they adopted and how emotional intelligence enabled them to utilise these.

The findings from the race focus on the 12 skippers whose yachts successfully completed the race around the world. These skippers, selected from 186 applicants, were all achieving at a very high level. However, for the purposes of this book, when comparisons are being made between the skippers they will be described as 'higher performing' and 'lower performing' relating to their overall position in the fleet.

For the purposes of anonymity the term 'he' has been used through-out the book in place of he or she. Quotes that have been included from the interviews with the skippers and crew are non-attributable.

Part III – Key business issues

You can dip in and out of Part III. It is designed as a series of seven stand-alone chapters. Each chapter addresses an issue that leaders are facing in business today. Vivid business and race parallels are given, and the relationship of each subject with emotional intelligence is dis-cussed. Each chapter finishes with a boxed summary of simple lessons for leaders.

Part IV – A Great Place To Be

This section draws together the lessons from the book. By applying these business lessons, you can create your own team culture. The way culture develops and the need for cultural flexibility is discussed. This is followed by a detailed analysis of the cultures developed in the podium teams who created 'A Great Place To Be'.

Part V – Summary

This section is a summary of the key lessons learned in the book and will provide you with a clear compilation of them all. This can be used for reference once you have read the book.

Our research over the past two years has taught us many new lessons. We hope that you, too, will take from our book the simple but essential lessons for leadership in turbulent times.

I

BACKGROUND

I

BT GLOBAL CHALLENGE AS A CASE STUDY

INTRODUCTION

On 10 September 2000, 12 identical yachts started 'the world's toughest yacht race' – the BT Global Challenge. With a professional skipper and a crew of 17 men and women of all ages and backgrounds, each team set out to race around the globe against the prevailing winds and currents, one of the toughest feats of teamwork, leadership and human endurance in the modern world.

Arriving back in Southampton in June 2001 after completing a 30 000–mile circumnavigation and stopping at six ports of call, these skippers and crews were proud to have finished the race and achieved a personal challenge of a lifetime.

Today, these individuals are recognised among an elite group of people who have tested themselves both physically and mentally in some of the most gruelling and extreme weather conditions. These extraordinary people have shown it is possible to conquer fear, push beyond known personal limits and work together to achieve something unique and seemingly impossible.

THE BEGINNING

Founded by Sir Chay Blyth CBE BEM and organised by The Challenge Business International, the first Global Challenge Round the World Yacht Race was sponsored by British Steel and took place in 1992/3. Ten identical 67ft steel yachts sailed from Southampton, following the westerly route taken by Sir Chay when he sailed single-handedly non-stop around the globe in 1971. Proving the critics wrong, these amateur crews completed their 30 000-mile circumnavigation, stopped at four ports of call and returned safely to Southampton. They proved that by working together, non-professional sailors could sail against the hostile and unpredictable conditions of the world's winds and oceans, overcome all obstacles and achieve a lifetime ambition.

Sir Chay's original concept for the race was seen to be successful and also very popular. Ordinary people wanted the sort of adventure that the Global Challenge could provide. The second race was launched and attracted hundreds of applications, from people from all walks of life. The second Global Challenge set off four years later, in 1996/7, this time sponsored by BT. The sponsorship was a huge commercial success and four years on, in 2000/1, BT sponsored the race again.

BT GLOBAL CHALLENGE 2000/1

Renewing title sponsorship of the Global Challenge race, BT worked with the race organiser, The Challenge Business, and the international organisations sponsoring the 12 race yachts to enhance the concept. Changes were considered and made to the following:

- route
- scoring system
- yacht design
- technology.

The route

The westerly direction that makes the race unique remained the same. However, the business markets of the sponsoring organisations were taken into account and a number of different cities were included in the new route. The race was divided into seven legs or stages that crossed four oceans and visited five continents (see Table 1.1).

TABLE 1.1   Race route (nautical miles)

Leg 1	Southampton to Boston	3200 miles
Leg 2	Boston to Buenos Aires	5840 miles
Leg 3	Buenos Aires to Wellington	6020 miles
Leg 4	Wellington to Sydney	1230 miles
Leg 5	Sydney to Cape Town	6200 miles
Leg 6	Cape Town to La Rochelle	5820 miles
Leg 7	La Rochelle to Southampton	300 miles

Three race marks indicated by waypoints were inserted into the route to ensure that the fleet remained below or above certain latitudes to minimise the chances of encountering ice.

Scoring system

A points scoring system was introduced to replace the former system where yachts were ranked on the basis of elapsed time. Points were awarded for each stage or leg of the race and these were accumulated over the seven stages. The scoring system was the same for every leg, despite the varying lengths. The first yacht to arrive in port received 15 points, the second 14, the third 13 and so on. The team with the highest number of points at the end of the overall race was awarded The Princess Royal Trophy. This system ensured that if a team fell behind on one leg, through gear failure or misfortune, they still remained in contention in the overall race. It also increased the competitive element and excitement of each leg. Yacht teams battled to finish ahead of others in order to gain an additional point that was critical to enhance their overall race position.

Yacht design

In May 2000, a new one-design fleet of Challenge yachts was launched. This second-generation yacht was built of steel, was 72ft in length and

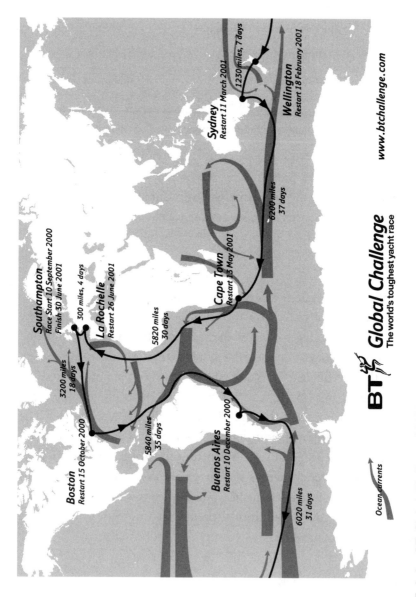

Southampton
Race Start 10 September 2000
Finish 30 June 2001

300 miles, 4 days

La Rochelle
Restart 26 June 2001

5820 miles
30 days

Boston
Restart 15 October 2000

3200 miles
18 days

5840 miles
35 days

Buenos Aires
Restart 10 December 2000

6020 miles
31 days

Cape Town
Restart 13 May 2001

6200 miles
37 days

Sydney
Restart 11 March 2001

1230 miles, 7 days

Wellington
Restart 18 February 2001

Ocean currents

BT *Global Challenge*
The world's toughest yacht race

www.btchallenge.com

FIGURE 1.1 BT Global Challenge 2000/1 Route Map

39 tonnes in weight. Having refined and improved the original design, these new yachts were 5ft longer and 4 tonnes lighter than their predecessors. To ensure that this fleet of identical yachts was built to the same specification, a system was developed using lasers to cut the steel parts. These were slotted together and then welded, so expensive mouldings and tooling were unnecessary and yachts could be built anywhere in the world. Of the 12 yachts, ten were built in Plymouth in the UK while two were constructed in Xinhui, China.

While the principles of safety, strength and seaworthiness remained the same, there were several significant differences in the design of the new yacht. The keel shape was modified to make it faster through the water downwind and lighter on the helm. Deck layout was altered to give greater protection to the crew in heavy weather conditions and the layout below was altered to accommodate 18 people.

Changes in the below-deck design placed the galley and saloon, where the crew cooked and ate, in the centre of the yacht. Here the pitching motion was less noticeable. Padded bunks were fitted – four in two cabins forward of the saloon and 14 in an open-plan arrangement at the back of the yacht. There were two toilets with showers. Water tanks containing up to 390 gallons were placed underneath the floorboards, together with fuel tanks with a capacity of 475 gallons. Each yacht had a watermaker capable of turning salt water into drinking water. Heaters were fitted to keep living conditions at a bearable temperature in the Southern Ocean and to assist in drying out wet clothing. A diesel generator provided power for the navigation equipment, lights, water pumps, computers and satellite equipment. Sails were stored in a watertight area at the front of the yacht and a fully equipped editing suite was built at the back of the yacht, where crew could prepare video footage for sending ashore.

Technology

Technological advancements over the previous four years provided the yachts with far more sophisticated satellite communications equipment than before. Skippers and crews were able to talk to the outside world from oceans around the globe, as well as send email, tap into the

World Wide Web and Internet, participate in video conferencing and transmit graphical video footage and digital still images from the yacht back to shore.

All the yachts carried identical equipment supplied by BT:

- Inmarsat C
- Inmarsat B
- Marine Mobiq.

Inmarsat C

Inmarsat C combined with the Global Positioning System (GPS) allowed race headquarters (RHQ) to monitor each of the yachts constantly and pinpoint their position to within a few metres. Both the yachts and RHQ could transmit important information via a two-way text messaging service. This included crucial weather reports and fleet messages. The Inmarsat C was also used for transmitting messages to the rescue authorities in emergencies.

Inmarsat B

Inmarsat B gave the crew high-speed digital dial-up access to the Internet for information such as weather and was also used for emails and video conferencing. The Inmarsat B's primary use was for the transmission of video pictures and high-quality digital still images from the crew back to shore.

Marine Mobiq

Marine Mobiq is a satellite telephone. The size of a notebook computer, it was effectively a satellite payphone and allowed the crew to speak to their families while out at sea. To avoid distraction, incoming calls were forbidden. The satellite system also provided a back-up to the Inmarsat B for sending digital stills and email.

See Chapter 9 for an overview of communications during the race.

CHALLENGE ETHOS

While changes were made to the route, the scoring system and the design of the yacht, the fundamental principles of the race remained the same. The ethos of creating a level playing field on which the teams could compete, initiated by Sir Chay at the outset, was endorsed and tightened.

Professional skippers who had previously skippered in a Challenge race were no longer eligible and the process of skipper selection was reviewed and enhanced. Management and leadership abilities were assessed alongside the necessary professional technical skills and racing experience. Crews from differing backgrounds and with varying skills continued to be recruited for their enthusiasm and determination and paid for the opportunity to take part in the race.

With a given route, a fair scoring system and identical equipment, leadership and teamwork, together with determination and endurance, remained the essential ingredients for success.

SKIPPER SELECTION

The role of a BT Global Challenge skipper is recognised as extremely complex and demanding.

- As an employee of The Challenge Business, the skipper is in charge of a project worth approximately £1.5 million, with a yacht, sails and equipment that need to be maintained constantly.
- As the only professional sailor on board the yacht, the skipper's technical knowledge, experience and seamanship are critical for leading and managing 17 fee-paying 'clients' and ensuring their safety.
- As a racing skipper on a sponsored yacht, the skipper is required to build and develop a racing team capable of competing in some of the worst conditions imaginable to achieve a prestigious position and raise the sponsor's corporate profile.

- As an ambassador of their yacht sponsor company, other subsidiary sponsors and race sponsor BT, the skipper is expected to be able to present to business audiences.
- As a PR spokesperson for the race organiser The Challenge Business and race sponsor BT, the skipper is expected to handle media interviews and utilise the sophisticated communications technology on board the yacht to publicise the race worldwide

As the race has evolved and expectations have been raised, the skipper's remit has become more and more complex. Sir Chay was aware that there were unlikely to be many professional sailors with the complex set of skills and attributes required for this role. As a consequence, he initiated an element of the selection programme that would assess the skippers' management and leadership skills and their potential for developing these.

Skipper selection programme

Phase 1

The process of skipper selection was started in the autumn of 1998 when more than 186 applications were received for the 12 race skipper roles. The initial application sorting was based on technical professional skills and qualifications, ocean mileage and racing experience. From this process, 90 applicants were selected and interviewed by The Challenge Business.

The professional qualifications required were:

- Royal Yachting Association (RYA)/Department of Transport Yachtmaster Ocean (sailing) with commercial endorsement
- Global Maritime Distress and Safety System General Operators Certificate (SOLAS)
- Basic Sea Survival Course Certificate
- DTp Ship Captains Medical Training Certificate
- RYA Diesel Engine Maintenance Course Certificate
- 25 000 miles' sailing experience
- Knowledge of International Sailing Federation (IsaS) Racing Rules

Phase 2

In June 1999, 41 of the 90 skippers were put forward for the second phase of the selection programme, a two-day residential event run by 12 external consultants at Calshot Activities Centre near Southampton. The programme was designed to assess the skippers' management and leadership abilities and their potential for development. Tasks and exercises were designed around four core elements and each task was assessed using a five-point rating scale adapted from the High Performance Managerial Competencies classified by Harry Schroder (1989).

- Leadership skills
  - influencing and inspiring
  - gaining followership.
- Team management skills
  - planning and delegating
  - teambuilding blocks (Woodcock 1985).
- Interpersonal abilities
  - interaction with others
  - dealing with conflict
  - motivation
  - flexibility.
- Communication skills
  - writing reports
  - handling media interviews.

Critical event interviews were conducted with each skipper and two interviewers. Skippers were questioned about their handling of a successful and an unsuccessful project. A number of psychometric instruments were used to help raise the skippers' awareness of their profile and the value of these instruments in building and developing their teams.

- preferred team role (Belbin 1999)
- motivational driver (McClelland 1988)
- leadership balance (Adair 1983).

Phase 3

The third phase of the skipper selection was conducted by The Challenge Business and took place in the summer of 1999. This phase focused on the sailing abilities of the 23 skippers taken to this stage. Sailing with representatives from The Challenge Business and a novice crew, the skippers were assessed on their competence in handling the yacht in a number of situations and their ability to lead and manage the amateur crew.

Phase 4

The fourth phase of the selection programme was held in September 1999 when 19 skippers undertook a five-day residential development programme run by eight external consultants. The programme was designed to provide management and leadership theory, as well as assess the aptitude of the skippers in understanding and utilising this knowledge in a number of simulated situations. At the end of the programme, reports were compiled on each of the 19 skippers, outlining strengths, weaknesses and development needs. Skippers were given personal feedback.

Reports and recommendations were submitted to The Challenge Business, who announced the final 12 race skippers and two reserve skippers in November 1999.

The 12 race skippers were:

- Will Carnegie
- Andy Dare
- Mark Denton
- Nick Fenton
- Manley Hopkinson
- Conrad Humphreys
- Neil Murray
- Will Oxley
- Lin Parker
- Alex Phillips
- Jeremy Troughton
- Stephen Wilkins.

The reserve skippers were:

- Richard Chenery
- John Read.

Both reserve skippers were called up during the race. John Read took over from Andy Dare at the end of leg 1 and Richard Chenery took over from Alex Phillips from leg 5.

SKIPPER ALLOCATION TO SPONSOR

In keeping with the Challenge ethos, the allocation of skippers to yacht sponsors was fair and honest. In a sponsor meeting held in November 1999, sponsor project managers were each asked to select a blank envelope containing the name of one of the 12 skippers. Not all the sponsors had been confirmed at this stage so an envelope was allocated to the remaining six yacht sponsors and given to them at the time their sponsorship was announced.

CREW COMPOSITION

Each yacht team consisted of 18 people. This was composed of the skipper, 15 core crew members and two leggers. Core crew members were recruited and paid to complete the entire race. The majority of

TABLE 1.2 Final allocation of sponsors and skippers

BP	Mark Denton
CGNU	Neil Murray
Compaq	Will Oxley
Isle of Man	Lin Parker
LG Electronics	Conrad Humphreys
Logica	Jeremy Troughton
Olympic Group	Manley Hopkinson
Quadstone	Alex Phillips / Richard Chenery*
Serco Group plc	Nick Fenton
InvestHK	Stephen Wilkins
TeamSpirIT	Andy Dare / John Read*
VERITAS	Will Carnegie

* Reserve skippers called up during the course of the race

leggers were employees of yacht-sponsoring companies or race sponsor BT and undertook one leg or stage of the race. Some of the sponsor companies invited journalists or celebrities to undertake a specific leg. Due to injury, illness or personal reasons, some of the core crew members were unable to complete the entire race and replacements were brought into the team.

CORE CREW RECRUITMENT

A total of 180 core crew places were available in the BT Global Challenge. These places were filled by men and women aged between 21 and 60, from differing backgrounds and of varying nationalities. Sailing experience was not required and 60 per cent of the crew had never sailed.

The recruitment process involved an initial deposit paid on application for a berth. An interview with Sir Chay was arranged and the individual was assessed on levels of enthusiasm, determination and self-motivation. Having support of family and friends was important, as well as the ability to raise the berth fee of £24,800.

Core crew training

A five-phase sail training programme, completed over a two to three-year period, was a requirement. Core crew applicants were assessed constantly by the Challenge training skipper and mate and reports were written at the end of each phase:

- induction
- continuation
- development
- consolidation.

Induction

The initial training phase of five days focused on the basics of sailing, safety, hygiene and emergency procedures such as man overboard and firefighting. One night was spent sailing and crew members were introduced to the system of being 'on' and 'off' watch, working and sleeping in short two to three-hour periods.

Continuation

The second phase of the training involved a further five days' sailing with two nights at sea. This session built on the basics and focused on the trim of the sails. The crew were introduced to sailing under spinnaker and given an insight into weather analysis.

Development

By the third phase of the training, crews were expected to spend seven days and six nights at sea, working in watch systems and interpreting the weather. They were introduced to the principles of sea survival. At the end of the week they undertook a written examination.

Consolidation

A final five days gave crew members full responsibility for running the yacht. They were also assigned sailing-related topics on which they had to give a presentation to show the necessary level of understanding. To supplement the core training, individuals had the opportunity to join the yachts on delivery trips throughout the training period.

Qualifying

The concluding element of sail training took place in the year preceding the race. Three sessions lasting four days had to be undertaken on board a race yacht and a final eight-day qualifying sail completed with the entire race team and skipper on board their own race yacht.

LEGGER RECRUITMENT

As part of the sponsorship package, the individual yacht sponsor companies were entitled to two berths on board their sponsored yacht. The majority of the sponsors allocated their berths to company employees who were asked to raise funds towards the race charity, Save the Children. Many allocated a berth on leg 4 to one of their senior executives. This leg became known as the 'executive leg'. Several sponsors gave berths to selected journalists and some captured the media spotlight by having celebrities on board. BT, as race sponsor, was allocated berths on five of the yachts and a total of 29 employees undertook a leg of the race.

Recognising the effect that two new people could have on the team dynamic, sponsors and skippers were careful that leggers were integrated into the core team as early as possible in the project, and many joined the teambuilding events and were allocated responsibilities to support the core team from shore.

Legger training

Legger training was a condensed version of the five-part core crew training programme. This was undertaken in two sessions lasting five days and run by the Challenge training skipper and mate. Leggers undertook additional training with their core team in the preparation period from January to September 2000.

CREW ALLOCATION TO TEAMS

In November 1999, the 180 core crew members were divided into 12 teams. Each team of 15 needed to be as equally matched as possible and a set of criteria was followed:

- average age of 37
- five females
- mix of nationality
- a qualified medic.

The assessment reports for each individual crew member were reviewed to ensure that each team had individuals with strengths in key areas. Personality was also considered and each yacht was assigned an individual who was considered to be a 'joker' – someone who would bring humour to the yacht.

Involving the training skippers as well as some of the race skippers in the process of dividing crew into 12 teams ensured that each yacht team was as equal in strength and ability as possible. At this stage no one knew which team would be allocated to which skipper or sponsor.

TEAM ALLOCATION TO SKIPPER AND SPONSOR

On 8 January 2000, at the London Boat Show, the race skippers, core crew members, leggers and sponsors waited to hear Sir Chay announce the race teams. As six of the yacht sponsors had not been announced, some teams did not have an immediate corporate identity. Consequently these teams did not have leggers and the skipper assumed a team of 15 core crew. Other skippers immediately assumed a team of 27 individuals. The leadership challenge had begun and the skippers left the London Boat Show with nine months to shape their team into a high-performing, racing crew.

PREPARATION FOR THE RACE

During these nine months the skippers had a complex and demanding task to accomplish. They needed to get to know the individual members of their crew, start to form and develop a cohesive team, organise and plan their race strategy, prepare their yacht, sails and equipment, learn how to use the new communications technology and organise the food for the ten-month race. This had to be balanced with meeting the corporate requirements of their sponsors and the media responsibilities of the race sponsor.

Most of the core crew members had full-time jobs and were still raising their berth fee. Many were unable to join the team permanently until late August or early September. Time together, as a full crew, was often difficult with team members spread around the world. When they did manage to get together, time was precious as there were a lot of things to be addressed.

Having learned the importance of teambuilding and development from the skippers of the 1996/7 race, all 12 skippers identified, as a priority, the need to get their team together at an early stage in the project. By the end of February, all teams had had their first team session. They had started the process of getting to know each other and agreed team goals and values.

With the new Challenge fleet still in build, the race teams had to sail-train on board the old 67ft Challenge yachts, with one three-day sail training session on board the prototype 72ft Challenge yacht. A delay in the building of the new race fleet added to the workload of the skippers and teams. Taking delivery in April, they worked with The Challenge Business to ensure the yachts were complete and ready to depart on the inaugural sail to St Katharine's Dock, London at the beginning of May.

Aside from team and sail training, there were a number of specialist courses for the skipper and a designated crew member to attend. Professional training was given in areas essential for the smooth running of the yacht. For each yacht team to be self-sufficient at sea they needed to have an engineer, an electrician, a plumber, a carpenter, a rigger, a sailmaker and someone responsible for servicing the safety equipment. Additional training was required for individuals assigned to collate weather information and interpret weather patterns. At least one person was required to act as yacht photographer, while others needed to be trained to use the communications and video-editing technology. One team member needed to be a qualified Ocean Yachtmaster.

Clothing and food were two vital areas that the teams had to get right. Skippers realised that being cold, wet and hungry could have enormous impact on crew morale and could affect the overall performance of a team. Most yacht teams assigned an individual or a project group to source the best technical clothing available. While the berth fee included special Musto HPX breathable oilskins, crew members had to pay for their own inner thermal layers and protection for their head, feet and hands. Food specialists and nutritionists were brought in by a number of teams to help them to plan varied and balanced meals. With weight a prime consideration for performance, teams were keen to use lightweight freeze-dried food.

THE RACE

Leg 1 – Southampton to Boston, 3200 miles

Early on the morning of Sunday 10 September, the crews said their goodbyes to family and friends as the yachts left the dock in Ocean Village, Southampton. At 11.05 GMT, in light wind, the 12 race yachts slipped across the start line in The Solent and headed off on their 30 000-mile race around the world.

Norwich Union crossed the line first and battled with Logica to be the first out of The Solent. The first night at sea, Logica was struck by a fishing trawler. Damage was limited, but the crew were shaken and performance suffered, with the yacht falling back to 11th position.

The weather was changeable for much of the leg, with light winds and fog at times. The fleet met their first storm with winds averaging 50 knots as the tail end of Hurricane Florence passed across their track. Both Spirit of Hong Kong and Logica were knocked down by squalls when wind speeds of 78 knots were recorded. Two crew members were slightly injured and the satellite communications dome on the back of Logica was damaged (see Plate 6). There was also damage to sails and equipment on other yachts in the fleet.

There was further drama on Logica when a crew member suffering from severe stomach pains had to be taken by air to hospital in Nova Scotia. She was diagnosed with a perforated ulcer and had to stand down for the second leg, rejoining her crew in Buenos Aires.

After 18 days, 2 hours, 17 minutes and 55 seconds Quadstone crossed the finish line in first position, followed by BP Explorer and LG FLATRON. Within 56 hours all 12 yachts had arrived in Boston (see Table 1.3).

The crew on board TeamSpirIT arrived with some issues regarding the team goal and strategy. After many hours of discussion with the crew in a quest to reach a solution, skipper Andy Dare resigned, stating he was more of an adventurer than a racer. Reserve skipper John Read flew to Boston where he took over for the remainder of the race.

TABLE 1.3 Leg 1 positions

Position	Yacht	Elapsed time
1	Quadstone	18d 02h 17m 55s
2	BP Explorer	18d 07h 00m 49s
3	LG FLATRON	18d 08h 10m 16s
4	Compaq	18d 09h 16m 21s
5	VERITAS	18d 12h 01m 56s
6	Isle of Man	18d 12h 16m 06s
8	Spirit of Hong Kong	18d 18h 29m 08s
9=	Save the Children	19d 07h 47m 43s
9=	Logica*	18d 18h 00m 13s
10	TeamSpirIT	19d 21h 46m 50s
11	Norwich Union	20d 07h 25m 57s
12	Olympic Group	20d 10h 29m 40s

* Seventh position bumped to ninth following judgement by the International Race Jury on use of motor during crew evacuation

Leg 2 – Boston to Buenos Aires, 5840 miles

Leg 2 was christened by Sir Chay as the 'gin and tonic leg', due to its normally light winds, warm temperatures and easy sailing. However, the BT Global Challenge fleet sailed into a tropical storm and then a hurricane, experiencing winds of up to 80 knots and suffering seasickness and minor injuries. As they crossed the equator, temperatures soared to over 100 degrees fahrenheit and dehydration became a major problem.

By the end of week one the fleet had crossed into the steadier and stronger trade winds of the Azores High, experiencing increasingly hot and stifling conditions. They soon reached The Doldrums, an area characterised by frustratingly light winds, major shifts in wind direction and sudden violent squalls. These unexpected squalls damaged many sails and crews took to mending them in the saloon which with the insufferable heat became known as a sweat shop as the crews rotated like a tag team to ensure a swift sail repair. The team on Olympic recorded 12 000 stitches as they completed one repair.

By the end of week two the fleet had separated by 242 miles. However, in some areas racing was extremely close and there were just one or two miles between the yachts. Trouble set in for the crew on Isle of Man as they experienced problems with their watermaker. The problem was resolved but, as a precaution, skipper Lin Parker took the decision to ration water for the remainder of the leg. The rest of the fleet were warned of this problem and other yachts soon detected similar problems.

The yachts crossed the equator in week three and the teams upheld the tradition on entering King Neptune's domain. Crew members who had already crossed the equator took great pleasure in dousing those who crossed for the first time with vile leftovers, supposedly cleansing them of their sins.

The final sprint up the River Plate to Buenos Aires was down to tactics and hard work. LG FLATRON was well ahead of the fleet, finishing in first place after 32 days, 22 hours, 13 minutes and 37 seconds, but Quadstone and BP Explorer battled it out to the very end, finishing within just seven minutes of one another (see Table 1.4).

Leg 3 – Buenos Aires to Wellington, 6020 miles

Leg three was the crews' first encounter with the notorious Southern Ocean, known for its huge seas and violent winds which build as a result of the oceans uninterrupted swirling around the globe. The leg was the longest yet encountered and the crews left Buenos Aires full of fear and trepidation.

After a light wind start with warm temperatures, the fleet was soon faced with winds of up to 40 knots and temperatures dropped rapidly. Many crews found it difficult to adjust from the sweltering temperatures of the previous leg.

While the rest of the fleet was battling down the coast of South America, BP Explorer was languishing at the back in light airs. Their

TABLE 1.4 Leg 2 positions

Position	Yacht	Elapsed time
1	LG FLATRON	32d 22h 13m 37s
2	Spirit of Hong Kong	33d 13h 11m 45s
3	Logica	33d 19h 19m 29s
4	Compaq	33d 20h 15m 05s
5	Olympic Group	33d 22h 07m 03s
6	Quadstone	34d 02h 29m 37s
7	BP Explorer	34d 02h 36m 46s
8	VERITAS	34d 04h 56m 24s
9	Isle of Man	34d 07h 00m 21s
10	TeamSpirIT	34d 10h 49m 57s
11	Norwich Union	34d 18h 44m 56s
12	Save the Children	34d 23h 57m 15s

restart from Buenos Aires had been delayed due to contaminated fuel supplies. After spending several hours cleaning the fuel tanks they finally set sail eight hours after the rest of the fleet. Their delay cost them more than just the eight hours as they entered a different weather system to the rest of the fleet and struggled to make up the lost ground.

On 18 December the fleet, led by Quadstone, began rounding Cape Horn. The crews felt a sense of great achievement yet at the same time fear and awe. Racing was still tight, despite vicious weather conditions – crew members were swept along the deck by huge volumes of water and suffered severe bruising and injuries that confined them to their bunks.

Preparations for Christmas gave the crews some relief from the hardship of the Southern Ocean. Some yachts hung decorations and played Christmas music. Many celebrated the day with a special meal and shared presents brought from home or that they had made for each other on board. The best Christmas present for the crew of BP

Explorer, struggling to catch up with the fleet, came in the fourth week when they passed Save the Children and moved into 11th position.

The finale of one of the hardest legs was just as dramatic as the previous five weeks. LG FLATRON and Olympic Group fought neck and neck for first position into Wellington. Battling against storm-force conditions, disaster struck for Olympic and they tore their headsail. This was the break LG FLATRON needed and they slipped past taking first position after 36 days, 10 hours, 53 minutes and 39 seconds (see Table 1.5).

Leg 4 – Wellington to Sydney, 1230 miles

Leg 4 was a quick seven-day sprint across the Tasman Sea. Several senior directors from sponsoring companies joined their yacht for this 'executive leg'. Alongside these executives were several celebrities: Jeremy Irons who hopped aboard LG FLATRON, Chris Serle who

TABLE 1.5   Leg 3 positions

Position	Yacht	Elapsed time
1	LG FLATRON	36d 10h 53m 39s
2	Olympic Group	36d 12h 52m 12s
3	Compaq	36d 13h 16m 12s
4	TeamSpirIT	36d 20h 30m 08s
5	Quadstone	37d 05h 18m 06s
6	Isle of Man	38d 03h 15m 39s
7	Norwich Union	38d 06h 40m 25s
8	Logica	38d 06h 52m 17s
9	VERITAS	38d 08h 31m 14s
10	Spirit of Hong Kong	38d 08h 53m 35s
11	BP Explorer	38d 12h 27m 46s
12	Save the Children	39d 19h 27m 25s

joined Compaq, Zinzan Brooke who accompanied VERITAS and Robert Powell who raced on board Logica against his wife Babs, a core crew member on board VERITAS.

The weather was not favourable during this leg and light winds delayed the fleet's arrival in Sydney. The combination of close racing and light winds put pressure on the crews to do everything they could to give them that extra knot of speed. To save weight, the BP Explorer crew took only the clothes they were wearing. To avoid slowing the yacht, the crew on Logica did all they could to keep movement aboard to a minimum. To keep the yacht well balanced, many of the crews slept and ate while sitting on the side rail. With fickle light winds, the leader board changed constantly as one yacht caught the wind and moved up a few places, only to lose the wind again and fall behind.

The finish in Sydney Harbour was breathtaking. Logica, which had been 20 miles ahead of the fleet, lost its lead position and LG FLATRON and BP Explorer slipped past. In very close quarters and with fickle winds, the two battled to cross the line. BP Explorer managed to slip through and after 7 days, 23 hours and 36 minutes crossed the finish line just 25 seconds ahead of LG FLATRON (see Table 1.6).

Meanwhile, an unfortunate collision between Quadstone and Save the Children just two hours after the start of leg 4 meant that neither of the yachts was able to complete the leg. Both yachts returned to Wellington for repairs while Nick Fenton, the skipper of Save the Children, received hospital treatment for injuries after being thrown from the helm. Alex Phillips, the skipper of Quadstone, took full responsibility for the collision. Upset by the fact that both teams were unable to complete the leg and that a fellow skipper had been injured, Alex resigned. The second reserve skipper, Richard Chenery, was flown to Wellington to take over and led the Quadstone crew for the rest of the race.

Quadstone was repaired and sailed to Sydney where the team rejoined the fleet for the start of leg 5. Save the Children had suffered more extensive damage and was unable to make the start of the next leg. The yacht rejoined the fleet in the Tasman Sea and sailed with them to Cape Town. As the innocent party in the collision, they were awarded average points for legs 4 and 5 and the status of having completed all legs of the race.

TABLE 1.6   Leg 4 positions

Position	Yacht	Elapsed time
1	BP Explorer	07d 23h 36m 11s
2	LG FLATRON	07d 23h 36m 36s
3	Logica	07d 23h 40m 26s
4	Compaq	08d 01h 52m 13s
5	TeamSpirIT	08d 05h 30m 21s
6	VERITAS	08d 06h 53m 00s
7	Spirit of Hong Kong	08d 06h 58m 51s
8	Isle of Man	08d 08h 58m 04s
9	Olympic Group	08d 09h 39m 59s
10	Norwich Union	08d 10h 12m 00s
11	Save the Children	Did not complete leg
12	Quadstone	Did not complete leg

Leg 5 – Sydney to Cape Town, 6200 miles

Leg 5 took the yachts back into the Southern Ocean for possibly the most testing leg of the entire race. The crews knew this leg was not going to be fun and were certain it would push them to their mental and physical limits.

Both BP Explorer and Logica got off to a poor start in Sydney Harbour – BP Explorer clipped the starter mark and had to effect a penalty turn and Logica arrived at the start line 10 seconds too early and had to bear away, which cost it four places. TeamSpirIT won the Wee Chay Trophy for being the first to pass the Wee Chay Buoy in Sydney Harbour, a mark set for fun to raise money for Save the Children. Quadstone spent the first half of the leg getting to know their new skipper, Richard Chenery.

On day two Compaq reported a huge breaking wave in the Bass Strait and just hours later VERITAS took a powerful knock by a rogue wave. Two crew members were thrown from the rail across the cockpit resulting in serious injuries. As a helicopter evacuation was not feasible, the yacht diverted to Port Eden where a team of paramedics was awaiting the injured crew.

Five days into the leg and LG FLATRON had a 69-mile lead on the fleet. Seeing an opportunity to head south, the crew dived down and extended their lead by up to 200 miles for most of the leg. As the fleet headed across the Southern Ocean they were battling with major wind shifts and wind speeds that would hit 45 knots without any warning, ripping sails and damaging equipment (see Plate 3).

Save the Children rejoined the fleet and, while not officially racing, battled at the front of the fleet for the duration of the leg. The leader board was constantly changing as racing was close and yachts were

TABLE 1.7   Leg 5 positions

Position	Yacht	Elapsed time
1	LG FLATRON	35d 17h 34m 08s
2	Norwich Union	36d 19h 10m 41s
3	Quadstone	36d 20h 03m 02s
4	BP Explorer	36d 20h 20m 21s
5	Save the Children	36d 21h 01m 15s*
6	Compaq	37d 11h 02m 11s
7	TeamSpirIT	37d 15h 00m 54s
8	Isle of Man	37d 16h 09m 05s
9	Logica	37d 20h 53m 05s
10	Spirit of Hong Kong	37d 21h 04m 01s
11	VERITAS	39d 19h 42m 25s
12	Olympic Group	39d 21h 11m 41s

* STC elapsed time for statistical purposes is calculated from the official start time in Sydney until the time they crossed the line in Cape Town

sailing within one mile of each other. Norwich Union experienced an accidental gybe that caused it to lose a sail over the side. This cost the yacht in miles and also in points as it incurred a penalty. The conditions were relentless and temperatures so low that crews could spend no more than 30 minutes on deck at a time. The yachts continued to battle it out and crews enjoyed some relief with the spectacular Southern Lights show.

LG FLATRON held the lead throughout the leg and arrived in Cape Town to finish first after 35 days, 17 hours, 34 minutes and 8 seconds. Norwich Union took second place, arriving 26 hours later. Only ten miles separated the second and fifth-placed yachts after 6200 miles of racing (Table 1.7).

Leg 6 – Cape Town to La Rochelle, 5820 miles

With the Southern Ocean behind them, the crews left Cape Town feeling a lot more relaxed about the leg. However, where leg 5 required physical strength and was more about survival, leg 6 tested the crews' mental stamina and the team dynamics. Many felt that for these reasons this leg was a lot harder than the Southern Ocean.

What made this leg even harder was the longevity of it. As the first yachts arrived after 36 days, leg 6 of the BT Global Challenge distinguished itself as the slowest leg – with one of the longest awaited finishes. Plagued by light air from the start, the challenge fleet fell behind schedule. As a result, the Race Committee announced the postponement of leg 7 from La Rochelle to Southampton by one week.

Leg 6 finally delivered Compaq as the leg winner after 36 days, 5 hours, 52 minutes and 8 seconds, a position the crew had fought for throughout the race. For the crew on-board LG FLATRON, it was a very different race. Accustomed to finishing in the top three, on this leg LG FLATRON finished in eighth place. Many of the yachts had a taste of success as the positions changed in the lights airs and the crews played a game of mental skill and tenacity. Logica was the first yacht to cross back into the Northern Hemisphere. Isle of Man started the leg well after a brave tactical move paid off. They fought right up until the finish line and watched in dismay as BP Explorer slipped across the line less than 2 minutes ahead (see Table 1.8).

TABLE 1.8   Leg 6 positions

Position	Yacht	Elapsed time
1	Compaq	36d 05h 52m 08s
2	Logica	36d 07h 58m 22s
3	BP Explorer	37d 08h 14m 20s
5	Spirit of Hong Kong	37d 14h 19m 17s
6	Isle of Man*	37d 08h 15m 46s
7	TeamSpirIT	37d 20h 36m 38s
8=	Norwich Union**	37d 18h 46m 10s
8=	LG FLATRON	38d 06h 44m 46s
9	Save the Children	39d 01h 50m 55s
10	Quadstone	39d 01h 59m 58s
11	VERITAS	39d 02h 00m 13s
12	Olympic Group	Retired

* Isle of Man incurred a two-point penalty for damaging a spinnaker 'beyond economical repair' during leg 5

** Norwich Union incurred a two-point penalty for losing their No 1 sail during leg 5

The decision of the International Race Jury was that these penalties would be applied in the leg where the yachts had the advantage of the new sails

Sadly for Olympic Group, the exceptionally lights winds and a poor forecast forced them to retire from the leg to ensure they reached La Rochelle for the start of leg 7. In what was described as a 'quiet and sombre' moment, they turned on the engine. They arrived in La Rochelle to be greeted by a big cheer from the rest of the fleet.

Leg 7 – La Rochelle to Southampton, 300 miles

Leg 7 was a fast and furious sprint home to Southampton in strong winds.

TeamSpirIT held the lead for the majority of the leg and led the fleet into English waters. In order to manage the arrival of the fleet for

Saturday afternoon, the course was extended by racing round buoys in The Solent. Many of the skippers were sailing in familiar home waters, making the competition exciting right up until the end.

The final battle was fought between Norwich Union, TeamSpirIT and LG FLATRON as they sailed towards Cowes under spinnaker, all jostling for first position. A further leg and a final buoy finalised the positions as they headed for the finish line in Southampton Water. LG FLATRON made a final sail change and stole the lead, taking first position for the leg after 4 days, 3 hours, 6 minutes and 13 seconds (see Table 1.9 and Plate 15). With the highest number of accumulated points, LG FLATRON was also confirmed as the overall winner of the BT Global Challenge 2000/1 and awarded The Princess Royal Trophy (see Plate 16).

TABLE 1.9 Leg 7 positions

Positions	Yacht	Elapsed time
1	LG FLATRON	04d 03h 06m 13s
2	TeamSpirIT	04d 03h 09m 18s
3	Norwich Union	04d 03h 10m 58s
4	Olympic Group	04d 03h 16m 16s
5	Compaq	04d 03h 16m 45s
6	BP Explorer	04d 03h 30m 30s
7	VERITAS	04d 03h 35m 32s
8	Logica	04d 03h 41m 23s
9	Spirit of Hong Kong	04d 03h 45m 31s
10	Quadstone	04d 06h 14m 25s
11	Save the Children	04d 06h 26m 13s
12	Isle of Man	04d 21h 27m 51s

BT GLOBAL CHALLENGE AS A CASE STUDY

The race provided a unique platform for a study on leadership and human performance. With 12 equally matched teams, using the same equipment, starting and finishing a project within the same duration and encountering the same hostile and unpredictable conditions throughout, the parameters of the study were clearly defined and comparable. The way the skippers handled their teams, managed their resources and ran their project gave an incredible insight into the leadership skills and attributes required to shape and sustain high-performing teams.

Financial support for the project was raised through the companies that formed the Inspirational Intelligence Research Forum. Representatives of these companies joined the Inspiring Performance research team in ports of call to collate, through interview, qualitative data on which the findings are based. Details of the IIRF companies are listed in the front of the book. The research methodology is set out in Chapter 4 and the research findings are given in Chapter 5 and supported with examples through each of the chapters in Part III of this book.

REFERENCES

Adair, J. (1983) *Effective Leadership*, Pan: London.

Belbin, M. (1999) *Team Roles at Work*, Butterworth-Heinemann: Oxford.

McClelland, D. C. (1988) *Human Motivation*, Cambridge University Press: Cambridge.

Schroder, H. M. (1989) *Managerial Competence: The key to excellence*, Kendall Hunt: Iowa.

Woodcock, M. (1985) *Team Development Manual*, Gower: Aldershot.

2

THE BUSINESS ENVIRONMENT OF TODAY

Your biggest competitor is your own view of the future, both in the running of your business and the maintenance of your career. The most elusive and therefore most desired quality of leadership is vision. Without it you simply cannot succeed.

Larry Hochman, European Business Speaker of the Year 2001

INTRODUCTION

The business environment is undergoing continuous change. At the start of the 21st century, the environment can best be described as competitive, challenging, turbulent and unpredictable.

Katzenbach (2000) researched more than 25 companies in North America, most of which had achieved superior competitive advantage, either financially or in the marketplace, over several years. The leaders of these enterprises were convinced that their people made the differences in performance, and the research supported this view. It was the commitment and energy of people that resulted in performance beyond the norm.

What does this mean for the leaders of today and tomorrow? It marks the start of challenging times for leaders who will need the right skills and attributes to capture the hearts and minds of their people in order to develop and sustain competitive advantage for their organisations in an environment of continuous change.

Two of the critical drivers for change are the technological revolution taking place and the growth of a global market economy. Successful leaders will recognise the need for a new mindset and skill set if they are to keep pace with the changes and be successful as a leader. In Gibson's words (1998), 'no one can drive to the future on cruise control.'

The opportunity to study leadership and teamwork during the BT Global Challenge Round the World Yacht Race provided an excellent parallel with business in the current environment. The race was highly competitive, the environment was hostile, at times dangerous, and conditions were uncertain. Faced with these pressures, and sailing identical yachts, the winners were the skippers who used their skills and attributes as leaders and who worked most effectively with their teams to achieve the highest performance. The skippers also needed to scan carefully the external environment to put together their strategy and tactics for each leg of the race.

The business leader, like the skippers in the yacht race, must be very aware of the environmental forces impacting on their business. This means constantly having an external focus, being responsive to the environment, and keeping one step ahead. This chapter outlines the environment in which organisations are operating today, the challenges faced by leaders and teams, and how these influence the skills and attributes needed by leaders to achieve and sustain high performance. The key changes will be discussed and the implications for leaders will be summarised.

THE TECHNOLOGICAL REVOLUTION

Leaders have been required to deal with radical change in the last few years and the one certainty today is change and discontinuity. There has been unprecedented change in the hi-tech industry. Technology has opened up opportunities to work independently of location and time, and has dramatically changed the way organisations do business.

Traditional organisations have had to reassess the way they harness IT to achieve business success. They have had to revisit investment in IT, explore new ways of communicating with customers and capitalise on market opportunities to meet competition from unexpected directions. New specialist players are attacking profitable parts of company value chains.

Leaders are likely to have already experienced a change of role as technology is applied to support areas and leaders are required to fill the gaps left by parts of the function that cannot readily be automated. Leaders will need to develop a broader business understanding to fulfil their role.

Although growth of the Internet has been slower than anticipated in the business-to-consumer market, after five years of web site use some paths to profitability are emerging, according to Green and Sharpe (2001). So far the problems experienced by the dot-com companies have been a cost issue, not a market demand issue. Very soon travel, financial services, healthcare and education will be distributed cost effectively in the US. Niche players are starting to make a profit and certain organisations are taking the opportunity provided by the Net to increase routes to market, helped by their solid brand name.

Vishwanath and Mulvin (2001) refer to the Internet continuing to be a perplexing new tool. While it can be intuitively useful, versatile and in some ways transformational, it was hugely disappointing to many business people and investors in 2001. However, it has exceeded expectations in some important areas. Large 'bricks and mortar' companies are starting to find ways to use the Internet as a source of revenue and as a means of cutting costs.

The more innovative organisations are finding ways of turning information into new services. For example, the industrial conglomerate GE is using the Internet to provide information on operating its engineering products such as turbines and engines. Customers can now compare GE machines with similar machines around the world. This service generates a profit for GE and improves the company's competitive position.

Use of the mobile phone will be very different in the future. According to Baker and Capell (2001), Chris Gent, chief executive officer (CEO) of Vodafone Group, is determined to grow market share to make Vodafone the world's dominant phone company. In 2001, the growth of the company was coming from voice customers; the next growth area will be more extensive use of the Internet via the mobile phone. In 2000, Vodafone formed a Net venture with Vizzavi to create a net portal which reaches customers through their PCs, digital TVs and cellular phones. Vodafone has bought a stake in J-phone in Japan to learn more about this market. In Japan there are 36 million mobile Net users, according to Kunii (2001). Gent is looking to grow through further acquisitions. There are 40 000 mobile Web sites offering a range of services, even alerting customers whenever they pass their favourite boutiques.

During the race the yachts were equipped with Inmarsat C combined with a Global Positioning System. This allowed race headquarters constantly to monitor the position of the yachts. The skipper and crew had high-speed digital dial access to the Internet most of the time. The yachts also had a low-cost satellite phone. This provided global coverage and acted as a back-up system to the Inmarsat Satellite B for live voice interviews, sending digital photographs and emails. The yachts were also fitted with video equipment and a full editing suite to capture situations on video throughout the race.

Managing in the new economy is different and requires new approaches. A survey conducted by Henley Management College (2000) found that traditional organisations have now recognised the importance of strategic planning, e-business knowledge and leadership to help cope with the demands of the new economy.

Four key needs were identified for leaders to help their organisations stay ahead of the competition:
1. to cope with change in highly uncertain environments
2. to develop skills in leadership and relationship building
3. to become more risk aware and take more risks
4. to adopt new working practices and be less detached from subordinates.

Additional skills and attributes were identified:
1. to develop a 'can do attitude'
2. to have a broader business perspective to cope with broader responsibilities
3. to be on the look-out for new business opportunities which become possible with advancing technology.

KNOWLEDGE MANAGEMENT AND COMMUNICATION

Technological change has also made an impact in the area of knowledge management and communication. While technology both helps and increases the intensity of information, it is the knowledge worker, through understanding and interpreting the information, who converts information to knowledge.

The acquisition and development of knowledge have become key components of competitive advantage, raising the profile of the knowledge worker and the importance attached to organisational learning. Competitive advantage depends on the ability of the organisation to create, transfer, use and protect difficult-to-imitate business assets.

The new knowledge economy requires organisations and their leaders to have certain skills and attributes. They must be entrepreneurial, highly flexible and able to make good decisions with limited information. In the age of innovation they must be able to work in collaboration with others to share and build positive relationships with customers to help understand their needs, and be responsive in markets that are changing at high speed. According to Teece (2000), converting information to knowledge requires a change of mindset of leaders and people, away from the concept that information is power towards a genuine desire to help others learn. This leads to the need for different ways of working, more cross-functional and collaborative, than the traditional form of organisation, and this is one of the drivers for restructuring.

Information and communications technology (ICT) is used in almost all organisations as an integral part of many systems. This technology facilitates globalisation, allowing communication worldwide at minimal cost. One cannot underestimate the extent to which technology has speeded up the rate and volume of communication impacting on the way organisations do business.

During the 2000/1 race the skippers had access to a wealth of information, including weather patterns, to help them navigate round the world. While the data was available, skills were required of the skippers and crew to convert this data to knowledge and sometimes to take decisions with only limited information.

What does this mean for leaders? Responding to the challenges of the knowledge era creates the need for leaders to possess a number of skills and attributes:

- be entrepreneurial and highly flexible
- have the ability to make good decisions with limited information
- work in collaboration with others to share and build positive relationships with customers
- understand and be responsive to the needs of customers
- have a change of mindset away from information as power and towards helping others to learn.

GLOBALISATION

Trade and business barriers have been reduced, opening up markets across a range of sectors, for example insurance, motor manufacturing and retailing, leading to a more integrated global marketplace. Developments in communications and IT have helped the management of organisations to lead very large business enterprises successfully. Leaders within organisations need to recognise the opportunities and respond to them.

Organisations have expanded worldwide to protect their market position in existing markets. Marketplaces are becoming increasingly competitive which means that organisations have to become better at what they are doing to stay in business in a much more complex environment. The survivors will be those businesses able to reinvent themselves to stay ahead of the game.

According to Deal and Kennedy (1999), more than 40 per cent of the market for companies such as Coca-Cola, Gillette, Lucent Technologies, Boeing, GE and ABB is located in Asia. These organisations have been shifting the balance of resources to the parts of the world where markets exist. Organisations like Coca-Cola and Gillette are so used to running global businesses that they can respond to fluctuations in the marketplace very quickly. Consequently at the start of economic problems in Asia in 1998, Gillette responded by announcing a significant reduction in staff in the region.

Operating globally can impact on leaders in a number of ways. Perhaps the most important is the requirement to work with others from a range of cultures. Leaders have to adapt very quickly to the diversity of cultural norms and customs to be able to work successfully in a global business. During the race skippers and crews had to work successfully across a range of cultures including Europeans, Chinese, Americans and Australians.

Apart from cultural differences there are local laws and regulations which must be understood and observed. From a personal perspective, leaders are likely to be required to travel extensively, communicate across time zones and accommodate different days of rest, for example Fridays in the Middle East. These factors impact on the work/life balance and add to the challenge and stress facing leaders.

To be successful as a global leader you must develop:
- a global mindset, open to the opportunities available
- a greater flexibility to be able to react fast to changes in the marketplace
- greater sensitivity to cultural differences and be able to work with a range of different cultures.

INCREASED COMPETITION RESULTING IN MERGERS AND ACQUISITIONS

Alongside globalisation we have seen the growth of mergers and acquisitions. The trend is away from 'small is beautiful' and towards 'domination' of the marketplace. Organisations either recognise the power of two organisations in the same marketplace coming together and the economies of scale possible if the organisations are similar in terms of products or services offered, or they may seek to broaden the business portfolio by moving into associated markets and gaining additional benefits through diversity of products and services offered.

The challenge from the people perspective is the merging of cultures and re-alignment of values and goals. Large bureaucratic organisations can clash with a smaller entrepreneurial organisation in a takeover scenario, destroying the passion and initiative of people from the smaller business. In reality 70 per cent of mergers fail, according to Clutterbuck and Cage (2001). They do not achieve the financial or strategic goals, or deliver the expected synergies.

The high-profile worldwide merger of computer companies Compaq, Digital and Tandem took place in 1996. In New Zealand the names of Digital and Tandem have been forgotten and Compaq is achieving a revenue increase of 15 per cent a year, according to Tapsell (2001). The key to success was building a common corporate culture very quickly so that everyone was heading in the same direction, and the people from the three companies united behind the one brand of Compaq.

The new CEO took over at the beginning of 2000, just after the new building for the merged organisation was built but in time to influence the interior. It was fitted out with glass walls to help nurture an open culture. Work stations and walls could be moved easily, giving the building a dynamic feeling. The company has created an environment where people feel it is a good place to be.

> The skills of leaders required following mergers and acquisitions are summarised as:
> - flexibility and resilience to survive and grow in a newly merged organisation
> - good communication skills to take others with you
> - a clear focus on aligning the values and goals.

THE DEMISE OF THE HIERARCHY – NEW FORMS OF ORGANISATION

The organisations of the past were designed for efficiency in a stable environment. The typical organisation was large, bureaucratic and with a command-and-control style of leadership. As the world changed in the 1980s, a number of issues emerged:

- How can cost be reduced?

- How can the organisation become more flexible to respond to change?
- How can organisations help staff become more innovative and creative?
- How can organisations react faster to change?

In the face of recession in the 1980s organisations were forced to downsize to help achieve and sustain competitive advantage. Layers were stripped out and organisations became leaner, meaner and flatter. Leadership with its emphasis on involvement and flexibility, became more appropriate in an era requiring speed of reaction and allowing staff greater freedom for innovation.

The new-style organisation has become boundaryless as strategic partnerships and outsourcing of certain activities have led to employment of staff on short-term contracts. This has led to the breakdown of organisations as we knew them, causing fragmentation and bringing greater inconsistency, a more diverse culture and more virtual team-working. All these changes require different styles of leadership, more flexibility and styles that give people more control over their lives.

Today many leaders are faced with project managing people without accountability for them. They may be contract workers or work for other organisations, or portfolio workers with commitments with a range of organisations. This requires a different set of influencing and communication skills, particularly when the team is located in a number of locations.

Flexible work patterns and the work/life balance

Traditionally leaders and their people worked in close proximity, putting in similar hours. Today many leaders have to lead virtual teams that come together when meetings are arranged. The people work at different times and are based at different locations, often working from home. Flexible working has increased as a result of:

- the shift in employment away from manufacturing towards knowledge work, which requires less office space
- the drive to reduce costs

- the growth of portable computers and mobile phones, allowing people to work any time, anywhere
- the growth of global companies
- the increase of dual-career couples with family commitments requiring more flexible work patterns.

According to IRS Employment Trends (2001), ICL, Abbey National and BT have experienced increased productivity and greater motivation, in addition to reduced costs, from flexible working schemes. Abbey National piloted a flexible scheme in 1998 for 20 employees working on group technology, enabling them to work from their own office, another Abbey National site or at home. The pilot scheme was very successful and Abbey National has developed a formal flexible working policy that will be available to all areas of the business.

Home working is not always the best option. According to Cole (2001), Sun Microsystems in the US has set up satellite work centres. These offer comfortable work areas, a series of cubicles with a high-speed network connection, ergonomic desk furniture and good lighting, and support office equipment such as fax machines and copiers. These office centres are more attractive than working from home, where there are distractions and where separating work and home becomes more difficult. The location of the centres cuts down on travelling time for people commuting in the heavily populated Silicon Valley, California.

The skippers in the race had to lead a 24-hour operation. In order to manage this they operated a watch system. This put pressure on them to ensure that all crew members were integrated. The crew also changed leg by leg, with two new members joining and two leaving at each port of call. In the early stages of the race the skippers experienced difficulty ensuring that the new members became integrated with the existing crew. As the race progressed, however, they developed mechanisms for integrating these new crew members. For example, skippers put more emphasis on communicating with the new crew members, and some of the yachts devised a system whereby the crew leaving would brief the incoming members.

One of the issues of the 21st-century is managing the work/life balance and this is helped by flexible work approaches. Barnett and Hall (2001) state that balance is not just a personal issue, it is a business issue. In the new economy, success will go to those businesses that win the war for talent, and work/life balance is a critical success factor. Telecoms company Motorola is a winner. Its strategy for entering China was centred on balance. Relationships came first, then work and then doing business. In the Western world the organisation's approach had been business first, then working together, then relationships.

Flexible working and establishing an effective work/life balance might have great benefits for business, but leaders will need to adjust to the challenges presented by these trends:

- **Communication**
  This needs to be carefully managed, supplementing audio and video conferencing and electronic communication with regular face-to-face meetings with the team and with people individually to ensure everyone is properly informed.

- **Performance management**
  This needs to place more emphasis on goal achievement rather than hours worked. Leaders need to develop monitoring and control procedures to ensure people do not work excessively long hours.

- **Leadership style**
  Leaders have to be flexible, build trust with people, and allow staff a high degree of control over their work.

- **Managing relationships**
  Leaders must work hard on building relationships with their people.

- **Integrating new team members**
  Leaders have a more difficult task building a cohesive team with flexible workers. Mechanisms must be put in place to ensure new people become a part of the team.

- **Managing the work/life balance**
  Leaders need to encourage a good work/life balance for their people by 'modelling the way' themselves. They will need to adopt a leadership style which allows people to control their work.

THE CHANGING PSYCHOLOGICAL CONTRACT AND THE WAR FOR TALENT

Human capital is now widely recognised as a key to competitive advantage in the new economy. As the economy has become more prosperous and talent more scarce, power has shifted away from the employer to the employee, resulting in a different relationship between the two – and giving rise to a rethink of the psychological contract.

In the past people joined an organisation with an expectation of a job for life, career progression and reward for service. In return they were highly committed to the organisation and had a strong work ethic. Today people no longer have the same attachment to their employer. They expect more responsibility and accountability, to be stretched and challenged. In turn people are expected to achieve results and are rewarded accordingly. The younger generations, known as X and Y, have never experienced difficulty in obtaining employment. Job security, which employers can no longer provide, may be less important to some younger people and they expect to move jobs more frequently than older people. The 'New Deal' therefore carries with it a range of different expectations on both sides. This has implications for leaders who need to operate in ways that will get buy-in rather than expecting automatic commitment.

The skippers in the race had to cope with a different relationship with their crews. As crew members had paid to take part in the race, they expected to achieve their personal goals and therefore the skippers needed to earn the crews' respect.

The 'New Deal' puts considerable pressure on employers, and coming at a time when talent is scarce, organisations and their leaders need to consider carefully the strategies they adopt to retain their talent. In particular, leaders need to ask themselves whether their staff experience satisfaction with their work, feel involved and self-fulfilled, and have an opportunity for development. One group identified as having a rather different attachment to work is referred to as Generation X.

Generation X – different times, different minds

The Generation Xers were born between 1965 and 1980. They constitute a significant proportion of today's working population, shaping attitudes and expectations of the workforce. A working paper for think-tank Demos by David Cannon (1995) entitled *Generation X and the New Work Ethic* summarises all the main research conducted on this group of people. The paper outlines why this generation are different, in essence being shaped by prevailing economic and social forces, and how they have developed with very different attitudes from their predecessors.

Factors influencing the development of Generation X include:
- Invasive media – including TV, VCR, DVD and satellite TV. This is a generation who do not read so much and are accustomed to receiving information at a fast rate in a simplistic form.
- The 'global generation' – described as the first global generation, joined together by a sophisticated knowledge of consumer products, for example Nike, Benetton and Windows. They also think more about global issues, having been sensitised to ethical issues as a result of working practices of brand leaders reported in the media. They are more likely to have travelled, which once more broadens their horizons.
- Accessible communication and computer tools – they are the first generation to use computers as children. They are very at home with the Internet and the mobile phone. This is the generation that communicates using text messages.
- New attitudes – the generation have different attitudes demonstrated by:
  - decline of trust – in the area of relationships, education leading anywhere, security of employment and personal relationships
  - 'it's up to me' – a self-reliant group who look after themselves
  - independence and choice – a generation who, if they don't like their work situation, will walk away. They are prepared to work hard but place a high priority on the leisure and social aspects of their life. They want flexibility, autonomy, opportunity to develop and a good balance to their lives.

The materialistic, ethical and disposable society

Some members of Generation X have a strong need for wealth and are not prepared to wait for things to come. They may be prepared to work extremely hard for high monetary reward. Their life plan is to work hard early in their working lives so that they can retire at 40. This group of people will place less value on the work/life balance and will treat their job in the same way as they would treat possessions – a short shelf life, discarded for a new model. Managers need to be prepared for an individual, flexible approach when dealing with Generation Xers.

This is also the generation with strong ethical views. Organisations are recognising the importance of business ethics and social responsibility and their impact on their reputation. BP takes corporate social responsibility very seriously and can be seen as motivational for employees, according to a report by Overall (2001). He quotes David Rice, director of BP's policy unit, as saying: 'CSR [corporate social responsibility] comes out of what we do. Policies drive the way we behave.'

So, as a leader meeting the needs of Generation X you will have to:

- encourage them to contribute their ideas
- create flexibility of work
- give them the opportunity to develop themselves
- enable them to thrive on a project-based approach where they can see a beginning, an end and a new beginning
- be flexible, have good interpersonal competencies, be able to deal with failure and mistakes, praising people where necessary and equipping them to deal with conflict
- respect and encourage the work/life balance
- be aware of corporate social responsibility.

Generation Y

Having come to terms with the Generation X workers, leaders are now encountering Generation Yers, born after 1980, the next generation to hit the workplace. What are the characteristics of Generation Y?

- They are motivated and goal orientated – they recognise the value of education and they are very focused on achieving personal goals.
- They need regular reinforcement – this was the generation that was brought up with video games (the 'Nintendo generation').
- They are technologically wise – they have grown up with the high-speed, high-tech revolution: technology is just part of their lives.
- They like to work in teams – unlike the earlier generations, including the Generation Xers, the Y Generation are strong team players.
- They are good at multi-tasking – they have been brought up bombarded with stimulation and as a result can multi-task.

Verret (2000) cites Eric Chester, who was the first to use the Generation Y categorisation, as emphasising that Generation Yers have not experienced unemployment. Managing by intimidation and threats will not work in the future. Managers and leaders need to be able to manage and motivate this generation if they are to gain their commitment.

What are the strategies? As a leader you need to:
1. Let them know that what they do matters – this requires communication and involvement to develop understanding.
2. Tell them the truth – hiding bad news is not a good strategy.
3. Explain why they are asking them to do it – giving a reason will help ensure buy-in, and people need to know what is in it for them.
4. Learn their language – speak the same language and take the time to talk to people on a 1–1 basis.
5. Be on the look-out for rewarding opportunities – give praise for a situation well handled.
6. Praise them in public – make people stars.
7. Make the workplace fun – look for opportunities for a little light relief.
8. Demonstrate model behaviour – lead by example and don't expect them to do something that they could not deliver themselves.
9. Give them the tools to do the job – this covers technical and general skills training.

These strategies are what good managers and leaders should be practising with all generations to attract and retain staff in a shortage.

WOMEN IN EMPLOYMENT, DIVERSITY AND VALUING DIFFERENCES

Women make up 50 per cent of the workforce in the UK and as organisations face a shortage of talented people they can no longer ignore this segment of the workforce. Yet women make slow progress in reaching the top positions. In 2001, only one CEO in the top 50 companies of the FTSE 100 in the UK was a woman. Two CEOs in the Fortune 500 in the US were women (Olian, 2001). Carly Fiorino, appointed CEO of Hewlett-Packard in 1999, has struggled to focus media attention on the business issues of the company instead of the fact that she is a woman (*Financial Times*, 2001).

Changes in demographics and a chronic skills shortage in the US have encouraged employers to face up to the importance of recruiting a more diverse workforce. Coy (2000) states that the manager of IBM's diversity programme claimed that in 2000 there were 350 000 unfilled jobs in the US technology industry. (Although subsequently there was a downturn in the IT sector, resulting in the shedding of jobs.) IBM has a range of projects to develop talent among women, blacks, Asians, homosexuals and other groups to fight the war for talent.

Eastman Kodak, based in Rochester, New York, tended in the past to retain its staff because people knew they could have a good career without having to move to another company. However, in the early 1990s Kodak was forced to cut back staff, thus losing the concept of loyalty from the employment package. Today it employs few people under 30, and many are nearing retirement. Yet despite an ageing workforce, Kodak retains a reputation of innovation and invention. This is applied to its approach to the war for talent and diversity. According to Cole (2000), the vision for diversity goes way beyond racial and gender profiles. Diversity is viewed as valuing each person for their unique skills and talents.

More and more women are returning to work after having children, putting pressure on organisations to develop family-friendly policies and give more help to staff managing the work/life balance. This is a category requiring a more personal approach with opportunities such as career breaks, part-time work or job-sharing schemes.

Skippers and crew were selected to achieve diversity, although the skipper population was less diverse. Of the skippers, two were Australian, and the age span ranged from the youngest skipper at 26 to the oldest at 38. There were two women selected, although one resigned after the collision coming out of Wellington Harbour. Greater diversity was achieved among the crew in terms of age, race and sex in comparison with the skippers.

WHAT ARE THE IMPLICATIONS FOR THE LEADERS OF TODAY?

The key drivers of technology and globalisation have resulted in critical changes that organisations need to address to achieve and sustain competitive advantage. Each of these changes prompts the need for certain leadership characteristics. These skills were very applicable to the skills required of the skippers in the race, managing in a hostile, turbulent and changing environment.

LESSONS

As a leader today you need to:

1. be able to cope with discontinuity and uncertain environments

2. be risk aware and able to take risks

3. be able to adopt new work practices and be less detached from your staff

4. be flexible to react rapidly to change

5. be prepared to help others to learn instead of viewing information as power

6. remain sensitive to people's needs and be able to create an environment in which people can enjoy their work, feel fulfilled and enjoy a good work/life balance

7. be committed to involvement and development of others

8. remain open to the ideas of others

9. be able to give feedback and recognition

10. be able to handle conflict.

REFERENCES

Baker, S. and Capell, K. (2001) 'Wireless warrior', *Business Week:* New York, 21 May.

Barnett, R. and Hall, D. (2001) 'How to reduce hours to win the war for talent', *Organisational Dynamics*, Vol. 29, No. 3, pp. 192–210.

Cannon, D. (1995) *Generation X and the New Work Ethic*, Demos: London.

Clutterbuck, D. and Cage, S. (2001) 'Communications in mergers and acquisitions: keeping the ship on course', *Training Journal*, May.

Cole, C. (2000) 'Kodak snapshots', *Workforce*, June.

Cole, C. (2001) 'Sun Microsystems' solution to traffic that doesn't move? Satellite work centers', *Workforce*, January.

Coy, P. (2000) 'The creative economy', *Business Week*: New York, 28 August.

Deal, T. and Kennedy, A. (1999) *The New Corporate Cultures*, Orion Business Books: London.

Financial Times (2001) 'A clear perspective from above the glass ceiling: The chief executive of Hewlett-Packard is confronting the issue of sexist stereotypes in business', 22 August.

Gibson, R. (ed.) (1998) *Rethinking the Future*, Nicholas Brealey Publishing: London.

Green, H. and Sharpe, R. (2001) 'How to reach John Q Public', *Business Week*: New York, March 26.

Henley Management College (2000) 'E.Business-Management in the New Economy', Henley Management College: Henley on Thames.

IRS Employment Trends (2001) 'Managing flexible workers', *Performance Management*: London, 723 March.

Katzenbach, J. R. (2000) *Peak Performance*, Harvard Business School Press: Boston.

Kunii, I. (2001) 'Look out, DoCoMo – someone's gaining on you', *Business Week*: New York, 21 May.

Olian, J. (2001) 'A woman's place', *Executive Excellence*, August.

Overall, S. (2001) 'Ethical cleansing', *Personnel Today*, 4 September.

Tapsell, S. (2001) 'Creating a can-do culture', *Management NZ*, May.

Teece, D. (2000) 'Strategies for managing knowledge assets: The role of firm structure and industrial context', *Long Range Planning*, 33, pp. 35–54.

Verret, C. (2000) 'Generation Y: Motivating and training a new generation of employees ideas and trends', *hotel-online.com*, November.

Vishwanath, V. and Mulvin, G. (2001) 'Multi-channels: The real winners in the B2C internet wars', *Business Strategy Review*, Vol. 12, Issue 1, pp. 25–33.

3

LEADERSHIP IN
TURBULENT TIMES

This chapter aims to give the reader an understanding of the different leadership theories and research. It will also demonstrate which skills and attributes are needed to be an effective leader in a turbulent and hostile business environment. The leadership theories will be presented from an historical perspective, to demonstrate the way thinking has developed over the years in response to the changing demands on leaders. Brief parallels will be drawn between the theories and the research findings. More detailed analysis of the research will be presented in Chapters 5 and 6.

Research was conducted during the BT Global Challenge race through interviews with the skippers and crew, using the critical incident method. Data was mapped onto a modified version of the Woodcock Building Blocks (1989) which gave a valuable insight into the management aspect of leadership and helped to differentiate between high and lower performance. It was also mapped onto the elements of emotional intelligence put forward by Higgs and Dulewicz (1999). Further analysis of the data and comparative analysis between high-performing and lower-performing skippers revealed further attributes associated with effective leadership and achievement of high performance. Leadership styles identified by Blanchard *et al.* (1985) were also tracked.

SITUATIONAL/CONTINGENCY APPROACH – WHAT IS THE MOST EFFECTIVE STYLE OF LEADERSHIP FOR A PARTICULAR SITUATION?

The situational or contingency approach to leadership took the view that successful leadership depended on the leader matching his style to the particular situation. This approach focused attention on the behaviour of successful leaders. Hersey and Blanchard (1969) conducted research to identify the most important variables in determining leadership style – their approach is appropriate for managing others on a one-to-one basis within the team rather than the team as a whole – and worked to the following definitions:

- Leadership: 'An influence process, working with and through others to accomplish the goals of the organisation.'
- Leadership styles: 'The pattern of behaviours that you use with others as perceived by them.'

For Hersey and Blanchard, leadership style is determined by two independent categories of behaviour: 'directive' behaviour that is task-focused, and 'supportive' behaviour which emphasises relationship building with a person.

When leaders use 'directive' behaviour they:

- set goals and objectives
- plan and organise work schedules
- communicate priorities
- clarify roles and responsibilities
- determine evaluation criteria and standards
- check work
- show or tell subordinates how to do a specific task.

When leaders use 'supportive' behaviour they:

- listen to problems (job or non-job related)
- give praise and encouragement
- invite input and suggestions
- give information about the organisation
- facilitate problem solving
- disclose information about themselves.

The level of directive and supportive behaviour used defines the leadership style. If a lot of the behaviour is used the level is high, if little or no behaviour is used the level is low.

There are four distinctive 'styles':
- directing style: high direction, low support
- coaching style: high direction, high support
- supporting style: low direction, high support
- delegation: low direction, low support.

The important question is, however, under what circumstances is it most appropriate to adopt a particular combination? Blanchard *et al.* (1985) state that no one leadership style is always correct. They believe each style can be effective according to the situation and must primarily be based on the manager's judgement of a person's willingness and ability to perform a particular task. This is referred to as the 'developmental level' of the individual. In fact, individuals progress through four stages of development (D1, D2, D3 and D4) according to their level of:

- competence – a function of knowledge and skills gained from education, training and experience
- commitment – a function of a person's level of confidence and motivation.

It is thus the individual's level of competence and commitment that dictates which style is most appropriate for the leader to use. Each leadership style is outlined below, identifying the development level of the individual and demonstrating how this assessment is reached. The Blanchard Model of Situational Leadership is shown in Figure 3.1.

The 'directing style': high direction, low support

For a person who is willing but lacks competence (Development Level 1). The leader who uses the directing style actively organises and directs the work of others and makes each person accountable for specific activities and outcomes. Motivation is achieved by clear objectives of what needs to be done, when and how.

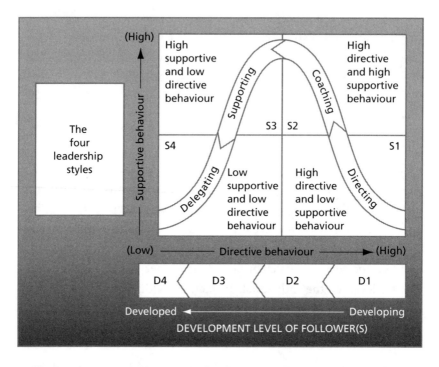

FIGURE 3.1 The Blanchard Situational Leadership Model
(Reproduced from Blanchard, K., Zigarmi, P. and Zigarmi, D. (1985)
Leadership and the One Minute Manager, with permission of HarperCollins Publishers Ltd)

The 'coaching style': high direction, high support

For a person who has developed some competence but where motivation or confidence is low (Development Level 2). Here, the leader sets high but realistic standards, explaining what needs to be done and why. People are motivated from receiving feedback and having a high level of personal involvement in the work.

The 'supporting style': low direction, high support

With the supporting style the leader recognises and praises good work. They are open, supportive and appreciative and motivate people by allowing them to structure their own work. This style is appropriate for the person who has high competence but whose motivation or confidence is low (Development Level 3).

The 'delegating style': low direction, low support

Here, the leader assigns tasks and responsibilities and allows people room to follow their initiative. The leader monitors results and motivates people by allowing them control and showing respect. This style is appropriate for the person who has high competence coupled with high motivation and confidence (Development Level 4).

Effective leadership means not only selecting the right style for the right situation but also executing the given style well. To achieve high performance, leaders must put energy into systematically developing each of their people to the stage where the delegating style becomes most appropriate. Here, leaders are most likely to attain the best performance from their team and are themselves freed from more routine tasks, allowing them to keep a broader perspective, be more inspirational and concentrate on 'value-added' work.

> *' I have changed my style as the race has progressed. I am now able to stand back more. I now have two very strong watch leaders, they manage their teams really well. The crews respond well to them. '*

The different leadership styles used by the various skippers were monitored during the race. By the end, the high-performing skippers had naturally recognised the need for flexibility of style and provided a good example of the situational leadership model being used well.

By leg 6, the last long leg of the race, 5 of the 12 skippers were showing evidence of using all four styles. This quote illustrates the awareness of the skipper to the leadership style they were using: 'If you can delegate early on and get a bunch of people to feel responsible, it makes the project a dream. In this stopover I don't have to be on the yacht, I can leave the boat preparation to the crew.'

The following quote represents the flexibility shown by all of the top four skippers: 'I feel I am strong on delegation. From the outset I made the decision not to sail the boat. I run the yacht through the watch leaders and support them in doing this, we discuss ideas and issues. I make the important sailing decisions. In the last leg I have spent time coaching people who were good at certain tasks to improve their performance.'

Some of the lower performing skippers placed far too much reliance on the directing style towards the end of the race. During the race these skippers had lost self-confidence and self-belief which had a profound effect on the way these skippers performed. One particular skipper used a directive style extensively: 'The skipper expects the crew to do what he says, there is no attempt to persuade the crew. Leadership only works when the skipper has gained the respect of the crew'.

> *' The skipper is still concerned with micro-managing. He doesn't know when to leave things alone. '*

Other lower performing skippers also failed to use the right style in the right situation. On leg 4 senior managers from sponsoring companies joined the race for one leg. On one yacht one of these managers took control of the situation in a crisis in the absence of any direction from the skipper: 'Following a critical incident an executive legger took control. The crew all rallied to the call and I realised the need for the use of a directive style and clear, positive instructions in a crisis'.

The situational leadership model represents an easy, common-sense approach and is still used by organisations to help develop people to manage individuals within their team on a one-to-one basis. While this theory helps leaders develop their team and adjust their leadership style to different situations, it is not enough on its own to account for outstanding performance. It sees leadership as a set of enduring personal characteristics rather than as a means of achieving longer-term goals of importance for organisational success.

ACTION-CENTRED LEADERSHIP – WHAT DO LEADERS DO?

John Adair (1983) focuses on what leaders actually do. The effectiveness of the leader, he argues, depends upon meeting three areas of need within the work group:

- need to achieve the task
- need for team maintenance
- individual needs of group members.

This is depicted by Adair in the form of three overlapping circles, as shown in Figure 3.2. Adair originally used this model in the 1970s for Sandhurst Military College where the environment was more predictable than the current business environment. The three circles were subsequently drawn inside a bigger circle representing environmental factors.

The leader needs to be constantly aware of what is happening in the team in terms of the three circles and maintain an appropriate balance. Adair more recently identified the concept of shared leadership on the one hand and, on the other, the importance of the leader maintaining distance from the team.

Like the situational leadership model, this model is still used by organisations today helping leaders meet the three sets of needs. During their selection, the skippers completed a questionnaire to identify the importance they attached to each of the three circles. They used the model when leading their teams during the race to ensure they achieved an appropriate balance between the three sets of needs. They received feedback after the selection process and were aware of the emphasis they gave to each of the sets. One skipper was quite surprised that he placed most emphasis on task needs; 75 per cent of the skippers focused on team needs.

FIGURE 3.2 John Adair (1983) Action-centred leadership

The example outlined below shows how one skipper used the Adair model to act appropriately after a traumatic accident. The skipper recognised the need to get people focused on a task and gave crew members jobs to do. He focused on the team needs by giving the whole team the chance to discuss the accident. He also spent time with team members on a one-to-one basis to take care of individual needs: 'Once out there I kept the crew busy with jobs but I knew these would run out. In the afternoon I sat down with the crew with tea and talked about what had happened. I had a quiet word with those I could see were suffering more than others.'

Other skippers recognised that they had lost the balance between the three sets of needs. One skipper had a problematic crew member on one of the legs. He realised he had spent so much time trying to sort out the issues that he had lost focus on the race and the team as a whole suffered: 'Emotionally it was quite draining with problems with crew members. I had regular briefings with the watch leaders to discuss how to handle the situations.'

Another skipper became very task-focused during one of the legs. He concentrated on the long-term goal of being in the top three and lost sight of the shorter-term goals. The crew were unhappy and felt the pressure was too intense. They started to look after just themselves and there was much less team spirit. The skipper noticed the lack of fun and switched the emphasis away from the task slightly to redress the balance: 'There were different vibrations from the crew. We made mistakes on board as a team. When things were going well, then they acted as a team. When things did not go so well they acted as individuals.'

MANAGEMENT AND LEADERSHIP

If one wishes to distinguish leadership from management or administration, one can argue that leaders create and change cultures, while managers and administrators live within them.

Edgar Schein, writer

In the 1960s, 1970s and early 1980s there was still no clear view of what actually constituted leadership and, as a consequence, the emphasis remained on developing managers. Zaleznik (1977), one of the early writers to differentiate between management and leadership, argued, however, that it was not possible to develop people to be both effective managers *and* effective leaders. He believed that managers and leaders were different types of people with different motives, different personal histories and different ways of thinking and acting.

Zaleznik differentiated between managers and leaders on the basis of four criteria:

1. Attitudes towards goals – managers view goals impersonally, aligning them with organisational necessities. Leaders, however, adopt a personal approach to goals, reflecting their own visions and strongly held beliefs.
2. Conceptions of work – managers view work as an enabling process, involving strategy formulation, decision making, planning, negotiating, rewarding and coercing. Leaders develop new ways of tackling problems and convey their ideas through images that excite and inspire.
3. Relation with others – managers like to work with people but prefer to maintain a low level of emotional involvement in their relationship with others. In contrast, leaders relate to people in a more emotional and intuitive way. As a result, leaders generate strong feelings, both positive and negative, in their people.
4. Sense of self – managers are those people whose early lives have been relatively straightforward and who have been required to make only minor adjustments to life in the process of growing up. Managers are therefore more suited to roles where they are required to strengthen the existing organisation and the exercise of duty and responsibility. Leaders, in contrast, have struggled in their early lives to achieve a sense of order and have developed through personal learning in the face of adversity. They are therefore individuals who seek change.

Identifying management skills

Woodcock (1989) identified 11 'building blocks' for team effectiveness:

- Balanced roles – blend of different talents and abilities.
- Clear objectives and agreed goals – clarity and commitment to goals and objectives.
- Openness and confrontation – team members able to state their views and differences of opinion.
- Support and trust – both can be achieved when team members feel free to talk and can receive help from others.
- Co-operation and conflict – working together and conflict are viewed as necessary parts of team interaction.
- Sound procedures – sound working methods and decision making give rise to achievement of objectives.
- Appropriate leadership – a flexible and appropriate style for the team.
- Regular review – on the way the team works together and gives feedback to individual team members.
- Individual development – giving attention to the development of individual team skills.
- Sound inter-group relations – relationships with other teams.
- Good communications – communication within the team and externally.

(The 11 building blocks for team effectiveness are reproduced by permission of Gower Publishing from *A Manual of Team Development*, 2nd edition. Woodcock, M. (1989).)

These building blocks are included because they were used to structure interviews to track team effectiveness during the race. Interviews were conducted with an appointed crew member from each yacht at every port of call and analysis of the data provided a useful insight into the management skills and attributes associated with management.

Although these building blocks were first identified in the late 1970s, the broad structure is still applicable today. For example, in 1996 Owen conducted case research into how the Red Arrows, the RAF aerobatics display squadron, developed their top-performing teams. Having observed and talked to the Red Arrows, Owen took Woodcock's 'building blocks' one stage further and created the synergy chain.

Table 3.1 identifies the categories of behaviour used in the BT Global Challenge research. Content analysis of the interviews conducted, using the critical incident method, produced extensive data on the way the skippers managed and led their teams.

As Table 3.1 demonstrates, 'management' is focused on having the right systems and procedures in place. To achieve high performance, of course, managers need effective management skills, including efficiency and the good use of resources. This contrasts with the passion, sense of purpose and ability to motivate others more characteristic of leadership. These leadership attributes are also important to achieve high performance in a different set of circumstances. Management and leadership are different, and within certain environments can be equally important.

TABLE 3.1 A comparison of management and leadership

Management (resource/process) HEAD	Leadership (creative/inspiring) HEART
Agreed goals	Vision
Preparation and planning	Values
Communication management	Recognition
Review	Motivation
Control management	Shared purpose
Roles	Support and trust
Discipline	Humour/fun
Feedback 1:1	Performance focus
Sound management procedures	Shared leadership

During the race the skippers encountered a range of situations and weather conditions which required different skills and capabilities to achieve high performance; sometimes the skipper's leadership skills were needed, at other times a management approach was more suitable. In the ports of call, for example, management skills were most important as the skippers had to review how the team had worked together during the previous leg and prepare the yacht for the next part of the race. The skippers also needed to ensure they had the right weather and navigational data to help prepare and plan their strategies for the next leg. Just prior to the restart, however, some of the skippers began to prepare their teams for the next leg. This involved sharing their vision for the leg and inspiring and engaging the team for what lay ahead. These are behaviours associated with leadership.

TEAM LEADERSHIP

When new teams come together they go through a process of development before they can become effective. Leaders need to be aware of this process and help the team move through the stages as quickly as possible to become an effective team. Tuckman (1965) identifies four main stages of team development.

Stage 1 – Forming

At this stage individuals are quite cautious towards one another, try to create an impression and tend to withhold how they are really feeling. Here the leader mainly makes the decisions and there is very little challenge by team members. Although the teams had met up prior to the race start, some were still at the forming stage when they started racing.

Stage 2 – Storming

At this stage the team start to get to know one another better and individuals will start to give opinions and express views more forcibly. Here there is potential for conflict. This is an important stage because if it is successful new arrangements will be made for working together and systems and procedures will be improved. It is a necessary stage if the team are to be able to handle conflict effectively in the future. The leader still mainly makes the decisions but will encounter more questioning.

Stage 3 – Norming

Once the conflict starts to be managed effectively the team start to develop their own norms of acceptable behaviour. This is an important time for the team to co-operate and identify common ways of working together, standards of performance and ways of achieving team goals. By this stage the leader begins to share decision making with the team.

Stage 4 – Performing

Once the team has progressed through the three earlier stages they are ready to become a high-performance team. At this stage they can focus on the shared goal and performance of the tasks to be successful. The leader here delegates some of the decision making to the team and assumes a role of arbitrator.

Data was collected throughout the race to determine the level of team development. High-performing skippers worked hard with their teams to ensure they were working effectively together. The lower-performing skippers were less successful at managing conflict that had a serious impact on team development. In the race the skippers had a big challenge in terms of team development because the composition of their teams changed every leg. This meant they had to focus on team building throughout the race if the team was to be effective. Findings related to team development will be discussed in Chapter 5 and the impact of conflict on performance will be discussed in Chapter 10.

TRANSACTIONAL AND TRANSFORMATIONAL LEADERSHIP

In the late 1970s there was a fundamental change in attitudes to effective leadership. This was due, in particular, to recession-struck businesses that were forced to reduce costs and increase flexibility to stay ahead of the competition. During this period, many companies were:

- delayering
- downsizing
- decentralising
- creating multi-functional teams
- focusing on closeness to the client or customer.

Front-line staff who interfaced with the customer were often in the best place to understand how well the organisation was meeting its goals and what the organisation needed to do differently to better serve the customer/client. As organisations committed themselves to quality, innovation and value, people had to work differently and the leader's power was eroded. In parallel, the rate of change in the business environment was escalating and leaders were needed who could help transform businesses. This demanded new and different skills of leaders.

The distinction between transactional and transformational leadership was first made by McGregor Burns (1978). Although he was writing about political leadership, the distinction is equally applicable to business leadership. Sadler (1997), in a comparison of transactional and transformational leadership, put forward the following definitions:

Transactional leadership occurs when leaders set clear goals, understand the needs of their people and select appropriate motivating rewards.

Transformational leadership is the process of engaging the commitment of employees in the context of shared values and a shared vision. It is particularly relevant in the context of managing change. It involves relationships of mutual trust between leaders and led.

According to Bass (1985), the transformational leader motivates followers to do more than originally expected, and the extent of transformation is measured in terms of the leader's effect on their followers.

Bass identifies four basic components of transformational leadership:

1. Charismatic behaviours – having a clear vision and sense of purpose, these leaders are able to win followers' trust and respect. They build a base for future missions by showing people they can achieve more than they felt possible and in turn obtain extra effort from their people.
2. Individual consideration – paying attention to the needs and potential development of individual followers using delegation, coaching and constructive feedback.
3. Intellectual stimulation – encouraging others to find new ways of doing things, to question basic assumptions and consider problems from new perspectives.
4. Inspirational motivation – the behaviour of the leader which gives meaning and challenge to the work of their people.

Bass's model gives a useful basis for understanding how to lead during times of change and much of his research was validated on senior managers. Soon after this, Kouzes and Posner (1987) identified leadership as a process that people could be taught. Leaders were seen as 'earning' their influence from their people and colleagues, while leadership came simply from a strong belief in purpose and a willingness to express that purpose.

They identify five practices of leadership:

1. Challenging the process – leaders encourage others to come up with new ideas and new ways of approaching their job, problems and processes in the organisation. They encourage experimentation and innovation, which also implies they are prepared to take judicious risks.
2. Inspiring a shared vision – leaders create a dream, a vision about the future. They have a desire to change the way things are and to inspire others by finding out what their dreams, hopes and aspirations are and articulating a vision which

enables others to see how all will be served by a common underlying purpose.

3. Enabling others to act – leaders realise that they cannot achieve the vision on their own, so they seek and enlist the support and involvement of others. They also encourage collaboration, co-operation, build teams and empower others. Others may not only include staff whom they manage but also their managers and customers and suppliers.

4. Modelling the way – leaders must encourage the management process of planning and reviewing how progress is going and taking corrective action. In so doing they must also behave in a way which gains the respect and trust of others. They have considerable integrity since they are clear about their values and act in a manner consistent with them.

5. Encouraging the heart – leaders realise that achieving the vision is exhausting and at times frustrating. They maintain morale by recognising and celebrating others' achievements and by signalling how much they believe in and value their staff. Their expectations are positive and their praise genuine.

(Reproduced from Kouzes, J. and Posner, B. (1987) *The Leadership Challenge*. This material is used by permission of Jossey-Bass, Inc., a subsidiary of John Wiley & Sons, Inc.)

Behaviour identified by Kouzes and Posner was observed during the race. The high-performing skippers, for example, continuously looked to find new and better ways of doing things, especially when they were performing less well. In the early part of the race they coached people to help perfect sail changes and gybing. The high-performing skippers also recognised the importance of a shared purpose and vision for the future. This helped give the teams focus and direction. Support and involvement in decision making was also critical.

The majority of skippers realised the importance of both planning and subsequently reviewing progress and the way the team had worked together. Any changes were made if necessary as a result of the reviews.

For example, in the early stages of the race the crew felt the skippers didn't always communicate well enough with the crews. Several of the skippers included daily briefings as a result of this feedback and ensured there was time for two-way discussion. This receptiveness to feedback helped earn the crew's trust and respect.

Although the Kouzes and Posner model dates back to the 1980s it is still a popular approach as it identifies the skills and behaviours needed to inspire others in times of change. The leader's main responsibility is to create an environment in which people can best apply their knowledge and skills. This model has formed the basis of leadership development programmes and gives practical behaviours that leaders can adopt to be 'transformational'. It gives a good summary of the behaviours needed to inspire others.

Transactional and transformational leadership and the relationship with change and complexity

Kotter (1990) maintains that organisations require both transactional and transformational leadership and that leaders should ideally be competent in both. The balance between the two modes of leadership, Kotter argues, varies depending on the complexity of the organisation and the amount of change it is experiencing:

- High-change environments increase the need for leadership (transformational).
- Very complex situations increase the need for management (transactional).

The relationship between management and leadership is summarised in Figure 3.3.

Kotter emphasises that a major problem for organisations in dynamic, fast-changing environments is that they are 'over managed and under led'. In uncertain times, organisations need people who will lead them forward with confidence. Unfortunately, many good managers fail to make inspirational leaders and the challenge for organisations today is to ensure the right people are in the right jobs to

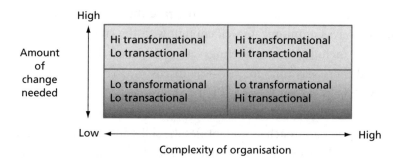

FIGURE 3.3   Relationship between change, complexity and leadership
(Adapted with the permission of The Free Press, a division of Simon & Schuster, Inc. from
A Force for Change: How Leadership Differs From Management by John P. Kotter.
Copyright 1990 John P. Kotter, Inc.)

achieve the right balance between 'managing' and 'leading'. Management
needs to ensure people can do what they have to do in the most efficient
way possible through:

- planning and organising
- resource management
- monitoring and controlling activities.

In dynamic, fast-changing environments leaders need to:

- provide vision and direction
- ensure people are aligned with the vision
- inspire and motivate people to act.

The BT Global Challenge research identified the need for both management and leadership skills and attributes. To compete in the BT
Global Challenge race with a novice crew, some members of which
changed after every leg, was a complex task. It required careful planning and organising, resource management, constant monitoring,
control and regular reviews.

Management skills

Overall the podium skippers exhibited all of the management attributes

' Prior to the start of the race I had a mindmap on the wall with all things I felt were important for the race. This helped me focus on what I had to do. '

listed on page 61. In contrast, by the end of the race there was very little evidence of most of these attributes being used by the skippers at the back of the fleet. Several skippers were very organised prior to the race, setting up project groups to handle the various activities including food, clothing, strategy, weather and team development.

Initially, the skippers were mostly task-focused and made more use of their management skills. They set goals with milestones on the way, allocating tasks and ensuring the right people were given the right roles. The high-performing skippers sustained a task focus throughout the race coupled with attention to the detail and meticulous preparation. One skipper described the preparation undertaken prior to the Wellington to Sydney leg: 'I knew this leg would be close, but no one would have believed that the first three yachts would be just four minutes apart. This is why a few days before we left Wellington I sent my No 2 to Sydney to discover as much as he could about the currents and conditions for sailing into Sydney Harbour. As a result we passed one yacht in the final approaches to Sydney to finish just 25 seconds behind the leader. Without the preparation and planning this may not have been the case.'

The lower-performing skippers tended to be less disciplined and lacked some of the management skills. In particular they did not use their resources so well or have shared goals. After criticism for a poor tactical decision one skipper said: 'The crew should realise that winning is not the only goal. It is about adventure and achievement.'

Some of the crew felt the skipper had downgraded the goal too much without debate. The skipper said on reflection: 'I wish I had pushed the goal to win harder at the start of the race.'

This example demonstrates the problem that some lower-performing skippers experienced in giving direction to their teams.

In addition, the physical environment was changing constantly and was sometimes quite hostile. These conditions required the skippers to use their leadership attributes to deal with a range of difficult and sometimes traumatic situations.

Leadership attributes

All the podium skippers demonstrated shared leadership, in other words they created an environment where pro-activity was encouraged, accountability shared and buy-in sought. They also maintained a focus on performance and inspired energy, drive and belief in the team that they could win the race.

One of the high-performing skippers described himself as very self-motivated and spent time encouraging the team to achieve the goals. He felt confident himself and inspired confidence and belief in others. Another skipper described how he left people to run their jobs on a day-to-day basis. As one crew member said: 'The skipper knows what he wants from people, he is confident, uses humour to good effect, and is trusted and respected by the crew. We all give of our best.'

The overall winning yacht very much attributed their success to getting the buy-in from the crew and shared belief: 'The single significant thing is getting the crew to be responsible for the outcome. They walk around this place with their heads held high because they are responsible for it. Everything we have done in the last two years has been the result of 30 people putting their heads together. Winning is the easy bit. But it's a battle to get there – whether you have got the stomach, the fight, the passion and the self-belief. On the last morning we had everyone on the rail and I looked at them and said, "We're going to win this leg." They looked back and I could see the self-belief click in.'

This feeling of self and shared belief separated the high-performing from the lower-performing yachts. At some stage during the race the lower-performing skippers lost this feeling of self-belief: 'I find it very difficult to influence the crew now. I have lost confidence and cannot motivate the crew or get my messages across.'

To lead in this dynamic, changing environment required leaders who could involve and highly motivate their team to ensure they performed at their best. The skippers therefore needed to be able to inspire the team with a clear sense of purpose, energise them and create an enthusiasm and desire within the team to give their best in what ranged from frightening to boring circumstances.

TRANSFORMATIONAL LEADERSHIP: A UK PERSPECTIVE

Much of the research discussed so far was conducted in the US. Alimo-Metcalfe and Alban-Metcalfe (2001), however, undertook a major investigation into the nature of leadership in the UK public sector, one of the first studies of its kind which included women in significant numbers. Analysis of responses from over 3500 managers and other professionals led to the identification of a model of transformational leadership that differs in complexity and tenor from the dominant US models. One reason for this difference may be that the study focused on 'nearby' leadership (i.e. the qualities and characteristics of leadership in 'bosses' with whom individuals had regular contact) rather than on 'distant' leaders, such as CEOs. From the model that emerged, a 360-degree questionnaire for assessing transformational leadership was developed.

More recently, Alimo-Metcalfe and Alban-Metcalfe (2001) have repeated the investigation in the UK private sector. There is a great deal of similarity between the public and private sector models, with three clusters of dimensions of leadership common to both, namely:

- leading and developing others
- personal qualities
- leading the organisation.

Specifically, Alimo-Metcalfe and Alban-Metcalfe identified the following factors as being fundamental to the nature of leadership:

- genuine concern for others
- empowers, delegates, develops potential
- political sensitivity
- decisive, determined, self-confident
- integrity and openness

- networker, promoter, communicator
- accessible, approachable
- clarifies boundaries, keeps others informed, involves others in decisions
- encourages critical and strategic thinking.

A further three dimensions emerged in the developmental model of the transformational leadership questionnaire (TLQ):

- intellectual versatility
- manages change sensitively
- risk-taker/entrepreneurial.

Alimo-Metcalfe and Alban-Metcalfe assert that the UK models of leadership share elements in common with US models, including qualities such as inspiring followers, encouraging them to challenge the status quo, creating an environment in which they are respected, valued and their aspirations and development needs take central stage. US models typically place 'vision' and 'charisma' at the top of the list of leadership qualities and suggest that the leader is a role model whom followers seek to emulate.

The UK public and private sector models, however, place the dimension of 'genuine concern for others' well-being' in the most prominent position in characterising leadership. This notion of leadership is much more akin to Greenleaf's (1970) notion of 'leader as servant'. Whether the difference in US and UK models of leadership is due to culture or methodology adopted, or the fact that the UK research included a substantial proportion of women as well as men, has yet to be investigated.

Alimo-Metcalfe and Alban-Metcalfe (2001) have also looked at gender and leadership style and found that the female bosses evaluated in their investigation were rated as significantly more transformational than their male counterparts. Other studies investigating the effects of gender on leadership style (e.g. Bass, Avolio and Atwater, 1996) found that women in general are significantly more likely to be rated as transformational, and men in general more likely to be rated as transactional or adopting a management-by-exception or *laissez-faire* style of leadership.

The two women skippers who took part in the race generally demonstrated similar behaviour to the men, adopting transactional leadership styles in common with many women in male-dominated sectors of business. They were operating in a very tough environment, and at least one had modelled her style on the male skippers who had taught her. One female watch leader, however, adopted a rather different style of leadership. She was described as very kind and caring, her team adored her and wanted to do well for her. She grew in confidence as the race progressed. Her team listened to her and respected her.

Alimo-Metcalfe and Alban-Metcalfe give a comprehensive overview of the factors associated with the nature of leadership and provide some interesting findings on gender and US/UK differences. There are also some interesting parallels between this work and the factors identified under the model of emotional intelligence put forward by Higgs and Dulewicz (1999).

UNDERSTANDING EMOTIONAL INTELLIGENCE

For many years psychologists have tried to identify those qualities other than IQ that determine success. In 1990 Peter Salovey and Jack Meyer were the first to adopt the term 'emotional intelligence' to describe the way people bring 'intelligence' to their emotions, and in 1996 Dr Daniel Goleman brought the concept to the attention of the world when he published his best-selling book *Emotional Intelligence – Why it can matter more than IQ*. Goleman partly supported his case for emotional intelligence being an important predictor of managerial performance by studying the physiological basis of emotional intelligence. He looked at three parts of the brain.

Neo-cortex

The neo-cortex is located at the top of the brain, overlaying the cortex, and is unique to man. It controls thinking, memory and reasoning functions – it allows people to think about their feelings and keeps feelings under control. It also appears to be at work when people experience fear or rage, stifling or controlling the feeling to enable the

person to deal more effectively with the situation. It brings more analytical or appropriate responses to emotional impulses modulating the
amygdala and other limbic areas of the brain. The left pre-frontal lobe
can switch off or calm down all but the strongest emotions. If an emotional response is needed, the neo-cortex works hand in hand with the
amygdala and other circuits in the emotional brain.

Hippocampus and amygdala

The hippocampus and amygdala are below the neo-cortex. The amygdala region is the brain's emotional memory. The amygdala helps
people recognise feeling. In an emotional emergency the amygdala,
with its extensive web of neural connections, allows it to capture and
drive the rest of the brain. A small bundle of neurons leading from the
thalamus to the amygdala allows the amygdala to receive impulses
direct from the senses and start to respond before messages have
reached the neo-cortex. The neo-cortex becomes swamped by the
amygdala. This is why people will sometimes say 'I can't think straight'.

The brain stem

The brain stem at the bottom of the brain controls the body and basic
instincts including survival.

Goleman's study is particularly appropriate in today's fast-moving and
often stressful business environment. When people are calm, he argues,
the neo-cortex functions at the optimal level – vital for understanding,
planning, decision making, reasoning and learning. Under these circumstances, people know how they are feeling and use these feelings to
guide their thinking and perform well. However, when people are
under intense pressure, the brain switches to 'survival mode' as energy
is directed from the neo-cortex to other sites to keep the senses hyper-
alert. At this stage, people may experience worry, panic, irritability,
anger and frustration, and will be incapable of operating rationally. In
extreme circumstances, emotions flood in and swamp the neo-
cortex – sometimes described as the 'amygdala hijack' – and this can
provoke an instant reaction with disastrous consequences.

Of course, people vary in their reaction to potentially stressful situations. More resilient people recover much quicker. These people are more action-orientated and start to think immediately about how to improve a situation. Others can take much longer to recover.

Higgs and Dulewicz (1999) researched emotional intelligence to help clarify exactly what the term means and help people understand its impact on performance in the work environment. They suggested the need for a new definition of emotional intelligence as follows:

Achieving one's goals through the ability to manage one's own feelings and emotions, to be sensitive to and influence other key people and to balance one's motives and drives with conscientious and ethical behaviour.

They went on to identify seven elements of emotional intelligence:

1. **Self-awareness** – awareness of one's own feelings and ability to recognise and manage these feelings in a way which one feels that one can control. This factor includes a degree of self-belief in one's ability to manage one's emotions and to control their impact in a work environment.
2. **Emotional resilience** – the ability to perform consistently under pressure in a range of situations and to adapt one's behaviour appropriately. The facility to balance the needs of the situation and task with the needs and concerns of the individuals involved. The ability to retain focus on a course of action or need for results in the face of personal challenge or criticism.
3. **Motivation** – the drive and energy to achieve clear results and to make an impact, and to balance both short and long-term goals with an ability to pursue demanding goals in the face of rejection or questioning.
4. **Interpersonal sensitivity** – the facility to be aware of, and take account of, the needs and perceptions of others when arriving at decisions and proposing solutions to problems and

challenges. The ability to build from this awareness and achieve 'buy-in' to decisions and ideas for action.

5. **Influence** – the ability to persuade others to change a viewpoint based on the understanding of their position and the recognition of the need to listen to this perspective and provide a rationale for change.

6. **Intuitiveness** – the ability to arrive at clear decisions and drive their implementation when presented with incomplete or ambiguous information, using both rational and 'emotional' or insightful perceptions of key issues and implications.

7. **Conscientiousness** – the ability to display clear commitment to a course of action in the face of challenge and to match 'words and deeds' in encouraging others to support the chosen direction. The personal commitment to pursuing an ethical solution to a difficult business issue or problem.

(The seven elements of emotional intelligence were adapted and reproduced from Higgs and Dulewicz (1999) *Making Sense of Emotional Intelligence* with permission of the publishers, the NFER-NELSON Publishing Company Limited, Darville House 2 Oxford Road East, Windsor, Berkshire SL4 1DF, England. All rights reserved.)

IS EMOTIONAL INTELLIGENCE THE KEY FOR LEADERS TO ACHIEVE HIGH PERFORMANCE?

Emotional intelligence is twice as important as IQ and technical skills in determining job success ... The higher up the organisation you go, the more important emotional intelligence becomes.

Daniel Goleman, BBC Radio 4, *Programme In Business*
(10 May 1999)

Goleman's strong belief in the importance of emotional intelligence over IQ and technical capability comes from his 1998 study which analysed competency models. These models captured what management believed were the skills and capabilities for excellence. Goleman worked with the Hay/McBer consultancy analysing the competency models from 188 companies, including global businesses such as Credit Suisse First Boston, Lucent Technologies and British Airways.

He determined which personal capabilities drove outstanding performance within these organisations and grouped them into three categories: purely technical skills, cognitive abilities and skills related to emotional intelligence. Goleman found that emotional intelligence was twice as important as the other two categories put together in predicting performance. Further work with the Hay/McBer company examining emotional competence for leadership showed that six emotional competencies distinguished stars from average performers:

- influence
- team leadership
- organisational awareness
- self-confidence
- the drive to achieve
- leadership itself.

Higgs and Dulewicz (1999), using data collected from a longitudinal study of general managers, also found evidence to support a relationship between emotional intelligence and career progression. Further organisational studies showed a link with performance.

During the race, there were interviews at every port of call focusing on the skipper's behaviour. These were conducted with both the skippers and the crew. Skippers were required to report on any critical incidents that had occurred during each leg and the way they had handled these incidents. The crew members interviewed also described critical incidents and reported back on the way the skippers had behaved. The behaviours were then mapped on to the seven elements identified by Higgs and Dulewicz to identify whether there was a relationship between emotional intelligence and high performance. The skippers were given ratings of high, medium or low for each of the seven elements based on the judgements drawn from the data collected from the interviews.

Overall, the ratings suggested a relationship between high performance and emotional intelligence. At the start of the race there was no clear differentiation. Towards the end of the race, however, the higher-performing skippers were rated higher on the elements than the lower-performing skippers. There was also data to show development of certain elements including self-awareness, emotional resilience and interpersonal sensitivity. In contrast, the lower-performing skippers were less able to access emotional intelligence behaviour with the loss of self-belief. A detailed analysis of the findings will be discussed in Chapter 5. Below is a sample of some of the evidence to support the findings that those rated high to medium performed better than those rated medium to low on the elements.

Self-awareness

A skipper who was rated low to medium was described as showing anger and frustration often and sometimes behaving without thinking.

> ❛ *The skipper's mood accounts for 50 per cent of the crew's mood.* ❜

After a tactical decision went wrong he retired to his bunk. He seemed unaware of the impact of his feelings on the crew. He had started to be aware of how he was feeling, but not aware enough. He was unable to control his feelings towards people he did not like or respect.

Emotional resilience

A skipper rated medium to high on emotional resilience was described as being very consistent and was open to being challenged. He was very level-headed and when sailing experienced no ups and downs. A crew member commented: 'In a crisis he is calm and collected and creates confidence in the crew, who respond well and maintain their performance.'

A skipper rated low on emotional resilience was described as having lost all consistency. He had difficulty handling tight situations and had lost every judgement and ability. When the racing was close he couldn't perform: 'He froze as he came into port. He panicked, fighting to hold the position.'

Interpersonal sensitivity

A skipper rated high on interpersonal sensitivity was described as being sensitive to others and a good listener and would listen to every viewpoint. He would use all the skills on the yacht and knew who to go to for input on issues: 'If there are any issues, the crew share problems with the skipper and "lance the boil".'

A skipper rated low on interpersonal sensitivity was described as insisting on doing things 'his way'. He didn't listen when suggestions were made and became defensive. Occasionally he discussed decisions but he was not necessarily consulting, just thinking aloud: 'He hasn't grasped he is dealing with professional adults with experience who could enhance performance.'

All examples of higher ratings were of higher-performing skippers, and those rated lower were lower-performing skippers, suggesting a relationship between emotional intelligence, behaviour and perform-ance.

Earlier research on the capabilities leaders need to be inspirational was conducted by Goffee and Jones (2000).

WHY SHOULD ANYONE BE LED BY YOU?

This is a question Goffee and Jones (2000) frequently ask executives while consulting with major organisations, and the result is usually a stunned hush. The question is pertinent – no leader can change or achieve much today without the support of followers. While they recognise that leaders need energy and vision, Goffee and Jones argue that there are four other qualities which can be honed by anyone prepared to dig deeply into their true selves. These qualities are not about results per se, but, vitally, they help leaders excel at inspiring people – capturing hearts, minds and souls. Goffee and Jones state that for leaders to be truly inspirational it is not enough to possess one or two of these qualities, they must possess them all.

1. **Showing vulnerability and selectively revealing their weaknesses.** When leaders reveal a weakness they show they are human, it builds trust and helps people get on board. It helps seem more

authentic. Leaders must be careful to be selective about the weaknesses they reveal. It would not look good if the finance director did not understand discounted cash flow. Weaknesses that are core to the leader's role should not be revealed.

2. **Relying heavily on intuition to sense the environment.**
When leaders are able to pick up signals in the environment, and sense what is going on without having to be told. They can easily gauge unexpressed feelings, can judge whether relationships are working or not and are sensitive to non-verbal cues. Leaders must, however, avoid becoming over-sensitive and projecting their own thoughts into the situation.

3. **Leading by showing tough empathy towards their people.**
Inspirational leaders empathise passionately and realistically with their people and care intensely about the work that they do. Those who show tough empathy are able to close the gap with their followers by identifying with the work of followers and entering their world by fitting in with the norms. Tough empathy is not soft: it is giving people what they need rather than what they want. It requires a balance between respect for the individual and for the task in hand, caring with detachment, which is not easy. Those who show tough empathy are more likely to show their true selves.

4. **Revealing differences.**
They dare to be different and in turn capitalise on what is unique about themselves. The difference is used to create a social distance and signal separateness. This may be represented by a different style of dress or differentiating on a quality such as creativity, loyalty or a particular expertise. Inspirational leaders use difference to motivate others to perform better.

(The qualities listed above were reprinted by permission of *Harvard Business Review* from 'Why should anyone be led by you?', Goffee, R. and Jones, G., September–October 2000. Copyright © 2000 by the Harvard Business School Publishing Corporation, all rights reserved.)

During turbulent times leaders need to hold their teams together. They must engage emotionally with their teams and reach the depth of understanding of themselves and others described by Goffee and Jones so that people do feel the person leading them is, in fact, the right one. This model appears particularly relevant for achieving high performance through inspiring leadership.

Analysis of the race data backs up these arguments, as the winning skippers all showed evidence of at least three of these qualities. The higher-performing skippers, for example, all showed evidence of sensing behaviour. By the end of the race, these skippers were recognising the importance of being a few steps ahead of their teams and keeping an outward focus to adjust their strategies for the race if necessary. They also knew how important it was to be sensitive to the emotional climate of the team at any moment in time.

The high-performing skippers were also able to keep themselves socially distant from the crew. They recognised the importance of building relationships with their teams but adopted strategies for keeping themselves a little bit separate – one of the skippers, for example, did not eat all meals with his team. Finally, these higher-performing skippers were more likely to show vulnerability than the lower-performing skippers. They were prepared to say they did not know the answer to something or to admit to having made a mistake. Tough empathy, however, was more difficult to identify from the data collected.

LEADERSHIP ATTRIBUTES FOR THE 21ST CENTURY

In his book *Organising Genius: The Secrets of Creative Collaboration* (1996), Warren Bennis states that a major challenge for leaders today is to encourage bright people to work together successfully and deploy their creativity. He describes his own difficulties as a university president, stating that trying to manage a group of individualistic academics was like 'herding cats'. Today's requirement is for creative collaboration and the ability to translate intention into reality – a strong contrast with the 20th-century mindset of control, order and prediction. Even today, though, Bennis feels too many organisations are overmanaged and underled, and stresses the need for leaders continually to reinvent themselves, their leadership roles and, ultimately, their organisations. Leaders today need to create an environment that embraces change, seeing it as an opportunity and not a threat.

In a more recent book Bennis (1999) identifies two types of people: 'inner directed' people who respond to internalised parental pressures and are rigid, unyielding and act on principles, and 'other directed' people who like to please others, are collaborative and adaptable. In today's world the leader needs, in particular, to develop the skills of collaboration to ensure understanding is captured. This, then, requires leaders to become 'other directed' people.

> Bennis emphasises the importance of four attributes:
> - to provide direction and meaning through purpose
> - to generate trust through integrity and authenticity
> - to create a sense of hope by providing optimism
> - to achieve results through a bias towards action.

For example, at the time Bennis was writing, unemployment rates in Silicon Valley, California, were 1.9 per cent. While these figures have changed since then, he warns that in such an environment collaborative skills are especially important. Very talented people need to be treated like 'volunteers' within the organisation and nurtured. Building collaborative relationships was paramount as these people could leave at any time for another employer.

The race posed similarly interesting leadership challenges for the skippers. The crews, for example, had volunteered and paid a significant sum to take part. Many had left positions of responsibility in which they themselves had been used to leading others. In addition, the very nature of the race – with tough climatic conditions and long periods in confined spaces – meant it was extremely important to build relationships with the crew and make them feel involved. Indeed, Manfred Kets de Vries in an interview with the Management Centre Bradford (MCB) in 2000 supported the importance of trust and emphasised the need for a strong leader in times of constant change when people get anxious and need a secure environment and guidance.

To increase understanding of leadership, Owen (2000) developed a model, the 'seven essences' of leadership:

1. Leadership is distinctly different to management and is not just something to be added to the job of a manager.
2. Everyone is born with some gift of leadership, be it great or small. It is part of the human spirit and should be expressed to the world.
3. Leadership is not the latest 'fad' but a timeless concept that has been studied and recorded for more than 3000 years in an attempt to understand this human phenomenon. We should use this abundance of knowledge.
4. Leadership starts with the individual and requires a journey of becoming your true self. This requires knowing and understanding who you are. Leadership begins with being.
5. Leadership requires us to understand and to listen to what is emerging in the world, share these experiences with others by connecting and then acting accordingly. This is the transforming part of leadership.
6. Leadership is expressed by everyone when people are connected and part of the whole rather than in separate components of a machine organisation.
7. Finally, leadership is about being followers as well as leaders; position or privilege is not what makes a leader.

(The seven essences of leadership were taken from *In Search of Leaders* by Hilarie Owen (2000) and reproduced with permission of © John Wiley & Sons Limited.)

This model is included because it brings together important aspects of leadership borne out by the research findings of the race that are not covered explicitly by other models discussed so far. Owen presents the view that leadership is a shared process, not just a role fulfilled by a few people. She gives an important focus on the leader as an individual with the need to tap into the inner potential possessed by everyone to become more effective as a leader. She also emphasises the importance of understanding oneself and being prepared to face the 'demons' that sometimes hold leaders back and impact negatively on self-belief.

LEADERSHIP IN TURBULENT TIMES – A VOYAGE OF DISCOVERY

This chapter has given an overview of the theories and research that help understand what makes an effective leader capable of achieving high performance. A certain blend of attributes and skills is clearly necessary for inspiring leadership, and being a skipper in the BT Global Challenge race provides a good parallel for leading in business. The skippers, just like many of today's business leaders, were in a highly competitive situation and had to achieve challenging targets. They also had to motivate their teams and ensure they achieved the best performance with the resources available to them.

Data collected during the race and subsequently analysed, comparing high-performing with lower-performing skippers, demonstrated a range of skills and capabilities that differentiated between these two categories. This section will pull together the various categories of behaviour that the skippers demonstrated. The categories needed by a leader today will be associated with the various parts of a yacht (see Figure 3.4).

The ballast in the yacht – the appropriate personal attributes and emotional intelligence behaviours

The ballast is needed in a sailing yacht to provide stability. In a similar way, a successful leader needs a number of fundamental attributes central to efficient management and effective leadership. These include self-belief, integrity, self-control and a sense of purpose. Emotional intelligence is also seen as a critical category of behaviour and is a part of other attributes and skills identified as being important for success.

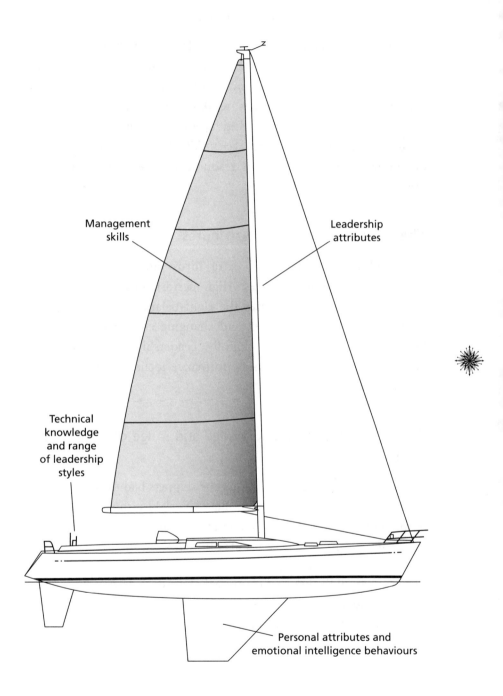

Management skills

Leadership attributes

Technical knowledge and range of leadership styles

Personal attributes and emotional intelligence behaviours

FIGURE 3.4 The yacht metaphor

The mainsail – the management skills

The mainsail does much of the work to drive the yacht forward and is particularly necessary to provide balance in heavy weather in a hostile environment – without it, in any conditions, performance would be mediocre. The mainsail might represent management skills. The review of previous theories and approaches and environmental circumstances suggests the necessary skills for today's leader include discipline, conflict management, resource management, planning and preparation.

The headsail – leadership attributes

The headsail gives the yacht extra thrust and power and could represent leadership attributes. High performance in a turbulent, complex environment requires the right balance of leadership and management. In this complex and changing environment different headsails must be deployed skilfully. Leadership attributes needed include a sense of purpose, a performance focus, shared belief and shared leadership.

The helm – technical knowledge and range of leadership styles

The helm gives the yacht direction. The skippers had to convert information into knowledge and then make the right technical decision to outperform the other yachts. Similarly, in business the right leadership style is important to achieve results through the team.

The next part of the book will outline the approach used to conduct the research and the major research findings associated with achieving high performance and inspiring leadership.

LESSONS

As a leader today you need to:

1. recognise the importance of management and leadership and the differences between the two

2. be sensitive to the needs of your team, and ensure you have flexibility to adopt the right leadership style in the right situation

3. understand and believe in yourself – leadership starts with your own sense of purpose and self-belief

4. be open to develop yourself as a leader and embrace change

5. be constantly on the lookout for new and better ways of doing things

6. nurture your team and build collaborative relationships with others

7. look out and read the external environment and be sensitive to the climate within the team

8. be committed to the involvement of all the team and sharing leadership with them

9. develop positive relationships with your team to build a climate of openness and trust.

REFERENCES

Adair, J. (1983) *Effective Leadership*, Pan: London.

Adair, J. (2000) Guru interview put on the Internet, MCB: Bradford.

Alban-Metcalfe, R. J. and Alimo-Metcalfe, B. (2000a) 'An analysis of the convergent and discriminant validity of the Transformational Leadership Questionnaire', *International Journal of Selection & Assessment*, 8, 3, 158–175.

Alban-Metcalfe, R. J. and Alimo-Metcalfe, B. (2000b) 'The Transformational Leadership Questionnaire (TLQ-LGV): A convergent and discriminant validity study', *The Leadership & Organisation Development Journal*, 21, 5, 280–296.

Alimo-Metcalfe, B. and Alban-Metcalfe, R. J. (2001) 'The development of a new transformational leadership questionnaire', *The Journal of Occupational & Organizational Psychology*, 74, 1, 1–27.

Bass, B. M., Avolio, B. J. and Atwater, L. (1996) 'The transformational and transactional leadership of men and women', *International Review of Applied Psychology*, 45, 5–34.

Bass, B. M. (1985) *Leadership and Performance Beyond Expectations*, Free Press: London.

Bennis, W. (1996) *Organising Genius: The Secrets of Creative Collaboration*, Addison-Wesley: Massachusetts.

Bennis, W. (1999) *Old Dogs, New Tricks*, Kogan Page: London.

Blanchard, K., Zigarmi, P. and Zigarmi, D. (1985) *Leadership and the One Minute Manager*, Willow Books, Collins: London.

Goffee, R. and Jones, G. (2000) 'Why should anyone be led by you?', *Harvard Business Review*, September/October.

Goleman, D. (1996) *Emotional Intelligence – Why it can matter more than IQ*, Bloomsbury Publishing: London.

Goleman, D. (1998) *Working with Emotional Intelligence*, Bantam Books: New York.

Goleman, D. (1998) 'What makes a leader?', *Harvard Business Review*, November–December.

Greenleaf, R. K. (1970) *The Servant as Leader*, Jossey-Bass: San Francisco CA.

Hersey, P. and Blanchard, K. (1969) *Management of Organisational Behaviour: Utilising Human Resources*, New Jersey: Prentice Hall.

Higgs, M. and Dulewicz, V. (1999) *Making Sense of Emotional Intelligence*, NFER-Nelson: Windsor.

Kotter, J. (1990) *A Force for Change: How Leadership Differs From Management*, Free Press: New York.

Kotter, J. (1990) 'What leaders really do', *Harvard Business Review*, May–June.

Kouzes, J. and Posner, B. (1987) *The Leadership Challenge*, John Wiley: New York.

McGregor Burns, J. (1978) *Leadership*, Harper and Row: New York.

Owen, H. (1996) *Creating Top Flight Teams*, Kogan Page: London.

Owen, H. (2000) *In Search of Leaders*, John Wiley: Chichester.

Sadler, P. (1997) *Leadership*, Kogan Page: London.

Tuckman, B. W. (1965) 'Development sequence in small groups', *Psychological Bulletin*, Vol. 63, pp. 384–399.

Woodcock, M. (1989) *Team Development Manual*, 2nd edition, Gower: Aldershot.

Zaleznik, A. (1977) 'Managers and leaders: are they different?', *Harvard Business Review*, May–June.

II
RESEARCH
FINDINGS

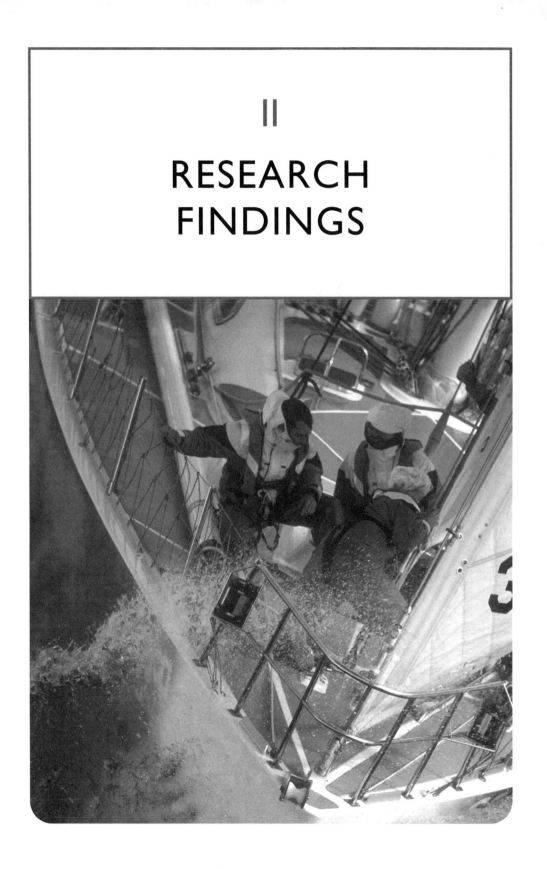

4

WHAT WAS THE CHALLENGE?

INTRODUCTION

This chapter provides an outline of the research study undertaken during the BT Global Challenge Round the World Yacht Race 2000/1. It will address:

- background and reason for the research study
- research models used
- research methodology
- process of data analysis.

Background

The BT Global Challenge 1996/7 Round the World Yacht Race provided an excellent environment in which to study the behaviours required for high-performing leaders in the 1990s, a time when leadership was paramount.

The study tracked the behaviour of the 14 race skippers using the high-performance managerial competencies classified by Professor Harry Schroder (1989). The findings showed that these high-performance behaviours were in fact differentiators for the leading skippers, as can be seen in the book *Global Challenge, Leadership Lessons from the World's Toughest Yacht Race* (Walters, Mackie and Bacon 1997).

Today

Four years on from the previous research study, the business environment has changed considerably and leaders face new challenges, as discussed in Chapter 2. While high-performance behaviours are still critical, relationships are increasingly essential for achieving success. Leaders of today need to be able to deal with people, to build, nurture and develop long-term relationships, show sensitivity and flexibility, and be more prepared to help others to learn.

With the leadership role as complex as the business environment itself, the skills required have changed as discussed in Chapter 3. The days when management skills were sufficient have gone; good leadership skills have become essential. With very different skill sets it can be exceedingly difficult for managers to combine the two.

RESEARCH CHALLENGE

The challenge for the research team this time was much wider. Taking the BT Global Challenge Round the World Yacht Race 2000/1 as the setting for their new study, the research team set out to explore some of the questions left unanswered by the study four years earlier:

- How did the skippers at the front of the fleet sustain their performance over the course of the race?
- Was there a need for a set of behaviours that would help to retain the cohesiveness and loyalty of a team for a specific project with a definitive timeframe?

Emotional intelligence has been widely discussed in the past few years and is outlined in Chapter 3. It is seen as a concept that balances the rational with the emotional. The research team were also interested to investigate the role emotional intelligence played in sustaining performance within the race. Recognising the changes in the business environment and the complex characteristics of a leader within that environment, the team designed their research around the following questions:

- What skills are required for management?
- What attributes are required for leadership?

- How important is personal performance?
- Are there other factors yet undefined?
- What is the impact of emotional intelligence behaviours on performance?
- How does a leader create 'A Great Place To Be'?

RESEARCH MODEL

The high-performing behaviours were seen to be essential in the high-performing skippers in the BT Global Challenge 1996/7. As such they were used as part of the selection criteria to identify the 12 race skippers and two reserve skippers from the 186 applicants in the BT Global Challenge 2000/1, as discussed in Chapter 1.

The research team set out to track the attributes, skills and behaviours of the skippers in the BT Global Challenge Round the World Yacht Race 2000/1. Interview questions were constructed around two models:

- team building blocks (Woodcock 1985)
- emotional intelligence (Higgs and Dulewicz 1999).

Woodcock looked at the raw materials of effective teamwork. At that time little had been written on the subject. Today much has been added. Woodcock's original building blocks formed the basis on which the findings were mapped (see Chapter 3).

Although there are several different models of emotional intelligence, the research team chose also to map their findings onto the seven EI elements identified by Higgs and Dulewicz (see Chapter 3).

During the research study, evidence was seen to support two further models:

- situational leadership (Blanchard 1985)
- developmental sequence in small groups (Tuckman 1965).

Blanchard looked at the different leadership styles required to manage different situations, while Tuckman argued that there are predictable stages every team goes through on its way to becoming a highly productive, efficient team and that members who are aware of this can improve the quality of their interactions during each stage (see Chapter 3).

RESEARCH METHOD

The research team conducted their qualitative research through a system of interviews designed to provide an in-depth profile of each of the race skippers. The interviews were conducted at intervals before, during and after the race.

- The first set of interviews focused on the skippers from their appointment in September 1999 until their teams were announced in January 2000. This was a time when the skippers were considering the enormity of the project and working on their race strategy. The questions asked were based around critical incidents that illustrated the skipper's preparation and planning, their organisational ability and their self-development. Only the skippers were interviewed at this time.

- The second set of interviews focused on the skippers from the time they were allocated their teams in January 2000 until April. This was a stressful time when the Challenge yachts were not fully built and the skippers had to galvanise new teams, many of whom were still trying to hold down full-time jobs. This time the skippers' questions were based around critical incidents that illustrated their use of emotional intelligence behaviours. Evidence seen was rated high, medium and low, based on judgements drawn from these interviews. The research team also reviewed the level of team development and the leadership style of the skipper. At this stage, the research team interviewed a crew representative from each yacht who had volunteered to be interviewed at each of the six ports of call. This interview was based around the

Woodcock team building blocks and the development of the team was tracked as the race progressed.

- The third set of interviews was conducted in July 2000. This was after the qualifying sail when the team completed their first off-shore sail together. Many technical and team issues were beginning to emerge at this stage. Questions were again based around critical incidents that illustrated the skipper's use of emotional intelligence behaviours, the team development and the skipper's leadership style. Only the skippers were interviewed at this time.

- Structured interviews of 1–1½ hours were conducted at the end of each leg of the race in Boston, Buenos Aires, Wellington, Sydney, Cape Town and La Rochelle. These were constructed around critical incidents and open-ended questions were designed to give an in-depth insight into:

  - the way the skipper managed and led his team
  - the skipper's use of emotional intelligence behaviours
  - the skipper's leadership style
  - the manner in which the skipper built and developed the team.

Interviews were conducted with the 12 race skippers, two core crew and two departing leggers (individuals undertaking one stage of the race) from each yacht. The core crew members interviewed were different in each port of call. The crew representative from each yacht was interviewed around the Woodcock team building blocks.

- Additional interviews were conducted around the business subjects that form the chapters within Part III of this book. This supplemented the forum member research on each of these subjects and formed part of their contributions to each chapter.

- Final interviews were conducted after the race where data clarification was needed.

- The research team also interviewed people who had been closely involved with the skippers both before and during the race. These included:

- race director
- race management team
- race support team
- skippers' partners (where possible)
- yacht sponsor's project managers
- senior executives from sponsor companies
- celebrities and journalists.

Over 550 interviews, totalling more than 825 hours, were conducted over an 18-month period. On average 80 interviews were undertaken at the end of each leg by members of the Inspirational Intelligence Research Forum who joined the research team in ports of call to collect data.

DATA ANALYSIS

At the end of each interview session the research team undertook a content analysis of the data collected. Through this stage-by-stage analysis, the research team were able to build a comprehensive profile of each of the 12 skippers as the race progressed. The final profile of each skipper was based on judgements drawn from their nine self-perception interviews and 40 observer interviews.

These profiles identified:
- personal attributes
- management skills
- leadership attributes
- utilisation of emotional intelligence behaviours
- style of leadership
- development of the team and culture.

Case studies, learning and quotes were drawn from each interview session and these were shared and debated by forum members at regular forum meetings. Business analogies and parallels were also sought and discussed.

As the skipper profiles developed, it was evident that there were certain attributes and skills shared by the leading skippers that seemed to indicate superior performance. There was also evidence that the level of utilisation of emotional intelligence behaviour varied and that the skippers' leadership style had significant implications on team development and effectiveness. All elements seemed to impact on the skippers' ability to drive performance and inspire their teams.

At the end of the race the research team undertook an eight-week in-depth analysis, comparing and contrasting the skipper profiles built up over the race. In addition, they considered data collected during the skipper selection programme. This included:

- preferred team role (Belbin 1999)
- motivational driver (McClelland 1988)
- leadership balance (Adair 1983).

The findings of this research study are set out in Chapter 5. Reference is made to the McClelland and Adair data in Chapters 6 and 3 respectively.

REFERENCES

Adair, J. (1983) *Effective Leadership*, Pan: London.

Belbin, M. (1999) *Team Roles at Work*, Butterworth-Heinemann: Oxford.

Blanchard, K., Zigarmi, P. and Zigarmi, D. (1985) *Leadership and the One Minute Manager*, Willow Books, Collins: London.

Higgs, M. and Dulewicz, V. (1999) *Making Sense of Emotional Intelligence*, NFER-Nelson: Windsor.

McClelland, D. C. (1988) *Human Motivation*, Cambridge University Press: Cambridge.

Schroder, H. M. (1989) *Managerial Competence: the key to excellence*, Kendall Hunt: Iowa.

Tuckman, D. W. (1965) 'Developmental sequence in small groups', *Psychological Bulletin*, Vol. 63.

Walters, H., Mackie, P. M. and Bacon, A. (1997) *Global Challenge, Leadership Lessons from the World's Toughest Yacht Race*, The Book Guild: Sussex.

Woodcock, M. (1985) *Team Development Manual*, Gower: Aldershot.

5

WHAT MADE THE DIFFERENCE?

INTRODUCTION

This chapter sets out the findings of the research study conducted through the BT Global Challenge Round the World Yacht Race 2000/1.

As shown in Chapter 3, leadership is a well researched and widely documented subject. In setting out to undertake our research programme we reviewed many books and articles written by leadership researches over the past few years. What we believe we have achieved is to synthesise leadership thinking with our own research findings to produce a pragmatic approach for leaders facing today's turbulent environment.

As outlined in Chapter 4, our research study focused on the skippers of the 12 race yachts in the BT Global Challenge. This was an elite group of skippers selected from over 186 applicants, following a lengthy selection programme outlined in Chapter 1. Leading their teams through the harsh conditions of the Southern Ocean, racing in extremely close contention, all were successful.

This comprehensive study focused on these 12 leaders, running parallel projects, using the same equipment, with amateur crew, facing unpredictable and hostile conditions over an 18-month period. These findings were drawn following detailed content analysis. Although it is accepted that knowledge and experience play a part in performance, this study focused on the leadership skills and attributes that make the difference.

For the purpose of this section, the findings do not include the skipper of Olympic Group. The reason will become evident in this findings section. While each section shows evidence of the findings, more detailed examples will be found in each of the seven chapters in Part III of this book. Reference made to high, middle and low performance in these examples is relative to the incident described.

SKILLS AND ATTRIBUTES OF A LEADER

The findings identified a number of key skills and attributes that were common among these 12 skippers to a greater or lesser extent. Many of these elements were in line with the thinking of leadership researchers discussed in Chapter 3. These skills and attributes fell naturally into three clusters: personal, management and leadership, as seen in Figure 5.1. Definitions can be found in the Glossary of Attributes and Skills at the end of this chapter.

Management and leadership

The findings showed the necessity for the skills and attributes of both management and leadership. Operating in a complex and changing environment, skippers showed there was a need for control and procedures of management, as well as flexibility and creativity of leadership.

> *' It takes more than management to get the full commitment of the team. '*

Podium skippers took differing approaches to combine these management and leadership skills:

- Skipper of LG Flatron appointed a second in command with complementary skills: 'He has more courage, I am more reserved.'
- Skipper of Compaq led in a calm and consistent manner with a strong management approach: 'You have to be so far ahead of the guys in organisational terms.'
- Skipper of BP balanced his management and leadership skills: 'Don't overlook the human factor.'

The podium skippers showed a balanced approach to managing and leading and led teams that were performance-focused, happy and united. Further evidence can be found in Chapter 13. Some skippers showed a stronger management approach to leading their teams. They led using systems and procedures. However, these skippers showed weaker leadership skills and led less motivated and united teams. Other skippers showed a stronger leadership approach and inspired confidence and belief in their teams. However, these skippers showed weaker management skills and led teams less focused on achievement.

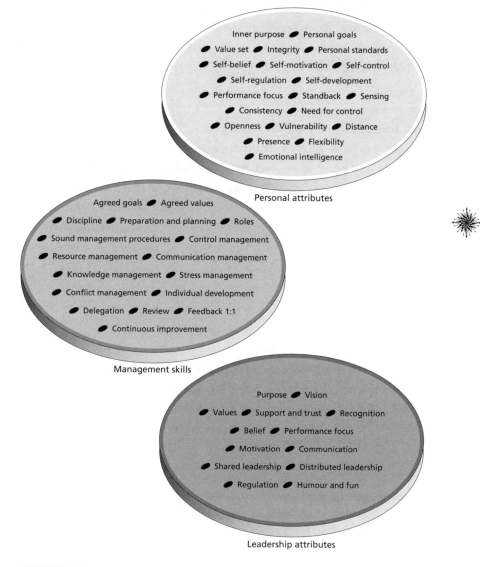

FIGURE 5.1   Personal, management and leadership clusters

Personal attributes

Personal attributes were identified as being important to anchor individuals in themselves. Skippers needed to have self-confidence, self-belief, a strong value set and an ability to cope with their emotions. Where personal attributes were evident the skipper was able to lead successfully. Evidence of the use of personal attributes among the podium skippers can be seen in Chapter 13.

Skippers with a strong inner purpose and a belief in their ability to handle the project were able to inspire belief among their crew. Their crews gained confidence early in the race and as their skills developed they showed strong belief that they could achieve their stated goals.

‘ *Self-belief is everything.* ’

One podium skipper realised during pre-race training that he couldn't sustain a high level of performance without regular sleep. Recognising the need for self-regulation he appointed a second in command and put in place a rota system that guaranteed a regular sleep pattern. Some skippers recognised their own shortcomings and were prepared to show vulnerability at times. By admitting mistakes or weaknesses they were often able to gain support and found their crews more willing to assist them in areas where they were not adept. One skipper admitted a weakness in organisation on shore. When the crew arrived in Boston they assumed the role and for the rest of the race they organised the team in ports of call.

On entering the Southern Ocean one skipper became overwhelmed by a feeling of technical inexperience and lost his self-control. This led to the loss of self-confidence and belief. As a result, this skipper's leadership capabilities diminished and performance of his team declined. Another skipper, with a personal goal to win, failed to align this with the team goal to sail around the world. As a result, he found it difficult to lead his crew as he faced a constant inner struggle. Without a strong value set and without a genuine belief, this skipper found it difficult to behave in a manner that was convincing.

‘ *If the skipper had been true to himself, he would have been happier.* ’

Utilising skills and attributes

The findings showed that real leadership ability was dependent on how the skipper utilised the skills and attributes of the three clusters. Personal attributes were seen to be important for both managing and leading.

Combining personal attributes and leadership attributes

Utilising personal and leadership attributes together produced a genuineness and openness of leadership that came from the heart. There was passion and commitment of purpose that inspired the team. A skipper who had a passion for the race, showed consistent behaviour, always did what he said he would and was highly sensitive to people, earned total respect from his crew and gained a 100 per cent following.

Combining personal attributes and management skills

Utilising personal attributes and management skills together produced a performance focus. There was discipline and commitment to success and this drove the team. For a skipper who had a performance focus, showed integrity and high personal standards, implemented clear, simple procedures, gave regular briefings, structured things well and paid meticulous attention to preparation and planning, the team put in 100 per cent effort.

Shared skills and attributes

The podium skippers utilised many of the same skills and attributes across the three clusters. They utilised them effectively and they were seen to make a difference in terms of achieving performance. At the end of the race, there was less evidence of these skills and attributes in the skippers in the middle and at the back of the fleet. The grid in Table 5.1 on page 106 is used to illustrate this.

The skills and attributes listed in Table 5.1 were those commonly observed among all the skippers during the race. However, by the end of the race there was evidence to suggest that some skippers were no longer using them. The decrease in the number of dark shaded boxes across the three columns shows that the middle and lower-performing skippers were using fewer of these skills and attributes than the podium skippers.

TABLE 5.1 Skippers' skills and attributes at the end of the race

	Podium positions (3)	Middle positions (5)	Back positions (3) excl. Olympic Group

Personal attributes
Inner purpose
Personal goals
Value set
Integrity
Personal standards
Self-belief
Self-motivation
Self-control
Self-regulation
Self-development
Performance focus
Standback
Sensing
Consistency
Need for control
Openness
Vulnerability
Distance
Presence
Flexibility

Management skills
Agreed goals
Agreed values
Discipline
Preparation and planning
Roles
Sound management procedures
Control management
Resource management
Communication management
Knowledge management
Stress management
Conflict management
Individual development
Delegation
Review
Feedback 1:1
Continuous improvement

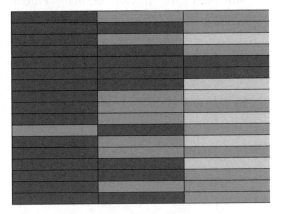

Leadership attributes
Purpose
Vision
Values
Support and trust
Recognition
Belief
Performance focus
Motivation
Communication
Shared leadership
Distributed leadership
Regulation
Humour and fun

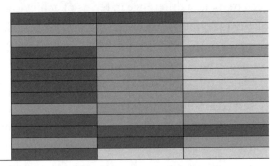

Dark shading (■) = Positive behaviour seen in all skippers in that column

Medium shading (■) = Positive behaviour seen in majority of skippers in that column

Light shading (■) = Positive behaviour seen in minority of skippers in that column

THE VITAL INGREDIENTS

Performance drivers

To determine the factors that were critical for performance, the profiles of the podium skippers were compared to each of the skippers in the rest of the fleet. The skipper of Olympic Group shared almost all the competencies of the podium skippers but was ranked at the back of the fleet. The competencies not seen were:

- performance focus
- discipline
- control management

- resource management
- conflict management.

These competencies were identified as critical for performance as the podium skippers were the only skippers seen to have all five. Skippers who ranked in the middle of the fleet showed evidence of some of these competencies, while those skippers at the back of the fleet showed no evidence at all. These competencies, together with self-motivation, were identified as performance drivers and classified as the X Factor (see Figure 5.2). The X Factor

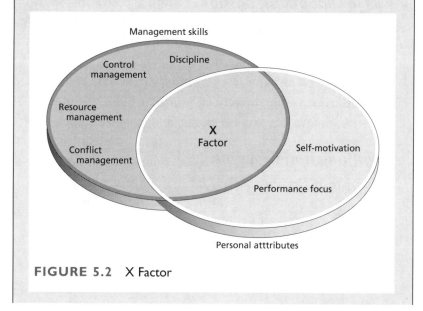

FIGURE 5.2 X Factor

was seen to be an important aspect of motivation and is discussed in detail in Chapter 6.

Performance enablers

Although the majority of performance drivers were seen to be missing from the skipper of Olympic Group, he had an exceptional leadership profile and was leading a cohesive, united, happy, loyal and supportive team. Despite coming last into Boston, narrowly missing first place into Wellington and having to use their engine and incur penalties, this team appeared completely loyal and supportive of their skipper.

> *I realised the race was not all a performance driver but a people issue.*

The research team took time to consider data on the way this skipper was leading and the effect on the team. The skipper's goal was 'to build a team that would learn and invest in the university of life'. He wanted his crew to learn from the race and take this learning back into their lives. This cultivation culture is discussed further in Chapter 13.

> *The concept for this race was for happiness, passion and maximisation.*

This skipper's purpose was to create an enviable team that could move on to other projects. He wanted to build relationships and trust to move forward. He created an incredible culture and team dynamic and since the race he has set up a company with members of his team.

> *Winning is not everything, crew dynamics come first.*

Comparison with all the other teams revealed that a similar culture and dynamic was evident on other yachts, though to a lesser degree. There were ten elements that were common among these skippers:

- integrity
- self-belief
- self-control
- sensing
- openness

- vulnerability
- purpose
- recognition
- belief
- shared leadership.

These competencies were identified as important for enabling performance through inspiring individuals and were classified as the Y Factor (see Figure 5.3). The Y Factor was also seen to be an important aspect of motivation and is discussed in detail in Chapter 6.

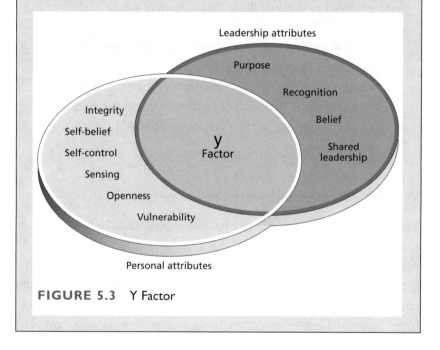

FIGURE 5.3   Y Factor

> ## KEY FINDINGS
>
> Evidence seen to support the X Factor (performance drivers) included:
> - The three podium skippers were the only skippers to share all six drivers of performance.
> - Skippers in the middle of the fleet showed some of the drivers of performance but the majority lacked discipline and the ability to manage conflict.
> - Skippers at the back of the fleet showed none of the drivers of performance.
>
> Evidence seen to support the Y Factor (performance enablers) included:
> - The three podium skippers shared eight of the competencies that inspired their team.
> - The majority of the skippers in the middle of the fleet showed evidence of more than 50 per cent of these competencies.
> - Skippers at the back of the fleet showed few of these competencies.

When performance drivers are important

Many businesses today work on a project-related basis. Individuals with specialist knowledge and expertise are brought together for a specific period of time to achieve certain objectives rapidly. In such situations, getting the best performance from team members and achieving results could be seen to be more important than building a cohesive team capable of repeated, long-term success. In such cases, it would be essential to appoint a leader with the attributes that ensure good leadership and the ability to deliver results. This leader would require the key drivers of performance and the ability to utilise his emotional intelligence behaviours to achieve success.

When performance enablers are important

Leaders need to inspire their teams in order to sustain their commitment and loyalty. This can be critical in times of uncertainty such as mergers and takeovers or when the environment is unpredictable. Inspiring individuals is also essential for retaining talent. Individuals need stimulation through recognition and continual learning. Leaders must build a strong culture and team dynamic and create an environment where people are inspired to perform consistently. By inspiring their team, leaders enable performance. To achieve this leaders require the competencies to enable performance and the ability to utilise their emotional intelligence behaviour.

Combining performance drivers and enablers

The podium skippers were seen to combine both the performance drivers and enablers. They had a clear purpose, focused on performance, showed high levels of discipline and set benchmarks against which they could measure processes and continually improve. They managed their resources well and recognised when they needed to ease on the discipline and focus on the needs of the team. These skippers had high levels of self- belief and inspired belief within their teams. They were open to share responsibility with their teams and this allowed them to regulate their own needs. Through balancing the performance drivers and enablers they were able to create a winning team that was united, happy and committed to success (see Figure 5.4).

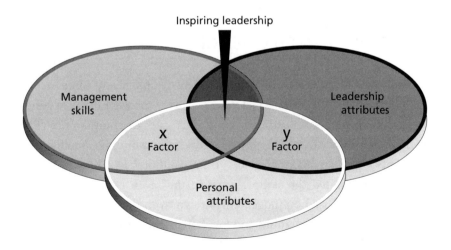

FIGURE 5.4 Model of inspiring leadership

LESSONS FROM THE RACE

As a leader today you need to:

1. recognise the need to balance both management and leadership

2. develop personal attributes to anchor oneself

3. realise that in order to drive performance in your team, it is important to have:

   - self-motivation
   - performance focus
   - discipline
   - control management
   - resource management
   - conflict management.

4. realise that in order to inspire performance in your team, it is important to have:

   - integrity
   - self-belief
   - self-control
   - sensing
   - openness
   - vulnerability
   - purpose
   - recognition
   - belief
   - shared leadership.

EMOTIONAL INTELLIGENCE

At the outset of the research study, the 12 race skippers and some members of their team were interviewed. The questions were based around critical incidents that illustrated the skipper's use of emotional intelligence (EI) behaviours. Mapping onto the emotional intelligence elements of Higgs and Dulewicz (1999) outlined in Chapter 3, the research team rated the skippers against the seven emotional intelligence elements based on judgements drawn from these interviews and using a scale of high, medium and low (where there was no evidence of the use of the behaviour this was noted):

- High indicated positive and frequent use of the behaviour.
- Medium indicated positive use of the behaviour.
- Low indicated negative use of the behaviour.

At every port of call, the skipper and five members of his team were interviewed and the emotional intelligence behaviours of each skipper were assessed and graded. The findings showed changes in the skippers' emotional intelligence behaviours and the relationship between emotional intelligence behaviour and performance.

Changes in emotional intelligence behaviours

At the start of the race, some of the seven emotional intelligence behaviours of the podium skippers were seen to be lower than those of other skippers. At the end of the race, all seven emotional intelligence behaviours were seen at a higher level than the rest.

The majority of middle-performing skippers were seen to have low emotional resilience, self-awareness and interpersonal sensitivity at the start of the race; at the end of the race, their emotional resilience and self-awareness were seen to have increased. Their interpersonal sensitivity remained the same. The other four emotional intelligence behaviours were seen to be lower than at the start.

The lower-performing skippers started the race with similar levels of emotional intelligence behaviour as the podium skippers. However, by the end of the race, the lower-performing skippers were showing lower levels of emotional intelligence behaviours than at the start.

As the race progressed, intuitiveness was seen to increase among the podium skippers but was seen to decline among the middle and lower-performing skippers. There was no evidence of an increase in motivation. This was high for all skippers at the start of the race and remained high among the podium skippers. However, motivation was seen to decline among the middle and lower-performing skippers. Emotional resilience, self-awareness and interpersonal sensitivity were the behaviours seen to increase most during the race (see Table 5.2).

The increase in emotional intelligence behaviour among the skippers was considered a result of the upward feedback received from their crews (see Table 5.3). The research team believe that this increase was

TABLE 5.2 Changes in emotional intelligence behaviour during the race

	Podium position (3)	Middle position (5)	Back positions (3) excl. Olympic Group
Self awareness	■ dark	■ dark	light
Emotional resilience	■ dark	■ dark	light
Motivation	medium	medium	light
Interpersonal sensitivity	■ dark	medium	light
Influence	■ dark	light	light
Intuitiveness	medium	light	light
Conscientiousness	medium	light	light

Dark shading (■) = emotional intelligence behaviour increased in majority of skippers in that column

Medium shading (■) = emotional intelligence behaviour remained the same in majority of skippers in that column

Light shading (▨) = emotional intelligence behaviour declined in majority of skippers in that column

TABLE 5.3 Increase in use of emotional intelligence behaviour

Emotional intelligence behaviour	No. of skippers who increased use of emotional intelligence behaviour
Self-awareness	5
Emotional resilience	6
Motivation	–
Interpersonal sensitivity	3
Influence	2
Intuitiveness	3
Conscientiousness	–

' The knocks don't hurt so much. '

accelerated by the intensity of the timeframe of the race. Crews were more willing to feed back concerns about the skipper's behaviour or style in which he led the team as they knew that their performance and finishing position on each leg had a significant bearing on their overall race position (see Chapter 9). Evidence of changes in emotional intelligence behaviour can be seen in the chapters in Part III.

KEY FINDINGS

- The podium skippers showed greatest increase in behaviours over the course of the race.
- All skippers were seen to have a high level of motivation at the start of the race and this remained high among the podium skippers throughout the race.
- Motivation was seen to decrease in all other skippers as the race progressed.
- Self-awareness, interpersonal sensitivity and influence were seen to increase more in the podium skippers than in the rest of the fleet.
- Emotional resilience was seen to increase more than other behaviours among the middle-performing skippers.
- Emotional resilience was seen to be the behaviour that increased most across the fleet, followed by self-awareness.
- Influence was seen to decline more than other behaviours among the middle-performing skippers.
- Conscientiousness showed greatest decline across the fleet.

RELATIONSHIP BETWEEN EMOTIONAL INTELLIGENCE BEHAVIOURS AND PERFORMANCE

Impact on leadership skills and attributes

There appeared to be an inter-relationship between emotional intelligence behaviours and the use of leadership skills and attributes. By the end of the race, the podium skippers showed an ability to use all seven emotional intelligence behaviours and demonstrated a positive use of 70 per cent of the leadership skills and attributes (see Table 5.2 and Table 5.1). All three skippers developed teams that shared responsibility for leadership. One podium skipper illustrated the level of shared responsibility on his yacht when he made the following comment: 'There are some huge decisions, sail changes and issues that have gone on during this race without my knowledge.'

The middle-performing skippers showed an increase in the use of self-awareness and emotional resilience. This was seen to enhance their ability to use certain leadership skills and attributes. One middle-performing skipper showed a significant increase in his self-awareness and a significant change in his leadership style. At the outset of the race this skipper was very single-minded, independent and overly distanced from his crew. Being a highly competitive individual, he pushed his own viewpoint and early on in the race took a strategic flier that didn't pay off. The failure had huge implications on the ability to achieve the team's overall goal. The skipper buried himself in analysing weather and looking for ways to improve their position. He brushed off the crew with cursory comments and cancelled the daily briefings. Without the opportunity to discuss the situation, the crew became very unhappy, heads hung low and they felt alienated. The skipper was totally unaware of the impact of his behaviour and failed to notice the crew's reaction.

Feedback from the crew at the debrief in the next port made this skipper realise his total lack of self-awareness. He spent time coming to terms with his feelings and on the following leg he dramatically changed his behaviour. He became more open, spent more time with the team, chatted through situations, listened, injected humour and encouraged learning through coaching. As the race progressed, this skipper learned to identify and manage his feelings and was constantly aware of his actions and the effect these had on the crew.

The lower-performing skippers showed a decline in the utilisation of all the emotional intelligence behaviours and a decline in the leadership skills and attributes. This seemed to be related to difficulties in dealing with interpersonal issues or leading in an inappropriate manner.

' The crew has a lot of respect for him but he needs to be more of a bastard. '

One skipper found it difficult to utilise interpersonal sensitivity and as the race progressed the impact on his leadership abilities became more evident. This skipper was sensitive to individuals and disliked any bad feelings or disagreement. He liked to involve crew and get their input when making decisions but was often too consultative. He didn't always like what he heard and would avoid addressing any real issues. He didn't like to delegate or implement a 'best person for the job' approach to roles. The crew began to lose respect for him as they felt he did not lead and almost abdicated responsibility in decision making and addressing conflict. This skipper also showed low self-awareness as he didn't realise the impact his behaviour was having on the crew. He struggled to motivate them and eventually lost his confidence and self-belief.

Impact of stress

There appeared to be an inter-relationship between stress, emotional intelligence behaviours and leadership. Where skippers were working outside of their normal sphere of knowledge or experience, or where they were under intense pressure with little or no regular sleep, their ability to utilise emotional intelligence behaviours and to lead was impaired.

A number of external environmental factors were recorded. Where a skipper was involved in an incident, faced with an unknown situation, exposed to prolonged periods of danger or challenging conditions or made a major tactical error, stress levels rose. With rational thinking impaired, emotions took over and as a consequence personal and leadership attributes were affected.

' As a skipper there is a need for perpetual containment of feelings. '

Recognising inappropriate behaviour

One high-performing skipper was seen to be outside his comfort zone towards the end of the race. He had taken his focus off the race while looking at possible future projects. He left the crew to carry out the maintenance and preparation of the yacht for the next leg. This skipper was a meticulous planner and liked to be well prepared and organised.

> **' You can change things that you have control of. '**

Not being involved in the yacht preparation unnerved him. Feeling out of control he became tense and difficult and started to lose his self-belief. He felt that the team was competent and cohesive and that his ability to influence had diminished. He started to dictate to the crew strongly and bicker about detail, which caused bad feeling. The crew recognised that his normal air of confidence had gone and they felt less confident in his decision making on the leg. The energy on the yacht decreased and the team's performance was the worst in the race.

This skipper showed self-awareness and was quick to recognise the signs that his emotions had taken over. He was aware of his inappropriate behaviour. He knew he needed to regain self-confidence. He took the step of revealing to the crew that he was having a tough time and asked for their support. Involving the crew in the tactical decision making, he regained respect, restored trust and started to regain his confidence and self-belief.

Inability to change behaviour

The decline in the performance of the skippers towards the back of the fleet could be attributed to a significant incident or specific period during the race. At this point, these skippers suffered considerable stress, were overcome by their emotions and were unable to continue to lead their teams effectively.

These lower-performing skippers were less able to recognise and manage their emotions, and there was less evidence of recovery from their setbacks. Some lost their self-belief, retreated inwardly, spent time on their own and physically removed themselves from their team. They lacked self-awareness and were unable to see the impact of their behaviour on the crew. The setbacks affected their motivation. With low self-confidence and belief they lost the drive and energy to pursue their goal. Decision making became more difficult as they lost their intuitive perceptions. Their ability to perform diminished consistently. They could not sense the needs of the team or balance these with the situation.

These skippers were seen to be less approachable and less open to the input and opinions of the crew. They were unable to accept feedback, questioning or comment from the crew without taking this personally. Their standards slipped, values were not upheld and they were not seen to be matching words and actions. As a result of their inability to utilise their emotional intelligence behaviours, their personal attributes suffered, they were unable to lead effectively, the atmosphere on the yacht was gloomy and crew support diminished.

> ‘ *The skipper's mood counts for over 50 per cent of the atmosphere on the yacht.* ’

Impact of stress on individuals

External and environmental factors can lead to stress. Stress inhibits rational thinking and the use of personal and leadership attributes. As a consequence individuals can be overcome by their emotions and lose the ability to utilise emotional intelligence behaviours.

The possible impact of stress on personal attributes includes:
- loss of self-control or self-regulation
- loss of vulnerability, consistency and flexibility
- loss of self-confidence, belief and motivation
- lack of purpose and goals
- loss of openness
- loss of reasonable distance and presence
- loss of ability to sense the environment and inability to stand back
- loss of value set, personal standards and integrity.

The possible impact of stress on emotional intelligence behaviour includes:

- inability to share feelings appropriately or to recognise basic needs; unaware of the impact of own behaviour on others
- inability to admit mistakes or accept feedback
- inability to continue to perform consistently or adapt to changes
- feelings of doubt, lack of energy, loss of drive and inability to pursue goals
- inability to recognise needs of others
- unwillingness to receive input and opinions of others in decision making; imposition of own solutions on others
- physical separation from team for long periods of time
- loss of presence and charisma
- inability to persuade others to change their point of view
- inability to use intuitive perceptions to make clear decisions when faced with incomplete information
- lack of commitment to a cause
- inability to match words and actions or to pursue an ethical solution to a difficult problem.

Importance of utilising emotional intelligence behaviours

At the end of the race, podium skippers were seen to use all seven emotional intelligence behaviours at a higher level than other skippers. While increased usage was aligned to the upward feedback received from the crews, it is also believed that the increase in emotional intelligence behaviours was related to success. The use of emotional intelligence behaviours was reinforced where performance was evident.

Using all seven emotional intelligence behaviours

The podium skippers had high levels of motivation and had the ability to make decisions using intuitiveness. They showed self-awareness and knew how their behaviour impacted on their crew. They used interpersonal sensitivity to involve their teams in decision making. They were able to utilise

' Keeping the crew motivated is the key to success. '

emotional resilience to perform consistently despite setbacks. These skippers used influence when necessary to change the viewpoint of their crew. They showed conscientiousness when upholding team values, were committed to performance and were seen to align their actions with their words.

Importance of emotional resilience

The performance of one of the yachts seemed to be related to the skipper's ability to utilise emotional resilience behaviour. The yacht ranked high in the fleet on incident-free legs. However, its ranking fell on legs where the crew were faced with a breakage, tactical error or incident. The skipper was unable to cope or to continue to perform consistently in such circumstances. He would retreat and remove himself from the crew. Some hours or even days later he would reappear and apologise for his behaviour. He would then refocus and involve the crew in making the best decisions to move forward.

Another skipper lost a leg podium position after letting his emotions take over. Being in close contention with another yacht at the end of a

' He let his emotions be his master. '

leg, he showed an inability to use emotional resilience to perform consistently. He took over on deck, tried to run the

crew, call the tactics and helm the yacht all at the same time. He took responsibility away from the watch leaders and in the confusion that ensued they were beaten across the line.

Importance of interpersonal sensitivity

In the unpredictable environment in which these skippers were operating they were constantly facing a high level of risk. The Southern Ocean legs were not the only ones on which the teams faced hurricane-force winds and 30–40ft waves. The skippers constantly had to weigh safety with performance and at times had to take calculated risks.

One skipper took such a risk early on in the race and chose to follow a more southerly course. He made this decision based on his instincts and without discussion with the crew. When the gamble didn't pay off, he was faced with a very unhappy crew. This skipper showed very low usage of interpersonal sensitivity in the early stages of the race, but as the race progressed he became more and more aware of the importance of this behaviour. As a result, the performance of this yacht increased from the lower half to the top half of the fleet.

Fear was heightened among the fleet following the horrendous storm in the Bass Strait that led to the evacuation of two seriously injured crew members on VERITAS. On one yacht the crew voiced their concerns to their skipper. They were unhappy about the planned strategy to go deep down south in the Southern

> **' The skipper has to work with us, not against us. '**

Ocean. Their skipper showed interpersonal sensitivity and listened to the crew before weighing up the situation. Although he knew that the southerly route was the shortest distance, he also knew the crew were scared. He reviewed his strategy, made the decision to alter course and took a more northerly route towards Cape Town.

Importance of intuitiveness

Another skipper calculated risk and reward following a bad leg start that left his yacht floundering at the back of the fleet. This skipper had shown a high level of intuitive-ness throughout the race, taking some of the more extreme routes that paid off favourably. Heading offshore,

> **' Intuition is the difference between the men and the boys. '**

he was the only one to round an island from the other direction. As a consequence the yacht moved from the back to the front of the fleet.

LESSONS FROM THE RACE

As a leader today you need to:

1. recognise that all seven emotional intelligence behaviours need to be utilised to achieve success

2. be aware of your feelings and understand the way they affect your behaviour

3. understand the impact your behaviour has on others

4. be aware that your ability to perform under pressure increases with practice and familiarity with a situation

5. achieve an appropriate balance between taking hard decisions and being sensitive to the needs of others

6. realise that when self-confidence and self-belief are lost you are less able to perform

7. be open to the views and opinions of others

8. be able to persuade others to your viewpoint

9. establish a code of conduct.

ADOPTING AN APPROPRIATE LEADERSHIP STYLE

The research team found that the successful skippers were those who could adapt their behaviour to meet the demands of the given situation. In order to track the adaptability of the skippers' behaviour, Blanchard *et al.*'s (1969) Situational Leadership Model was used (see Chapter 3).

' He is leading us where we want to go. '

Leadership style before the race

During the early preparation for the race the skippers were very relaxed in the way they led their teams. However, those skippers who were having problems, either with a lack of sponsor or lack of crew commitment, very quickly began to adopt a directing style in order to galvanise the crew. This style may also have reflected the particular stress that these skippers were under.

Leadership style during the race

Directing

The first leg was an eye-opener for many of the skippers who found sailing with amateurs a new experience. Many adopted a consultative style of leadership that was not very directive, but soon realised, given the lack of knowledge and readiness of the crew, that this style was inappropriate. The crews at this early stage were looking for direction.

A directing style of leadership was often the hardest style for the skippers to adopt. At times it meant being respected but not necessarily liked. Skippers sometimes felt very isolated when they were endeavouring to make decisions that they felt uncertain about or where information was insufficient. They had to keep up their energy even when questioned on their decisions. They were coping with amateur crews who were looking to them for direction and confidence. Their behaviour had to be exemplary.

Following an unfortunate and damaging collision, one skipper found his position very lonely. He realised that the event had been physically and mentally draining for the crew and that the team dynamic had changed. He went to his bunk to think through the event and realised that he would have to overcome his feelings. The skipper then talked through his feelings with the crew and persuaded them to adopt his plan for the next leg. The skipper held a debrief day on arrival at the port of call and discussed the incident at an emotional level. The crew pulled together and felt they had become a strong unit, able to cope.

> ‘ *Direction needs self-assurance.* ’

One skipper felt like the CEO, encyclopaedia, mentor and weatherman all rolled into one. 'He relies on his confidence in knowing what he is doing and this filters down. He takes command, is not challenged and his leadership is never questioned.'

Feedback from the crew on some of the yachts provided the catalyst for the skipper to adopt a more directing style. As a result of upward feedback, more than half of the skippers showed a directing style by leg 2. One skipper, having moved to a coaching and supporting style of leadership on legs 4 and 5, adopted a directive style of leadership in leg 6 to overcome complacency that had set in among the crew.

Coaching

When the skippers were coaching the crews they had to take into account the fact that these crew members were amateurs who were very often new to sailing. It required patience and self-control when jobs were taking longer than predicted.

> **' Predictive ability needs to be greater as with amateurs it takes longer to do things. '**

The skippers needed to be able to balance the need to coach for individual development with the need to race the yacht. They had to decide when racing positions were required and when they could take time for learning. They had to be aware of the needs of the learner and their individual learning styles when coaching. It was a time when the crew could be lacking confidence and were looking for encouragement from the skipper.

> **' See how easy it is when you know what to do. '**

The coaching style was rarely observed in the early stages of the race. Only four of the skippers in the fleet demonstrated it on leg 1. By leg 2 it was still not evidenced in the podium skippers but was seen in the majority of the other skippers. Where the skippers were able to coach and develop the individuals in their teams, the crew felt valued. There was renewed energy and commitment within the team.

> **' Our skipper is very calm, thoughtful and has a coaching attitude. He has a very approachable style. '**

One skipper set up a competition for the best trainer to encourage a culture of coaching. Each person was awarded points for the amount of coaching given to another person and a prize was awarded. On another yacht the skipper had named helms for each watch, but would coach others when time and conditions permitted. This skipper tried to ensure that everyone had a turn at doing other jobs for their own development and the overall development of the team.

On leg 5 one skipper spent time coaching individual crew members to fulfil their aspirations. This was usually in helming or navigation. One skipper coached only those who were enthusiastic and showed real potential.

Supporting

Some skippers left supporting style out of their leadership. However, this style had a great impact on the development of an individual's learning. At this stage they were looking for an approachable and supportive leadership style as they were still lacking in confidence and ability to do the task on their own. It was a time

> *We have confidence he will always be there if we need him.*

when the skipper had to show patience as he may have felt that the individual should be capable of working alone. He needed to be able to listen to new ideas and ways of doing things without feeling threatened and he needed to be able to show that he was 'practising what he was preaching'.

There was evidence of supporting in two skippers on leg 3 and leg 4. Some skippers felt that their teams had not developed sufficiently to be able to use this style of leadership, others went straight from a coaching style to delegation. By leg 5 seven skippers were displaying a supporting leadership style.

One skipper allowed the individuals to choose the area they wanted to be involved in and let them evolve in it. He was keen to listen to them and to filter out new ideas from them about the different work areas. Another skipper felt that having brought the team together to perform well as a team he was able to support them through their development on the latter legs. Having trained his watch leaders well, he was able to stand back from the overall running of the yacht and give more time to individual development.

Delegating

The skipper often had to justify his decision to delegate particular tasks to specific individuals. Sometimes crew members felt that the wrong person was being asked to take on a role or that the person being asked was not ready to do the task. It was by listening to those concerns before acting that gained the skipper respect. On occasion the skipper did not have all the facts before delegating a task but had to be decisive in his approach in order to build the necessary confidence.

> ' *Delegate, as you get so much back and achieve far more than you can ever do on your own.* '

Delegation had been an integral part of the leadership style of most of the skippers from leg 1. Eight skippers had started to delegate by the end of leg 1, nine by the end of leg 2, and by legs 5 and 6 ten skippers could delegate effectively. On one yacht the crew felt, from the outset, that the skipper trusted the crew and was happy for them to get on without questioning what they were doing.

> ' *I feel very strongly that if someone has a specific job, they must be allowed to complete it.* '

Another skipper also felt it was important to delegate early on and to give people responsibility so that there was a strong feeling of the project belonging to them all. The skipper felt that by the time they reached Sydney he didn't need to be on the yacht at all.

KEY FINDINGS

The research revealed the following findings:

- The podium skippers all adopted a supporting/delegating style on leg 1.
- The podium skippers all adopted a directing/delegating style on leg 2.
- On leg 2 all the skippers were either directing/delegating or coaching/delegating.
- The top four skippers were all working in all four styles by leg 5.
- The majority of skippers were working in three styles by leg 5 – supporting was missing.
- Two skippers were using only directing for the last 3 legs.
- Those skippers that began with a supporting/delegating style of leadership found it very difficult to utilise a directing style later on. Their crews also found it difficult to accept the harsher regime implied.
- The skippers were all able to be directive in a crisis, but many found it difficult to be directive otherwise.

Impact of leadership style

The ability to adopt a leadership style that was both appropriate to the situation and the individuals concerned had significant impact on the skippers' performance.

The ability to move between leadership styles

The podium skippers had all moved from supporting/delegating on leg 1 to directing/delegating on leg 2. They were devolving a lot of responsibility to their watch leaders. This was an inappropriate style as it was high on the task but low on relationships at a time when building the confidence of the crew was important. The podium skippers quickly realised the need to balance the needs of their teams. By the end of the race there was greater evidence that the skippers were able to adapt their style to the situation.

Six skippers were showing an ability to use all four styles when appropriate. The result was a culture of trust, development and learning. The teams had a confidence and belief that their skipper could handle all situations. By leg 6 the crews were able to sail the yachts efficiently and time was given to learning new skills before returning to Southampton. Those skippers who were able to adapt their style of leadership to the situation were also able to direct their crew as they began to learn a new skill. They

> ' *He is directive in key decision making, supporting through watch leaders and coaching when doing new things.* '

were able to coach them to improve on skills that individuals had been using but not well, such as helming. They were able to support them as they tried new ways of doing sail changes and delegate the tasks that individuals had proved they were well capable of doing themselves.

The inability to move between leadership styles

Where skippers were inflexible in their leadership style, the effect on the teams was often quite demoralising. There was an adverse effect on performance.

Directing missing

Skippers who lacked the confidence to adopt a directing style of leadership at the beginning found it increasingly hard to move to it during the race. Some skippers lost control over their teams and crew behaviour was adversely affected. Faced with confusion and a lack of direction, the crews lacked drive and that lowered performance.

> ' *People want direction as well as communication.* '

On one yacht there was an issue over a crew member who was in charge of food but was not handling it well. Although the crew felt strongly that the

> ' *He doesn't give us the direction that would make the difference.* '

skipper should address the situation, the directive style of leadership needed to deal with the situation was not evident and it continued to be a major issue.

Coaching missing

During leg 2 there was little coaching. The skippers were task-orientated and performance-driven. There was a lack of mutual understanding between skippers and crew. This lack of relationship resulted in a lack of recognition. On one yacht, where a culture of in-fighting and internal politics had developed, coaching became almost impossible, motivation dropped and the desire for improvement virtually disappeared.

> ‘ *The skipper can be too diplomatic and avoids confronting difficult situations.* ’

Supporting missing

Towards the end of the race four of the skippers were successfully adopting three styles – support was missing. Without this important element of leadership, the crews found there was little trust in their abilities and insufficient encouragement for the input of ideas and suggestions. On one yacht, crew opinions were disregarded that later proved to be right.

> ‘ *He doesn't respect and recognise the efforts of the crew.* ’

This led to real frustration within the crew and a disappointment that they knew they could have done better. Sometimes there was a tendency for skippers to expect that their crews should know everything by now. Crews were left to get on with things without the critical support of their skipper and the crews felt let down.

> ‘ *It doesn't work just to ask people who are already trying hard to try harder.* ’

Delegation missing

By the end of leg two there was evidence of delegation in all the skippers bar one, who showed no evidence of this until leg 6. This left him very stressed and the crew frustrated at the lack of trust in their ability to do tasks without being supervised. This breakdown in trust affected performance.

One skipper tended to overrule any decision made by the watch leaders. The crew wanted responsibility, but any time the skipper tried to give it to them, they were then closely supervised. The delegation he tried to give was always on his terms, telling people exactly how the task had to be completed. He struggled to let go of things.

Appropriate leadership style

The skippers who were able to sense the readiness and ability of individual crew members and adapt their leadership style to meet those needs built a culture of nurturing, learning and understanding. All skippers handled crisis situations well and were able to adopt an effective directing style. After a serious incident one skipper galvanised his dysfunctional crew with authoritarian behaviour. Throughout the ensuing leg the skipper's behaviour adapted to the need for direction, support and delegation, a style he had not adopted previously. The crew responded well to this flexible leadership and there was a determination and commitment to do well in the leg.

Inappropriate leadership style

There was a correlation between the skipper's leadership style and self-confidence. When confidence was lacking or the skipper was not in control, both coaching and supporting were missing. An inappropriate directing style was often adopted to compensate.

The research showed that two skippers were using only a directing style of leadership during the last few legs of the race. Both skippers had lost their self-belief and were compensating with an inappropriate controlling style. The teams lost confidence in them. The

' He leads by intimidation. '

skippers tended to overrule decisions made by their watch leaders. They expected their crews to do as they were told and there was no attempt to persuade crew members to their way of thinking. This inappropriate style led to a breakdown in the relationship, with a resulting loss of motivation and enjoyment – they had only the end of the race in mind. The drive and energy required to sustain performance was missing.

LESSONS FROM THE RACE

As a leader today you need to:

1. adopt the right style of leadership at the right time

2. remember that when people are learning they want to be told what to do

3. remember, if you fail to direct at the beginning of a project it will be harder to direct later on

4. use a directing style of leadership in a crisis situation

5. use a supporting style of leadership when learning is in progress

6. beware of hiding behind an inappropriate directing style of leadership when your confidence is dented

7. support people as they develop

8. stand back and allow people to get on with the job you have delegated to them

9. remember, flexibility is the key to being able to use every style

10. use the appropriate elements of emotional intelligence to enhance the style of leadership in any situation.

TEAM DEVELOPMENT

One of the important lessons from the 1996/7 race was the value of structured team development. As a consequence all the skippers of the 2000/1 race ensured that there was some form of teambuilding before the start of the race. Several of the teams involved external facilitators and activities ranged from outdoor training on Dartmoor, working with a trained psychologist, sailing, to sitting in a classroom pooling ideas. In all cases this proved to be a worthwhile way of focusing the team early on. They learned about each other and their individual aspirations as well as their strengths, weaknesses and motivational drivers.

> *It was a challenging but rewarding three days, during which our enthusiasm and belief in ourselves have been enhanced further. We're still going to be the ones to beat!*

One skipper divided his team into groups to accomplish several outdoor tasks during his teambuilding session. He was interested to learn what made them tick: 'The different characteristics of the individuals came through as they rotated through each of the exercises over the first two days. There were out-and-out achievers and there were those who wanted to reach consensus before acting, and there was the laid-back lot who bucked the trend with an astonishing final-day performance.'

Most teams were generating their own value systems and goals and these proved to be a vital part of the early development of the team. Those teams who agreed achievable goals at the beginning prevented many problems later on. Where goals were unrealistic, teams were demotivated by having to change them. Those who did not change them lived with false optimism.

> *The crew's common purpose was established painlessly and in remarkably quick time... the result was inspiring.*

The amount of team development during this race varied. Some skippers felt that what had been done before the race began was sufficient. Others had decided from the outset that teambuilding at stopovers was essential. One crew joined up with a team from the Cape Town office of a global organisation to climb Table Mountain. The aim was for the teams from these very different backgrounds to learn from each other. In the debrief following the climb, they discussed risk taking and the risks associated with performance. For both teams, the teambuilding experience proved to be a great motivator and they learned from each other's feedback. The yacht crew realised that they had to increase risk and adopted the slogan of 'Dare We Must'. The yacht team's values became:

> ‘ *The team-building thing has really been beaten to death.* ’

- maintain focus
- have fun
- be honest
- don't step over a job
- we can win.

The team went on to achieve their best leg position in the following leg.

Others used the facilities of their sponsor, where possible, for team meetings and debriefs. This was often a time when skipper's had feedback from their crew. There was no doubt that where the teams took time to work together in ports of call the effects could be seen in performance. After significant review sessions in a port of call, three yachts had their first win on the following leg; another came second.

Those who gave each other feedback in an open and constructive way enhanced their performance and realised their potential. The simple framework, Johari's Window (1970), shows how potential can be realised through feedback. As shown in Figure 5.5, by reducing the size of the hidden box through self-disclosure and the blind box through feedback, the transparent box is increased and potential is realised.

1. *Critical planning and preparation in Southampton before the race start*
   BP Explorer watch leader briefs his team using verbal and visual
   communications for deaf crew member

2. *Fundraising for Save the Children around the world*
   A Save the Children crew member hands over a cheque to John Parma
   Scholl in Nyanga Township, Cape Town

Photo: LG FLATRON © BT 2000/I

3.   *Maintaining performance focus despite severe conditions*
     LG FLATRON encounters severe weather in the Southern Ocean

Photo: Mark Pepper/Marinepics

4.   *Preventing and controlling risk is vital for long-term strategy*
     Under minimal sail Olympic Group battle against 70-knot winds and
     huge seas as they approach Wellington

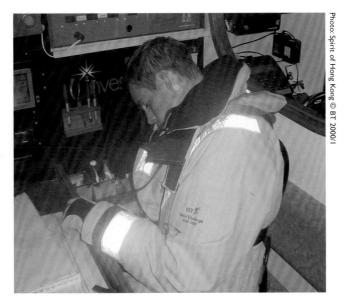

5. *Fatigue takes its toll*
   Spirit of Hong Kong crew member falls asleep at the chart table

6. *Skipper celebrates team's success over adversity*
   Logica skipper Jeremy Troughton arrives in Boston with a severely
   damaged satellite dome

Photo: Compaq © BT 2000/I

7. *Converting information to knowledge to make the best tactical decision*
    Compaq skipper Will Oxley wades through a mass of weather
    information

Photo: Isle of Man © BT 2000/I

8. *Finding a balance between ocean racing and fun*
    Despite racing mid-ocean the crew of the Isle of Man support Red Nose
    Day

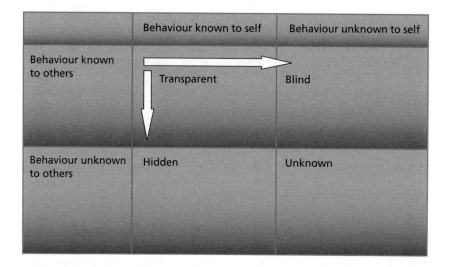

FIGURE 5.5 Johari's Window

(Luft 1970)

The skippers who were prepared to listen to feedback from their crews and act upon it appeared to develop several elements of emotional intelligence behaviour, especially self-awareness and emotional resilience. This led to a change in behaviour and performance. The fact that the crews were fee-paying and keen to get 'value' for money meant that they felt more able to give upward feedback to their skippers. This is difficult in business, but the outcome in performance is a key lesson for leaders today.

Appropriate team development on the yachts produced a culture of:

- focused activity
- creativity
- open communication
- integration.

STAGES OF DEVELOPMENT OF TEAM EMOTIONS

Success in passing through the Tuckman (1965) stages of the team development (see Chapter 3) is achieved by the leader having a clear understanding of what the stages are. Only then can he lead his team through each stage. It is also important for the leader to understand the emotions of the team during each stage of team development. Figure 5.6 shows the different emotions experienced at each stage of team development.

Forming – identifying emotions

At the outset the crew members were motivated by the challenge ahead but were unsure of themselves, their technical ability and their ability to cope with the enormity of what they were facing. There was a lot of self-interest, little questioning, and a certain amount of confusion. The crew members were only just beginning to identify their emotions and were feeling a lack of confidence, anxiety and concern. At one team-building session the crew had a discussion about their fears and concerns. At this stage there was fear about the structure of the yachts and their ability to withstand the pressures of the Southern Ocean. There was fear about not being able to cope in dangerous conditions and letting the team down. There was also fear of injury. Although these fears were put on the table, there was a feeling that there was far more unsaid than said at that time.

Storming – understanding emotions

At this stage the crew members were becoming more competent and were starting to challenge the skipper on his appointment and role as a

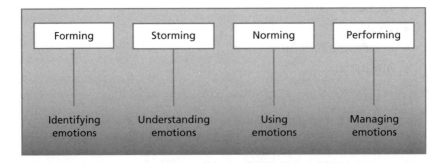

FIGURE 5.6 Stages of development of team emotions

‘ People need to be true to themselves. After 1500 miles we stopped giving the benefit of the doubt to the skipper. ’

leader. There was increased dissatisfaction with rules and procedures established initially. There was a juggling for position within the crew. Tolerance was limited. Most of the decisions were still being made by the skipper. At this stage the crew members were beginning to understand their emotions and they were better able to appreciate differences in style, motivation, need for change and diversity. Feelings were being discussed and personal animosities dealt with. More traumatic encounters with crew members were happening.

Norming – using emotions

At this stage the teams were consolidating, confidence was building, ideas were being shared and there was a willingness to change if there was a better way. There was a more systematic approach to things. Procedures were agreed by the team members. There was shared responsibility and a clearer understanding of strengths and weaknesses. There was a collaborative approach to decision

‘ The happier the crew, the faster they sail. ’

making. Team members were beginning to develop trust and were starting to solve problems together. On one of the higher-performing yachts the skipper felt that the team were relaxing more and more each leg and that by Wellington they were really having fun and enjoying the race. He was ‘giving power away’, the team were self-running and he didn’t need even to be there. There was an openness as a result of the issues resolved in the storming stage.

Performing – managing emotions

At this stage the crews were highly committed to the task and to each other. There was a feeling of well-being, and self-interest was put aside. There was openness, honesty and conflict handling. There was a healthy degree of tolerance. There was good feedback, debriefing was a way of life and there was flexibility in the procedures. Values were upheld and leadership was distributed. The team were beginning to look beyond themselves.

' To start with I was concerned with bringing the team together. I now want to focus on their individual development. '

They were managing their emotions and were focused on performance, making the best decisions and continually striving to improve. The openness and improved relationships from the storming stage and the improved approach of the norming stage now led to a mature team.

For some teams, although teambuilding had taken place, the forming stage of development happened on the first leg. It was the first time for many that the whole crew had been together, including the leggers. It was also the first time they had been racing for real and the culture on board was very different from training. As new crew members and leggers arrived, a further storming phase sometimes evolved.

A final stage, adjourning, was added to the Tuckman model as it was realised that as a project is accomplished, the members of a close team need to pass through a 'mourning' process as they look out for new challenges. On some yachts the skippers were proactive in dealing with the end of the race. Some started openly to discuss the future as early as Sydney. Many spent the long leg from Cape Town to La Rochelle helping people to come to terms with their feelings. On a few yachts the subject was never openly discussed.

Some crews never reached the performing stage, some never left storming. The lesson for the skippers was to acknowledge the stage the team were at and the state of their emotions and for the whole team to work through that stage together with the aid of their emotional intelligence behaviours.

One crew member likened the four stages to being seconded to a work-related project:

- Phase 1 is being excited.

- Phase 2 reality sets in and you think, 'what am I doing and I am depressed'.
- Phase 3 is beginning to like it and 'I am going to miss it'.
- Phase 4 is 'I have done it for the experience and achieved it'.

The change in dynamic effected by one person

There was a great deal of evidence to suggest that one person's behaviour could hugely change the dynamic of the crew. Sometimes a crew member just did not fit into the team or a legger who joined never managed to fit in properly. On several occasions leggers suffered through a lack of proper integration into the team. The dynamic was also affected when a particularly valued team member or legger left.

On one yacht a crew member was unable to start the race for medical reasons. This person was seen as significant because of his personality and ability to keep everyone's spirits up whatever the situation. On another yacht a legger brought a tremendous strength to the team through his ability to generate team loyalty and team spirit. His motivational encouragement was missed on the next leg. Another legger on the first leg of the race had been a real joker. The banter and laughter were greatly missed on leg 2. The team dynamic on both yachts changed when they left.

On several yachts there was a crew member who had an adverse effect on the dynamic of the crew. Their behaviour alienated them from their skipper and produced a negative feeling within the crew. By keeping themselves away from the rest of the team, they generated less support than there might have been. Sometimes the dynamic of a watch could be changed by swapping people around. Sometimes the issue with these individual crew members remained unresolved even at the end of the race. Some skippers felt in hindsight that they should have dealt more strongly with the individuals in question early on in the race.

On one yacht a crew member's behaviour caused the skipper to spend far too much energy and time trying to handle the situation. The skipper was very aware of the imbalance of his time between the team and the individual but was committed to trying to turn the situation around. The crew member left before the end of the race.

Fear often affected the behaviour of leggers joining a yacht. Several of them appeared to be ill for most of the leg. On one yacht a legger was seasick for the whole leg. On another yacht the legger became introverted. No one had taken the time to sit with him and find out his real feelings.

LESSONS FROM THE RACE

As a leader today you need to:

1. remember that team development is essential to high performance and the bottom line
2. take time for team retreats. They are vital for success
3. agree goals with your team
4. realise your team performance relies on 360-degree feedback
5. guide your team sensitively through the stages of development
6. understand the dynamics of the team.

REFERENCES

Blanchard, K., Zigarmi, P. and Zigarmi, D. (1985) *Leadership and the One Minute Manager*, Willow Books, Collins: London.

Higgs, M. and Dulewicz, V. (1999) *Making Sense of Emotional Intelligence*, NFER-Nelson: Windsor.

Luft, J. (1970) *Group Processes: An introduction to group dynamics*, 2nd edition, Mayfield Publishing Company: Mountain View, CA.

Tuckman, B. W. (1965) 'Developmental sequence in small groups', *Psychological Bulletin*, Vol. 63, pp. 384–399.

Woodcock, M. (1979) *Team Development Manual*, Gower: London.

GLOSSARY OF ATTRIBUTES AND SKILLS

PERSONAL ATTRIBUTES

Inner purpose   Having passion, energy and drive towards your personal mission.

Personal goals   Setting goals to achieve your personal mission.

Value set   Living by an inner set of ethical standards.

Integrity   Having a virtue of honesty and ethics.

Personal standards   Setting high standards for yourself.

Self-belief   Having confidence in your own ability to achieve.

Self-motivation   Generating drive and energy from within to achieve a course of action.

Self-control   Having the ability to keep emotions and feelings in check.

Self-regulation   Discipline to regulate all aspects of your life e.g. spiritual, mental, physical and social.

Self-development   Readiness to learn and develop yourself.

Performance focus   Being performance orientated in all you do.

Standback   Taking the time to review and reflect on the situation.

Sensing   Sniffing out the signals in both the environment and in people.

Consistency   Behaving in a dependable way.

Need for control   Having the appropriate level of control over others.

Openness   Being approachable and open to discuss issues, ideas, feelings and opinions of others.

Vulnerability   Selectively admitting weaknesses and mistakes in order to show authenticity; showing team that you are genuine and approachable.

Distance	Keeping a respected distance from the team.
Presence	Having physical power, charisma and confidence to be different.
Flexibility	Adapting to changing circumstances.

MANAGEMENT SKILLS

Agreed goals	Collaboratively agreeing project or team goals.
Agreed values	Collaboratively agreeing team values.
Discipline	Being strict with team members. Setting up appropriate rules and regulations.
Preparation and planning	Designing and organising things in advance.
Roles	Understanding job definitions.
Sound management procedures	Establishing a management process that is relevant, understood and used. Having the freedom to input on management process effectiveness.
Control management	Measuring processes against agreed benchmarks.
Resource management	Capitalising on all forms of resource.
Communication management	Establishing an effective system for the exchange of information, ideas and feelings.
Knowledge management	Effectively turning information into knowledge.
Stress management	Agreeing effective methods of stress relief.
Conflict management	Providing an effective forum for the discussion and resolution of opposed ideas and interests.
Individual development	Adopting appropriate systems to ensure individual growth.
Delegation	Having the ability to entrust tasks to another person.
Review	Adopting effective methods to constructively re-examine events.

Feedback 1:1	Establishing an effective system for the constructive assessment of individual performance on a one-to-one basis.
Continuous improvement	Having the ability to create an environment where new and better ways of working are constantly sought.

LEADERSHIP

Purpose	Inspiring passion within the team to achieve the agreed team mission.
Vision	Inspiring the team to buy into a concept by being able to paint a clear picture of the desired future outcome.
Values	Inspiring the team to live by the agreed value set.
Support and trust	Creating an environment where support is ingrained and trust is implicit.
Recognition	Giving genuine praise to inspire the team to do more and recognising everyone as an individual.
Belief	Inspiring optimism within the team and inspiring others to believe in themselves through building confidence.
Performance focus	Creating an environment where performance is at the centre of everything.
Motivation	Inspiring energy and drive within the team.
Communication	Creating an environment where information is the life blood of performance.
Shared leadership	Creating an environment where pro-activity is encouraged, accountability is shared and team buy-in is sought.
Distributed leadership	Passing the leadership baton to another member of the team for a specific task.
Regulation	Creating an environment where the team take responsibility for their own well-being.
Humour and fun	Injecting appropriate humour into the team and inspire a fun loving culture.

III

KEY BUSINESS ISSUES

MOTIVATION IN BUSINESS
Tesco Stores Ltd

Tesco managers have always recognised that well-motivated people (individuals and teams) are essential for sustained success.

In the mid-1990s, with the pressure to sustain increased levels of productivity while dealing with the demands of an increasing range of products and services, a review of work methods was started known as 'FUTURE', aimed at 'freeing up our people so that they can do more'. It was recognised that there was a danger of rising costs and increased complexity in the business which would make it more difficult for staff to stay motivated and focused on customers' needs. 'FUTURE' would inevitably impact significantly on staff, creating an environment of uncertainty during this period of intense change. To ensure that the changes implemented were effective and that staff felt motivated, everyone had the opportunity to voice their opinions and identify which tasks could be simplified or stopped (as they added no value for the customer).

The consultation and involvement process, combined with additional communication, resulted in a release of energy and enthusiasm in staff as they became aware that their views were appreciated and ideas actioned. The process was really making a difference. As well as identifying opportunities to simplify work methods and make jobs more interesting through a focus on the customer, feedback highlighted that leadership style and involvement through regular communication was critical in maintaining high levels of motivation and productivity. The introduction of situational leadership helped managers to implement the changes in their stores by identifying when they should flex their style to meet specific individual needs. This has since been integrated into the performance management process.

Routines and tools that encourage more face-to-face communication on an individual basis and team meetings to brief and consult staff on issues relevant to them, the store/department and organisation as a whole, have helped ensure staff remain motivated even in times of intense change.

The learning from 'FUTURE' in the stores was utilised subsequently in all parts of Tesco and has demonstrated how the Tesco values create a climate of motivation to sustain and build on success.

6

MOTIVATION – STAYING AHEAD OF THE COMPETITION

At Tesco, we look after our people so they take care of our customers. This simple, but effective equation is at the heart of our success. It is through our people that we have become the UK's leading retailer and this investment in them is helping us become a global player. Underpinning the success of the Tesco Team are core values, which ensure our people stay motivated and committed. Our One Team continues to be number one for customers. We value our staff through trust and respect, make their work more satisfying and enable them to progress and share in our successes.

Sir Terry Leahy, Chief Executive, Tesco Stores Ltd

Contributions to this chapter have been made
by the following Forum member:
John Metherell, Tesco Stores Ltd

INTRODUCTION

Those who have received training for management and leadership have learned about motivation. Most leaders will also believe they are good at motivating their people. How many leaders, though, have thought deeply about the challenges of motivating in today's changing times? This chapter will stimulate readers to think more carefully about motivating their people and will demonstrate some new ideas to help them stay ahead of the competition.

The purpose of this chapter is to use parallels from the BT Global Challenge race to help leaders to understand motivation and management of performance and give practical advice on how to achieve a motivated workforce and sustain high performance during turbulent times. It will explain the nature of motivation and summarise relevant theories and research. Particular emphasis will be given to motivational drivers and the different leadership approaches to motivation.

WHAT IS THE NATURE OF MOTIVATION AND HOW CAN THEORIES AND RESEARCH HELP LEADERS MOTIVATE OTHERS?

According to the Industrial Society (1999), the task of motivating others is one of the most difficult challenges for business leaders. Motivation is certainly a complex concept, as what motivates one person may very well not motivate another. Few would dispute, however, that well-motivated people are far more likely to perform better in their jobs than those who are less motivated. However, although motivation continues to be of ongoing interest for researchers, no significant theory explaining the nature and process of motivation has been advanced in the past 20 years.

According to Steers and Porter (1979), most definitions for explaining motivation have focused on three factors:

1. The driving forces: where does the energy come from to drive behaviour?
2. Goal orientation: what is it that directs and channels behaviour?
3. Feedback mechanism: what are the internal and environmental factors that help sustain this behaviour?

Theories of motivation have sought to provide answers to three questions:

1. **What needs do people seek to satisfy?**
   Knowing the 'needs' people are seeking to satisfy will help leaders match people to those jobs where their needs are most likely to be met. Individuals do not, however, always know the needs they

seek to satisfy – they are internal to the individual. An unsatisfied
need drives behaviour.

2. **What external factors influence human behaviour?**
   Leaders have more control over the external environment. An
   understanding of the particular extrinsic factors, for example financial incentives, or intrinsic motivators such as meaningful work will
   help the leader to develop the appropriate motivation strategies.

3. **How does a person choose between various courses of action?**
   This approach helps leaders understand the process people use to
   decide how to behave. For example, when faced with a certain
   task people may say to themselves, 'is the reward worth the effort
   I need to put in to achieve it?'

WHAT NEEDS DO PEOPLE SEEK TO SATISFY?

Understanding the needs people seek to satisfy is critical for motivating
others. Leaders who understand their people are better able to maximise their potential and set goals that will motivate the whole team.
They can also ensure that people are actively involved and will give that
bit of extra effort on a task rather than becoming alienated and not
'pulling their weight'.

According to Murray (1938) there is a range of needs people seek to
satisfy:

- achievement
- autonomy
- order
- aggression

- affiliation
- endurance
- power
- harm avoidance.

An individual may be described as having a high need for achievement and power and a low need for affiliation all at the same time. This
makes Murray's theory much more specific and it has retained great
popularity over time.

Maslow's (1987) hierarchy of needs seeks to explain what goals motivate people (Figure 6.1). He describes needs in terms of a hierarchy and
states that people are always seeking to satisfy needs, which in turn

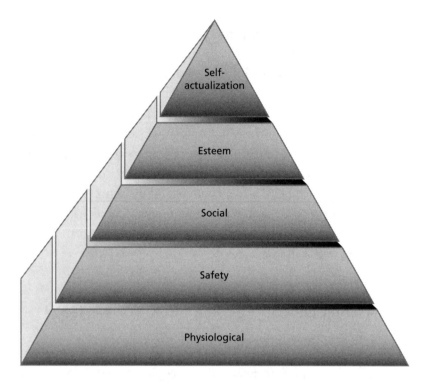

FIGURE 6.1 Maslow's hierarchy of needs

directs their behaviour. A person must first have satisfied what he terms the 'lower-order' factors – starting with basic physiological needs – before 'higher-order' needs such as self-esteem become a motivator.

As a model of motivation, Maslow's hierarchy is still widely used to help leaders understand the range of needs people seek to satisfy, although individuals may not follow through in the logical order suggested by Maslow. In business today people strive to move up the hierarchy to achieve self-actualisation, although few actually make it. In reality, situations occur which mean that 'lower-order' needs often become a priority. For example, a person may have a well-paid, secure job with high status and is motivated by the need for self-actualisation. They are made redundant and suddenly survival becomes much more important. People can of course satisfy needs at work or outside of work and people vary in the extent to which work is a central life interest. Many enjoy their work and may seek to satisfy most of their needs in the workplace. In contrast, others may have a very full life outside work and therefore come to work to satisfy a different set of needs. It can be summed up by the quote: 'Living to work or working to live.'

This issue is presenting a challenge to organisations today as individuals struggle to restore the work/life balance.

Alderfer (1969) developed a 'three factor' theory of needs, closely related to Maslow's hierarchy of needs but described as a continuum of behaviour. The three factors are:

1. existence – similar to Maslow's physiological and safety needs
2. relatedness – similar to Maslow's social needs
3. growth – similar to Maslow's esteem and self-actualisation needs.

Alderfer, like Murray, states that people can seek to satisfy more than one set of needs in parallel. People may want a stimulating job and at the same time be well paid. He also states that if people cannot satisfy the need for personal growth, social or existence needs will assume far greater importance. Leaders should ask themselves whether they are meeting the needs of their people. If they are losing highly talented people it suggests that these employees are not getting their intrinsic needs satisfied at work.

People who volunteered to take part in the BT Global Challenge race arrived with a wide variety of motives, partly related to their careers and partly to their personal lives.

These differing motives included:
- to have a once-in-a-lifetime experience with potential for development of self
- to satisfy a sense of achievement, to have sailed around the world
- to attain sense of personal power and importance from this major achievement
- to satisfy a need for challenge and adventure
- to get out of a rut
- to take a change of direction in their lives
- to find a new partner or make new friends
- an opportunity to make a fresh start either job-wise or in terms of a relationship.

The skippers had the challenge of pulling together a wide set of needs and coming up with goals that would satisfy all the needs of the team. One skipper recognised that some of his crew were not highly competitive. Therefore setting a goal to win the race may not have motivated them, so he focused on having a 'life experience', sailing round the world, developing sailing expertise, and themselves as people. In this way the race took on a deeper, almost spiritual importance and the crew, through the skipper, developed a broader purpose beyond the race itself.

The race offered the opportunity to satisfy many of the needs listed above. It also clearly challenged people, but at times forces in the external environment took away some of the basic physiological needs and meant that people became more focused on the need for survival. For example, food was carefully rationed and if yachts took longer than planned to complete a leg, the crew ran short of food. One or two yachts actually ran out of food. Under these circumstances the basic needs assumed far more importance than is normally the case.

The needs of leaders must also be taken into account. According to McClelland (1961), three types of need motivate leaders:

- achievement
- affiliation
- power.

The need that motivates the leader may tend to influence the way he seeks to motivate others. If a person is motivated by the need for achievement he is likely to be task-focused and always looking for ways to do things better. If a person is motivated by the need for affiliation he is likely to be more focused on people and sensitive to the needs of others. Those who are motivated by the need for power are likely to focus on situations which enable them to persuade, influence and ultimately control others. The skippers completed a McClelland questionnaire prior to the race to measure which of the three needs was dominant.

People in the team will also have their own, individual set of needs. If these are aligned with those of the leader they are more likely to be motivated. The approach that the skippers adopted to motivate others was partly a reflection of their own motives but also took into account the motivational needs of others.

WHAT EXTERNAL FACTORS INFLUENCE BEHAVIOUR?

Leaders need to know the external factors that will help act as motivators and factors that will give rise to dissatisfaction and be demotivating. Herzberg (1968) identifies two sets of external factors (see Table 6.1) which influence motivation at work. The 'hygiene' factors are the 'dissatisfiers' and relate to conditions surrounding the job. They are the extrinsic factors that Herzberg says will not motivate individuals but which can determine people's attitudes in either a positive or negative way, depending on how satisfactory they are. They are important – without them people will not be motivated. Working conditions, for example, are a hygiene factor and although good working conditions may result in positive attitudes, they do not necessarily lead to higher performance.

The 'motivators' are 'intrinsic' factors and are more closely job related, such as recognition for a job well done. According to Herzberg, high motivation is achieved only when both the 'hygiene' factors and motivators are met. Controversially, pay is included as a hygiene factor – Herzberg states that it is probably the most important 'hygiene factor' but on its own it is not a motivator.

The theory has been challenged on the basis that not everyone, particularly at different stages in the life cycle, is motivated by intrinsic factors – hygiene factors can become motivators themselves. For example, many

TABLE 6.1 Herzberg's hygiene factors and motivators

Hygiene/maintenance factors	Motivators
Company policy and administration	Achievement
Supervision	Recognition
Salary	Work itself
Interpersonal relations	Responsibility
Physical working conditions	Advancement

young people leave university with large debts and are more likely to be motivated by money to reduce their loans. Indeed, some businesses have recognised this financial motivator and are even offering 'golden hellos', including complete repayment of an individual's debts, as a way of attracting the most talented graduates. The theory is still relevant for helping leaders in business to recognise the importance of the motivational factors such as challenging work and taking care of the factors which, according to Herzberg, could be demotivational.

During the race, skippers had to motivate their crews under quite difficult physical conditions. The yachts were confined and during the Southern Ocean stretches people were often wet, cold and tired. However, those crews that were highly motivated through a sense of achievement and satisfaction from doing a job well were able to ride above the difficult working conditions which could be demotivating for those crews doing less well. Today organisations are recognising the importance of office surroundings in achieving a motivated workforce.

The high-performing skippers all paid attention to intrinsic motivators. They made the work on-board meaningful by giving explanations as to why individuals were doing a particular task. They gave people a feeling of achievement by setting a series of milestones and through shared leadership gave their teams a sense of responsibility, commitment to what they were doing and ownership.

In contrast, some lower-performing skippers made people feel demotivated by treating the team unfairly, particularly by having favourites. Some gossiped with certain crew members and they did not always uphold the values agreed by the team.

HOW DOES A PERSON CHOOSE HOW TO BEHAVE?

Leaders need to know how people will react when they attempt to motivate them. Expectancy theory put forward by Vroom (1964), and adapted by Nadler and Lawler (1979), helps to answer two questions:

1. How much effort are people prepared to put into a task?
2. How do people go about performing their work?

It is based on a set of assumptions about the way that an individual makes decisions about their behaviour.

Expectancy

Expectancy is the relationship between a chosen course of action and achievement of the desired outcome. In the first instance the outcome may be money or high productivity. However, through performance a second set of outcomes may be achieved such as praise, promotion or friendship with work colleagues.

Valence

Similarly, each outcome has a valence, or in other words an anticipated satisfaction for a particular outcome, to an individual. For example, while one person might have a need for power, someone else might have a need for achievement and someone else a need for financial reward. If an individual is offered a bonus for achieving a target and they have an overdraft at the bank, the bonus will have perceived value to that person. Someone else with different financial circumstances may find the prospect of time off more attractive.

Effort

Effort relates to the amount of energy a person exerts on a particular activity. The amount of effort put in depends on the value of the reward and the effort–reward relationship, i.e. that certain rewards are dependent upon a given amount of effort. People will be motivated if:

- they are confident of achieving high performance based on realistic expectations
- the reward is highly valued and they feel it is worth the effort to achieve the reward
- they feel they will receive the reward if they perform
- they perceive the rewards as fair.

In contrast, when individuals are having difficulty performing, their motivation level may drop, particularly when the likelihood of achieving a certain goal is not high. They will also be demotivated when the reward is not worth the effort required or they are not confident of receiving the reward.

The expectancy model supports Herzberg in saying that intrinsic factors are more likely to lead to satisfaction than extrinsic factors. As a model it provides a useful way of understanding why some people work harder than others and the fact that performance gives rise to satisfaction.

Expectancy theory was particularly applicable to the race. For example, those skippers who were performing less well started to lose motivation as their confidence in achieving a podium position dropped. However, when a yacht came first in a leg, the skipper and crew were highly motivated because their confidence in their ability to achieve a winning position had risen. It also explains why success breeds success. If people had the expectation that they would achieve a winning position they were more likely to work harder than those who had less belief in their ability to achieve the goal.

GOALS AS A MEANS OF MOTIVATING OTHERS

According to Locke (1968), the primary determinants of people's actions are the goals they set themselves. If certain rules are followed, setting goals can also be a useful tool for motivating others.

- Goals need to be challenging to stretch people, but achievable to be motivational. If goals are too easy people will not be motivated.
- If they are too difficult people will be demotivated.
- Working to goals that are unattractive to people is also demotivating.
- A lack of alignment between an individual's goals and those of the organisation should also be avoided.

In the race, clarity, focus and alignment of goals clearly helped to achieve high performance. Goal setting is discussed later in this chapter.

As a leader you need to remember:
1. Motivation is individual; what motivates one person may not motivate another.
2. A 'need' becomes more important if it is not satisfied.
3. More than one 'need' can drive behaviour at the same time.
4. Goals can be motivational, but they must be shared by the team and should be challenging and achievable.
5. Understand your people and you will be more able to maximise their potential and set goals that will motivate the whole team.

MANAGEMENT, LEADERSHIP AND MOTIVATION

Leaders have a major impact on motivation, and this will vary depending on whether management or leadership attributes are being used.

Transactional leadership – management and motivation

The leader can ensure he motivates people by using the appropriate leadership style with each person. According to Blanchard *et al.* (1985), when a person is inexperienced and new to a particular job they start as an enthusiastic beginner; a task-focused, directive style enables them to perform. Later on, however, the person may experience difficulty mastering a particular task and become less motivated. At this stage the leader needs to maintain the task focus but combine it with relationship building and a coaching style. Motivation and increased performance are achieved through encouragement and praise.

A further method, the supporting style, becomes appropriate once the person has mastered the task but still lacks confidence and motivation. Encouragement and praise maintain motivation at the appropriate levels and shared decision making acts as a further motivator. Finally, delegation gives maximum freedom to the person to operate. Here, a person's motivation comes from intrinsic factors such as responsibility, meaningful work and involvement.

Using intrinsic motivation

According to Thomas (2000), those who are intrinsically motivated:

- genuinely care about their work
- look for ways of doing things better
- feel energised and fulfilled by doing a job well
- have lower stress levels than those lacking intrinsic motivation.

Thomas goes on to recommend lessons about intrinsic motivation:

- **Encouraging self-management by directing activities towards a common purpose** – leaders need to ensure they communicate a sense of purpose to their people as those who feel commitment to a certain task are motivated.
- **Pursuing something worthwhile and enjoying the journey** – many jobs provide people with meaningful work. Those who are intrinsically motivated are able both to enjoy their work and experience pride and involvement. Rewards at regular intervals are also important to keep people alert and involved.
- **Self-management requires logical decisions powered by emotion** – decision making is a logical process and works best when people are emotionally involved.

Where does this feeling of involvement come from?

- **From having a sense of meaningfulness** – when the person is pursuing a worthwhile purpose, they find it easy to focus and will find ways round obstacles.
- **Having choice** – this gives the person a sense of ownership and a feeling of personal responsibility for outcomes. The person is more able to experiment when they have choice.
- **A sense of competence** – this gives the person a feeling of pride in their performance, a sense of mastery and confidence they will be able to perform in the future.
- **A sense of progress** – this gives the feeling that things are working and the person feels enthusiastic and eager to continue.

Overall motivational health can be judged by signs of emotions. If people are experiencing negativity they will feel distracted, uninvolved, dissatisfied with lack of achievement, discouraged and unenthusiastic. Intrinsic motivation is built by shaping people's interpretations of tasks. Leaders need to help people make these interpretations meaningful. People develop habits that skew interpretations, for example, focusing only on what has gone wrong rather than reviewing what has gone well.

During the race the high-performing skippers used their skills and attributes to inspire people to perform. They had positive emotional health, were enjoying themselves and were able to feel a sense of fulfilment. In contrast, the lower-performing skippers were less able to motivate people as the race progressed. Much of this lack of motivation could be attributed to the way the team was led.

Attitudes towards people

The attitudes leaders develop towards their people is another important factor in motivation. According to Norgaard (2001), the beliefs and opinions leaders have of their people dictates their leadership style and ability to motivate them. Leaders who view their staff as inherently stupid or lazy will, for example, be more likely to act as the ultimate authority and direct others. In such a relationship of low trust the leader is more likely to adopt a controlling style and performance decreases. Fair and equal treatment of people is also important and leaders with favourites lose the respect of the rest of the team.

However, those leaders who recognise individual talent and who do not have the need to control others, are more likely to engage in an interdependent relationship by sharing information and supporting others. In a trusting and egalitarian environment, people will see themselves as valued and be motivated. Those leaders who adopt such a positive attitude towards their people are, unsurprisingly, much more likely to achieve high performance.

During the race the high-performing skippers developed very positive attitudes towards their teams and treated the team members fairly. They talked about their team with pride. As the race progressed, however, some of the lower-performing skippers had a less positive relationship with their teams and there was a lack of support and trust on both sides. This was demotivating for both the skippers and their teams.

> As a leader you need to remember:
> 1. Motivation comes from intrinsic factors such as responsibility, meaningful work and involvement.
> 2. Transformational leaders satisfy the need for belonging, achievement, recognition, self-esteem and a sense of control.
> 3. Decision making works best when people are emotionally involved.
> 4. Leaders can inspire others by building energising visions and celebrating success.
> 5. People who are intrinsically motivated are able both to enjoy their work and experience a feeling of pride and involvement.
> 6. Leaders who adopt a positive attitude to their people are more likely to achieve high performance.

MOTIVATION IN TOUGH TIMES

Motivation is an important and difficult aspect of leadership under all conditions, but especially in times of great uncertainty and insecurity. During the race, for example, the skippers had to contend with tropical storms on the Boston to Buenos Aires leg, extreme heat while passing through the Doldrums, and the notoriously dangerous seas while rounding Cape Horn.

Today's business leaders face the challenge of motivating their people in very competitive circumstances. To stay ahead requires new and innovative ways of behaving and unless people are well motivated, businesses can lose out to the competition. Business leaders also need to ensure they maximise the potential of each of their people to meet targets that are becoming more challenging with increasing competition.

When people are faced with these challenges they either perform well or their performance drops because of the excessive pressure and they become demoralised and unable to cope. When motivating in difficult times, the leader must hold the team together to help people cope with uncertainty and insecurity. Focusing people on the right goals is very necessary at such times to prevent demotivation and excessive stress.

A number of factors are especially important to remember.

1. **Being able to build relationships based on respect and trust.**
   Kennedy (2001) stresses the importance of the leader being emotionally connected with his people to keep them motivated and cohesive as a team. This means building a relationship of trust and respect. The leader is then in a better position to harness people's energy and build the commitment of the team.

2. **Having a high probability of winning.**
   Kennedy also suggests that to sustain motivation people need to believe they have a high probability of winning. Winning can be defined in different ways, but people need to be goal directed to be motivated and they need confidence that their leader will bring them to the goal. This requires careful objective setting to ensure goals are achievable. When a team is experiencing tough conditions, the confidence which comes from success helps it weather the difficult times.

3. **The need for empathy.**
   Emmerich (2001) emphasises that to increase motivation and performance, leaders need to create a forum for people to share feelings during difficult times so that they can release their feelings and move on. During the race some of the skippers recognised the importance of building an open culture and creating opportunities for feelings to be discussed. In business, leaders must ensure they have an open approach and encourage their people to say how they are feeling.

4. **Shifting the focus to making a difference.**
   Emmerich also states that to instil passion in a team, the shared vision needs to focus on making a difference for others. This will stretch the team rather than them doing just enough to cope or get by. People who have emotional commitment to what they are doing are more likely to put in extra effort. Today many leaders

are involved in the service industry. Those people who can see how their role fits into the bigger picture and the way they make the difference are more likely to be motivated. During the race skippers who explained how each task contributed to the overall goals achieved a more motivated crew.

5. **Handling a lack of success – appreciate the steps along the way.** Emmerich also feels that when things are not going well, frustration levels rise, confidence is lost and performance lowers, spiralling ever downwards. However, showing appreciation for people and their efforts can break the cycle. Goal setting at this stage becomes important to boost people with small wins. Introducing fun also relieves the tension and raises motivational levels. During the tough parts of the race skippers looked for ways to maintain an element of fun and took opportunities for celebrations such as birthdays and special occasions.

6. **The importance of having fun and the occasional celebration.** Sometimes when businesses are experiencing a downturn, leaders feel celebrations are costly and cut them out. Successful leaders, however, recognise their importance and in this way are more able to sustain motivation.

Dealing with boredom

When people are required to undertake routine work, boredom can set in. The yachts that had a strong performance focus experienced less of an issue with boredom and these teams were continually driving the extra bit of performance from the yacht. This kept their energy levels higher. One of the skippers became conscious of boredom creeping in during long periods of inactivity and created word exercises to keep people mentally focused.

Another example from the race illustrates how managing well in adversity can enhance motivation and help develop a high-performance team. Just before a race restart at one of the ports of call a crew discovered that the fuel in their yacht was contaminated. This meant siphoning it off and refuelling, but not in time to restart the race. At first the team were very despondent, but the skipper gathered them together and explained they could either stay this way or make the best of the situation. He left the team to discuss how they felt and how they wanted to handle it. Having had the chance to offload their feelings, the team handled the situation in a positive way. They left the port about eight hours after the rest of the fleet. The skipper then used the leg to develop the team to work well. They enjoyed the leg and the skipper set a realistic goal, to come in 11th out of the 12 yachts. The team achieved the goal, were highly motivated to perform well in the next leg and went on to win it.

Effective leaders thrive in turbulent times because they rise to the challenge and know that if they can motivate people and sustain performance in the tough times, they will do even better in the good times.

Dealing with low morale

Low morale usually results from a lack of satisfaction and leads to reduced motivation. Communication and active listening are two of the important skills needed to restore morale. Initially, some one-to-one discussions are helpful to ascertain causes of dissatisfaction. Once the leader has a feel for the situation, open two-way discussion will give the opportunity to dispel frustrations and leave people in a position to move forward. Here, leaders need to assess their style of leadership – 'Am I part of the problem and if so what changes need to take place to rectify the situation?'

Causes of dissatisfaction need to be addressed. Steps need to be taken to build team commitment. This will be discussed later in the chapter.

> As a leader you need to:
> 1. connect emotionally with your team to help build a relationship of respect and trust
> 2. set achievable goals – the confidence from achievement of the goals will help people survive the tough times
> 3. encourage people to be open and say how they feel

4. show people how their role fits into the bigger picture and explain why they are doing things
5. remember the importance of having fun and celebrating
6. remember that communication and active listening are two of the important skills to help restore low morale.

THE MOTIVATION OF THE SKIPPERS

The motives, personal goals and the motivation element of emotional intelligence all had an influence on the ultimate performance of the yachts. Personal motivation influenced the leadership style and approach the skippers adopted to motivate their teams. Depending on their personal needs, the skippers demonstrated different behaviour towards their teams. Personal goals were important and impacted on the goals that were set for the team and the extent to which the skippers drew attention to the team goals. The majority of skippers were demonstrating a high level of motivation behaviour on the emotional intelligence element at the start of the race. This meant there was evidence of drive and energy among the skippers and a focus on achievement of goals.

McClelland motivational needs

As mentioned above, the skippers completed a McClelland questionnaire as part of the selection process for the race. The purpose of this questionnaire was to obtain a profile of the three motives – the need for achievement, affiliation or power – identified by McClelland, which would help predict how the skippers were likely to behave and what would give them satisfaction. The results showed:

- **A high need for achievement.** The majority of skippers had a high need for achievement. This meant most were task-focused and accepted responsibility for the success or failure of the task. They also sought continuous improvement. While all these factors were very motivational for the crew, some skippers who became too task-focused could lack sensitivity to people. The other downside of a dominant achievement need is that the skipper could be reluctant to delegate, wanting to do everything himself. At least two of the lower-performing skippers had a problem delegating to others.

- **A high need for affiliation.** Three of the skippers had a high need for 'affiliation' and thus focused strongly on relationships. They were sensitive to the feelings of others and these skippers were more likely to inspire their crews. They also valued the companionship of others and were very aware of achieving a good work/life balance, but like other skippers they had difficulty striking the right balance. A confident skipper was able to achieve a spontaneous co-operative approach with his team. However, a less confident skipper wanted to be liked by others and found it hard to take unpopular decisions or deal with conflict.

- **A high need for power.** The need for power was the main driver for two of the skippers. They valued their influential and prestigious role and enjoyed the opportunity to influence and persuade others. The upside of this driver is that in an emergency situation, having a strong personality to take charge could be motivational. However, these two skippers also needed to be aware of the potentially harmful effects of power as a motivator. For example, once people had developed a level of competence in certain tasks they would want to be given responsibility. In this context, an over-bearing skipper, unable to relinquish control, may well demotivate his team. Another effect of the need for power being the main need was that there could be a higher tendency to take riskier decisions 'to be noticed'. Both the skippers at certain times in the race did take different and riskier decisions than the rest of the fleet.

Examples of skippers using their personal motivation well

The motivational profiles of the skippers sometimes worked in their favour. One skipper with a high achievement drive was always looking for ways to maximise the performance of the yacht. The crew timed sail changes and they knew when they had done a good gybe. The team had set themselves benchmarks for continual improvement and reviewed good and bad sail changes.

Another skipper similarly motivated was viewed as very task-focused by the crew and would take a lot of time planning and making preparations. He also insisted, even during calm and relatively boring periods, that none of the crew were to read novels or focus on anything other than the race.

A skipper who had a high affiliation need was very sensitive to the needs of others and able to resolve potential problems. Even before the race had begun this skipper had become aware that one of the crew members had become demotivated and unsure why they were taking part in the race. The skipper discussed the problem on a one-to-one basis and was able to help restore the person's motivation. Another skipper motivated by high affiliation needs was able to create a good team dynamic on his yacht. The team had undergone a teambuilding event prior to the race. An external facilitator had been used and he had helped the skipper create a very open culture within the team.

Examples of skippers using their personal motivation less well

The motivational profiles of the skippers sometimes worked against them. One task-focused high achiever, for example, was so focused on the preparation of the yacht in the port of call that he insisted on the whole crew being present for a three-day period to prepare the vessel. In fact, there was clearly not enough work for all of them and this was potentially demotivating, especially as it impacted on the crew's relaxation period in port. Nor did the same skipper socialise with his crew in this port. Another high-achieving skipper, sometimes too task-focused, needed to switch a person from one watch to another. He made the swap without any consultation with the crew, showing a lack of sensitivity towards the feelings of others.

A skipper with a high need for affiliation was reluctant to address the difficult interpersonal issue of one particular crew member who remained detached and isolated from the others. This person did not always pull his weight on-board and had a difficult relationship with the skipper. The skipper was prepared to deal with the situation but each time backed away because he disliked conflict and wanted to be liked.

Finally, one skipper with a high need for affiliation lost the task focus in the port of call. After focusing his attention on helping the two new leggers feel part of the team, he celebrated success in the previous leg with the crew. He then realised that he had spent insufficient time on preparing the yacht for the next leg.

Personal goals

Personal goals are defined as those goals set by an individual to achieve a personal mission. These had a critical influence on performance in the race. Prior to the race start the skippers identified personal goals and also spent time with their crews agreeing a shared goal. Even at this stage the higher-performing skippers were already more performance-focused than their lower-performing counterparts. The higher performers identified finishing in the top three as their goal. Some of these skippers wanted to progress their careers as professional skippers and a good position was therefore very important to them. The lower-performing skippers did not identify winning as their ultimate objective, instead they were more focused on building the team and enjoying the experience.

In seeking to establish a shared goal the biggest split within the crews was whether people were there to race competitively around the world with the intention of winning or to enjoy an interesting challenge and the adventure of sailing round the world. The podium skippers quickly addressed the issue of this being a race and constantly reminded the crew that the shared goal was to win. One of these yachts, however, went halfway round the world before the skipper and crew really believed they could win the race, and then were able to win a leg.

**' It's all down to expectations, it is so different from how I imagined. '**

If goals were to act as motivators, the biggest challenge facing the skippers was how to manage the crews' expectations. The skippers found it was one thing to sit in a classroom environment and discuss goals and another to be out at sea working towards achieving those goals. Once the crews were at sea they found the goals were far less achievable than they had expected, and the whole experience different from what they had anticipated.

MOTIVATION AS AN ELEMENT OF EMOTIONAL INTELLIGENCE

Higgs and Dulewicz (1999) identified motivation as one of the elements of emotional intelligence. A high level of the motivation element is demonstrated by the following behaviours:

- consistently focusing on performance
- looking for ways to overcome obstacles to attain goals
- setting challenging goals or encouraging others to set challenging goals.

A low level of the motivation element is demonstrated by the following behaviours:

- dislike of committing to goals personally
- unwillingness or inability to encourage others to commit to challenging goals
- willingness to accept barriers to achieving goals
- lack of belief in being able to achieve stretching objectives.

In this research the skippers' behaviours were mapped onto the motivation element. It was found that at the start of the race all the skippers were demonstrating behaviour indicative of a high level of motivation. The higher-performing skippers sustained this motivation behaviour throughout the race. These skippers were confident and believed they could succeed. They sustained their goal-directed behaviour, regularly reminded the crews of the goals and had commitment to achieving challenging goals.

In contrast, the lower-performing skippers, at some stage during the race, experienced a loss of self-confidence and self-belief which raised their stress levels and had a negative impact on performance, causing a downward spiral. By the end of the race the lower-performing skippers were demonstrating behaviour indicative of low motivational behaviour. They lost focus on the goals and did not remind the crew of the goals. There was less evidence of these skippers and their teams reviewing to improve the way they did things.

USE OF DIFFERENT LEADERSHIP STYLES AS A MOTIVATOR

Chapters 3 and 5 described the leadership styles used by the skippers and gave the overview of findings. The four styles that can be used according to Blanchard *et al.* (1985) are the directing, coaching, supporting and delegating styles. When leaders tailor their leadership style to the person and the situation, this is motivational. This capability proved to be essential for high performance during the race and all the higher-performing skippers used a full range of leadership styles by the end of the race.

This section will illustrate with a series of examples how the good use of different styles helped the skippers motivate their teams and achieve higher performance. There are also examples of when the skippers used different leadership styles less well that in turn demotivated the team.

Examples of leadership styles being used well include:

- **Spending time during the latter part of the race to coach those who showed potential.** During a particular leg one skipper worked hard to raise the sailing capability of those showing interest and potential and who were enthusiastic to develop further. This helped to sustain motivation at a time when energy levels could have dropped and paid off when the yacht won the next leg of the race.
- **Using a blend of directive leadership, support and delegation after a traumatic situation.** One skipper operated well in a crisis, taking control and giving the crew confidence. He then delegated

responsibility to others and provided support to those having difficulty performing under the circumstances. Through using this range of styles appropriately, team motivation was sufficiently high to ensure performance.

- **Using the directing style, followed by the coaching style, in the early stages of the race to build confidence.** One skipper in a crisis situation with a spinnaker took charge to avoid damage to the sail or his people. Once the crisis was over the skipper, who was very keen to develop his team, took the crew through the procedures and the reason for his particular action.

- **Using the delegating style to give people a sense of involvement.** All the higher-performing skippers used the delegating style quite extensively, particularly during the latter part of the race. Increasing a person's autonomy in tasks where they have achieved a certain level of mastery gives them a sense of responsibility and involvement. For example, one or two of the skippers delegated the task of sailing the yacht to the crew while they focused on taking navigational decisions. Some of the crews also took responsibility for the preparation of the yachts at the ports of call. This both motivated the crews and removed some of the burden from the skippers, helping to keep their stress levels down.

Examples of leadership styles being used less well:

- **Switching between the delegating and directing style.** Several skippers would delegate sailing responsibilities to the crew before going below to work at the chart table. Some time later they would return to deck and revert to the hands-on directing style that both annoyed and demotivated the crew. This is a very common leadership style in business. Blanchard *et al.* (1985) describe it as 'seagull management': fly in, make a lot of noise, 'dump on everyone' and then fly out! Instead, the skippers should have focused on building relationships and using the supporting style if things were not going right, particularly after they had delegated a specific task to an individual.

- **Overuse of the directing style.** While some leaders switched too much between the delegating and directive styles, some concentrated too much on one or the other. In particular, the lower-performing skippers made too much use of the directing style, especially when they had lost their self-belief, had high stress levels and felt the need to control others. Used inappropriately, the directing style can be extremely demotivating and performance can suffer as a consequence. One crew, for example, was left to learn from their mistakes and waited until the skipper was out of sight to try new ways of doing things.

- **Overuse of the delegating style before the crew were ready.** It is also dangerous to delegate too quickly. For example, during the first leg of the race most of the skippers were already making extensive use of the delegating style, having clearly underestimated the level of inexperience of their crew.

- **Underuse of the coaching and supporting styles.** These two styles require a high relationship orientation. But as most of the skippers were of the higher-achiever mould, they tended to be more task-focused and did not adopt a coaching or supporting style when the crew became demotivated during the tough times. However, the high-performing skippers, particularly towards the end of the race, had begun to make more use of these methods. The lower-performing skippers who had lost self-belief and self-motivation and found it much more difficult to sustain relationships with their crews were unable to use these leadership styles. Consequently, the crew suffered from a lack of recognition and encouragement.

These examples demonstrate that leaders must be prepared to be highly responsive to the needs of their people and develop flexibility of style to suit both individuals and particular circumstances.

MOTIVATION THROUGH MANAGEMENT OF PERFORMANCE – THE X FACTOR

Motivation through the management of performance is achieved by group norms and pressures. With the right systems and procedures in

> ‘ *Maybe the difference in the ultimate performance is that one should never let things go and always look to make people do better.* ’

place, the team could deliver results consistently. The findings were analysed in Chapter 5, where reference was made to the X Factor, a group of attributes and skills referred to as the drivers of performance (see Figure 5.2, page 107).

The high-performing skippers all showed evidence of using these attributes and skills well. They were able to focus the team on achieving high performance and ensured the necessary systems and procedures were in place and adhered to by the team. The lower-performing skippers towards the end of the race were showing little evidence of using these attributes. We will now discuss the attributes, demonstrating the impact that they had on the skippers' and teams' behaviour and on the ultimate performance.

Discipline

This required the skippers to be strict with team members and set up appropriate rules and regulations. In a race such as this, discipline is imperative. At an early stage one of the high-performing skippers expected every one of the crew to adhere to his own high standards. The crew were very disciplined in every respect, including the way tasks

> ‘ *Walk the talk or lose respect.* ’

such as sail changes were organised and executed. They were also always disciplined to think one step ahead and a strong task focus dominated on deck. The yacht was viewed as a working environment – novels and music were not allowed on deck. This discipline helped them achieve high performance.

In contrast, another skipper who was less disciplined disliked using a controlling leadership style and was less rigid in enforcing discipline. He also disliked confrontation and handled issues indirectly, which usually did not have the desired effect. This approach at times had a negative impact on the yacht's performance, although watch leaders were able to support the skipper by enforcing discipline. For example, towards the end of the race when competition became stronger it was necessary for the crew to sit on the rail for long periods as the weight distribution made the yacht sail faster. This particular skipper could not get the crew to sit on the rail, although one of the watch leaders, better at enforcing discipline, made it happen.

Control management

This required the skipper to measure the processes against agreed benchmarks. The high-performing teams all ensured that once management procedures were in place they were monitored and controlled. One of the skippers who had extremely demanding standards would monitor what was going on and when systems were working well he would relax a little. The skipper and crew developed procedures for head sail changes and improved the process. Sail

' Come on guys, don't give up. '

changes were timed as a method of monitoring and control. Checklists were used to ensure people knew what was expected from them. Working to this level of precision meant the team had to be prepared mentally. The skipper always made sure the crew knew what was expected of them in advance so that they worked efficiently together as a result of the forward planning.

The lower-performing skippers nearly all had sound management procedures but were less meticulous about maintaining and monitoring these procedures. One yacht experienced a lack of mental preparation for the race after a stopover and the whole way of working, including control, was lost.

Resource management

Skippers who used the skill of resource management were able to get the best from the people available. This was an interesting attribute from a motivational perspective. The high-performing skippers adopted a policy of high-level specialisation, i.e. they had the person most suited for a particular task doing the job. This helped the yachts achieve peak performance and proved an efficient way to manage resources. For example, most of the crew wanted to develop their expertise at helming, the most popular activity on-board. However, the high-performing skippers assessed the capability of their crew and allowed only those really capable at the task to helm. The people

> ‘ *The best resource you have is the people around you.* ’

at the helm were instructed to stop helming if they were not performing at their best and hand over to someone else who might enhance the performance of the yacht. On high-performing yachts, each crew member had a specialist position and all were very motivated towards continuously improving their contribution and the performance of the vessel.

High-performing skippers were also able to gain the commitment of the crew to undertake the more unpopular activities – such as sitting on the rail and sleeping on the high side – when off watch. They achieved this by explaining to the crew the contribution this made to overall yacht speed and this is an important lesson for leaders: never assume people know why they are required to perform a task. Its purpose – obvious to the leader – might not be so clear to the employee.

Lower-performing skippers often took the view that people should be able to do what they wanted and one skipper was keen to ensure his crew developed the skills they had wanted to develop. Although this crew may have been less efficient, the skipper took the view that rotating people around the various positions would be more interesting and motivational. The cost was loss of efficiency.

Conflict management

Conflict management involved using conflict positively to encourage discussion and debate and resolving any negative conflict when it arose. Higher-performing skippers also had

> ‘ *Deal with the issue and let it go.* ’

a solid appreciation of conflict management and often encouraged 'positive' conflict. They usually had mechanisms in place for open communication, for example one skipper had the daily meeting, another the 'kangaroo court' (see page 221–2), both of which stopped problems being allowed to fester within the team and enabled crews to confront problems rather than ignore them. This had a motivational effect on the whole crew. Some of the lower-performing skippers, however, had a natural dislike of conflict and shied away from confrontation. Their failure to deal with issues led to a loss of respect and they were less able to motivate their crews (see Chapter 10).

Performance focus

Performance focus has been defined as 'creating an environment where performance is at the centre of everything the team does'. It was very much a part of the culture in high-performing yachts. The skippers who possessed this attribute were constantly looking at ways to improve performance, attending to the little things which, ultimately, made a big difference. This emphasis on performance, if conveyed properly, proved to be infectious and the crews from the high-performing yachts were all similarly looking for areas of improvement. The skipper identified and conveyed to the crew the responsibility for achieving high performance.

> *If the individuals remain focused and motivated, the team will do well.*

One high-performing skipper, for example, set very high standards from the start and kept demanding more of his crew, who in turn asked to be pushed harder. Another yacht set the performance bar at an achievable level and then raised the bar each time the crew felt ready to achieve a higher level. On this particular yacht 90 per cent of discussion was performance-related – idle chat was not encouraged.

This performance focus was missing in the lower-performing yachts, sometimes because of a lack of shared goals – if people were there more for the thrill of the adventure and not the actual race, winning and high performance were, of course, less of an issue. Leaders need to recognise the

> *I have learned in the race, you can't force people to want to win.*

importance of identifying their own goals in performance terms and take steps to influence the needs of others if they are to achieve a performance focus within their team.

MOTIVATION THROUGH INSPIRING BEHAVIOUR – THE Y FACTOR

People are motivated through inspiring behaviour to achieve the vision. It energises individuals through satisfying the needs for achievement, belonging, recognition, self-esteem and feeling in control. Again in Chapter 5 a group of attributes was identified which was referred to as the Y Factor (see Figure 5.3, page 109). Skippers who had these personal attributes had an open style and were receptive to the ideas of others. They were prepared to admit to mistakes and were able to create a motivational culture. The inspirational skippers who had these leadership attributes were able to create a vision which stimulated an inner drive within the team to achieve the vision. This energy, combined with the skippers' use of motivating behaviour, created an environment on the yacht which built a committed and highly motivated team.

When skippers used these attributes they became inspiring leaders. The teams developed a high level of commitment and were more able to sustain performance for the duration of the race. Inspiring behaviour is very important in turbulent

' This is a crew that is really motivated and wants to win. '

times because it gives individuals the passion and energy needed to find new and better ways of doing things. It helps to hold the team together and builds emotional commitment and a passion to perform well.

Self-belief

The skippers who had high self-belief had developed confidence from past performance and believed they could sustain or improve performance in the future. All the high-performing skippers shared a feeling

> **‹ Leadership requires the courage of convictions. ›**

of self-belief. One had such strong self-belief, for example, that he reported that even when things were not going well he always believed they would come right, and they did. Such self-belief of course had an important motivating effect on the crew.

On one occasion another crew did not believe that it was possible to take down the mainsail in bad weather. The skipper, however, had confidence in the crew's abilities and used those crew who had done it before to help those who hadn't. The skipper then stayed at the helm giving the crew confidence they could do the task, and they successfully took down the sail.

Although all the skippers started the race with feelings of self-belief, the lower-performing skippers began to lose their self-confidence as the race progressed. Once they had lost their self-motivating behaviour, they had great difficulty inspiring their crews.

Integrity

Skippers who had high integrity were honest and upheld the values of the yacht. They respected their crew and in return were well respected

> **‹ Respect by example is the best way to lead. ›**

themselves, leading to good motivation levels. These yachts operated with a 'no-blame culture' and the skippers also prepared people for difficult sea conditions ahead, such as special plans for rounding Cape Horn.

Certain skippers, however, demonstrated a lack of integrity by paying lip service to the shared values of the yachts or reprimanding crew for eating at the chart table and then doing the same themselves. Some skippers also lacked integrity when communicating with individual crew members, saying different things to different people, which inevitably led to friction. Certain crew members felt that some of the skippers sometimes gave priority to sailing performance over safety of the crew, for example, sending people onto the foredeck in very rough weather. This showed a lack of integrity.

Openness

One of the high-performing yachts had established a value of openness through teambuilding before the start of the race. They sent journals to the BT Challenge website (an open website on the Internet) during the race, showing a willingness to share feelings on and off the yacht. The culture of the yacht created by the skipper demonstrated a democratic leadership style. People did not bottle up issues and as a result the crew felt very motivated.

> ❛ *One thing you can always do is ask.* ❜

Another skipper from one of the lower-performing yachts disliked confrontation. As a result issues were not brought out into the open, there were unhealthy undercurrents and interpersonal issues were not resolved. Ultimately, the crew became quite alienated from the skipper and were less motivated.

Vulnerability

Showing vulnerability means the leader can selectively admit to weaknesses and mistakes. This demonstrates authenticity and shows the team that the leader is genuine and approachable. Skippers who showed vulnerability were able to have a motivational effect on their team rather than showing weakness. For example, on one of the legs one high-performing skipper was really struggling with a problem. With the changing weather patterns he was having difficulty with the routing and tactics. About 48 hours before the finish of the leg the skipper felt pressurised and finally decided to share his despair with the crew. He asked them for some 'out of the box' thinking, ideas came out of the blue and the pressure lifted. This situation actually motivated the crew, both through a feeling of involvement and from respect for the skipper who was willing to share his vulnerability. By contrast, one lower-performing skipper attempted to cover up his weaknesses after making an incorrect navigational decision, which had an adverse effect on the crew's motivation.

Purpose

Skippers who showed purpose had the ability to inspire passion within the team to achieve the agreed mission. One high-performing skipper was looking for performance beyond just the goal of winning, encouraging the team to be outstanding. They would use motivational statements such as 'I really want it' and would back this up with energy and enthusiasm. In contrast, the lower-performing skippers failed to convey such a strong sense of purpose to their crew. One crew member, for example, commented that they were unclear about what their skipper really wanted from the race.

> *Even the cruisers will kill to win.*

Recognition

Recognising a person's achievements is a well-known motivational action. The majority of skippers were high on achievement drive and quite task-focused. Consequently, even the higher-performing skippers did not always give crew members proper recognition. For example, it was said of one skipper that he was 'not quick to compliment people', although others were quicker to pass on their congratulations. Skippers who gave recognition gave genuine praise to inspire the team to do more and recognised everyone as an individual.

> *Praise gives people self-confidence and allegiance – the cheapest way to improve performance.*

Sometimes, however, skippers made remarks that showed a lack of recognition for the efforts of others. After the crew had spent three days cleaning out the bilges one skipper complained that it should have taken them just half an hour! One of the lower-performing yachts had a value of respect and recognition that was not upheld. This skipper had a tendency to put crew members down if they challenged a decision he made.

Belief

The shared belief in the achievement of a goal was critical during the race. Indeed, the winning skipper stated clearly that he felt self-belief was an important element of his yacht's motivation and success – his crew really believed they could win. High-performing skippers were also able to convey a positive message to their crews. For example, another skipper built the crew's self-belief by always being out on deck and involved, particularly in difficult situations. His presence gave the crew added confidence and motivation.

Once a yacht had achieved success in a leg it greatly increased the feeling of self-belief. Conversely, it was far more difficult for those skippers at the back of the fleet to inspire belief in their crews, particularly towards the end when several had, in fact, lost belief in themselves. Whereas the winning skippers were buoyed by their successes, so the self-belief of the lesser-performing skippers was dragged down after failure.

Shared leadership

Skippers who showed shared leadership created an environment where proactivity was encouraged, accountability was shared and team buy-in was sought. All the high-performing skippers realised the importance of this attribute. Sharing control and seeking the crew's input led to increased commitment and motivation for the yachts' members. The feedback from one yacht stated that as all the crew were responsible for sail changes and the performance of the yacht they should make collective decisions on these matters. For example, the amount of weight carried on the yachts was viewed as critical for performance. During one leg a team decided to pour the high-energy drinks overboard as they were adding to the

> *Followership isn't about telling them what to do. It's about recognising they're all leaders and they're all responsible for the yacht's performance.*

load and not being consumed. Another skipper said that by involving the crew in everything and having built up their trust, they were able to be confident in decision making and take more calculated risks.

Some skippers in the lower-performing yachts, although often aware of the potential benefits of shared leadership, were unable to relinquish control and preferred to use the directive style. One skipper expected his watch leaders to check with him each time even a small change could be made. Although he realised the crew needed to be given responsibility, he was uncomfortable with delegating to others and ultimately demotivated his team.

OTHER WAYS TO INSPIRE MOTIVATION IN OTHERS

The race provided challenging conditions for the skippers and crew. Although the crew were often very active, in very calm waters long periods of inactivity meant boredom could become a powerful demotivator. Over the race the skippers used a number of different tactics to motivate others.

Humour and fun

Most skippers were aware that humour and fun helped generate a climate of enthusiasm and energy. Humour, for example, was a good way to defuse tension arising from potentially demotivating conflict. There were also parties held in ports of call, birthdays were celebrated and significant events were marked, such as crossing the equator. The high-performing skippers, however, were careful to differentiate between times when the crew were required to be performing and times when they could relax and enjoy themselves. One yacht had the 'above deck' culture, which could be viewed as the workplace. When the crew were on watch they were expected to be fully focused on performance. Once they were off watch, they enjoyed the 'below deck' culture, where they could relax and enjoy themselves.

In the early stages of the race some skippers failed to strike a balance between performance and having fun. One skipper in particular realised he had become far too intense and directive and needed to relax a little, recognising that humour was a saving grace on a number of occasions.

Communication

Several of the skippers also recognised the value of communication as a motivator. They held regular briefing meetings, discussions on a one-to-one basis and on occasions gave motivational speeches. One skipper who recognised the need to keep up his crew's energy levels during the latter part of the race made a passionate speech just prior to a restart. Their words touched a chord with the team and they really seemed to pull together better, going on to do extremely well in the next leg. The ways the skippers used communication to manage and inspire their teams will be discussed fully in Chapter 9.

THE RELATIONSHIP BETWEEN MOTIVATION AND EMOTIONAL INTELLIGENCE

The emotional intelligence behaviours were rated high, medium and low, based on the judgements drawn from the data collected from the interviews. All seven elements of emotional intelligence were seen to be important for skippers motivating to stay ahead of the competition. The behaviour is important both in terms of the motivation of the leader and for motivation of their teams.

Self-awareness

Those more aware of their feelings and able to share their feelings with others can build a climate of openness and trust that is motivational. In developing awareness of their feelings and the impact these have on others they may be able to control their feelings if necessary. This will stop feelings disrupting performance, which will help self-motivation.

Control of negative feelings when necessary will also prevent these feelings demotivating others. The higher-performing skippers reported being aware of such feelings and the need to control them if necessary. One high-performing skipper became very aware of the impact his feelings could have on the crew. If possible he tried to control them, but in extreme cases he explained how he was feeling and told the crew not to take it personally if he shouted.

A lower-performing skipper who was demonstrating a lack of self-awareness behaviour was described as dictating to the crew. He involved the crew in decision making when it was imposed on him by the crew.

Emotional resilience

This is an important element for self-motivation and the motivation of others. Some skippers were able to perform under pressure and did not let criticism affect performance. They were also able to balance the needs of the people with the needs of the task in a sensitive way. When the behaviour was mapped onto this element it became clear that this is particularly important for achieving high performance.

One skipper, who showed evidence of high emotional resilience, had to balance the needs of his crew with the issue of starting the engines to reach port in time for the next leg restart. He handled the situation by exploring all possibilities and delayed starting the engine as long as possible for the sake of those wanting to sail round the world. This same skipper was able to handle criticism and maintain performance under pressure.

In contrast, several of the skippers performed less well under pressure. It was said of one skipper, 'he takes his eye off the ball' – he concentrated on trivial activities rather than taking a decision about the bigger picture. Another tended to panic under pressure.

Motivation

This element is critical for the self-motivation of the leader and for motivating others. The high-performing skippers set challenging goals and ensured that these goals were shared by others. They were also more likely to achieve high levels of performance through their drive, energy and enthusiasm and were continually looking for ways to do things better. The lower-performing skippers started the race with equal energy and enthusiasm but even at this stage showed less focus on setting challenging goals. As these skippers experienced difficulty getting to the top of the fleet in each of the legs there was less evidence of motivation behaviour as the race progressed. The teams also showed evidence of lower motivation behaviour, for example no longer trying to find ways of doing things better. They were also less focused on goals.

Interpersonal sensitivity

Being able to listen and understand the needs of others and take these into account during decision making is vital to build commitment to decisions and buy in. The higher-performing skippers who showed evidence of this behaviour had regular discussion sessions with their crew, listened carefully to their views and took these into account before taking decisions. This impacted upon the way roles were allocated to crew members and navigation decisions.

The lower-performing skippers involved their crews far less. One skipper was described as wanting to organise everything and not wanting any input from anyone else. Another crew described the frustration of having a skipper who would not involve them in decision making and would not listen to them. These skippers were far more comfortable with a directive style of leadership.

Influence

Having the capacity to influence others to accept one's ideas and opinions in a way that responds to the needs of others is more likely to be motivational. Having the capacity to changing people's perception of a situation is also necessary. The high-performing skippers were all able to take their teams with them, for example sitting on the rail for weight distribution to make the yacht sail faster.

Towards the end of the race the lower-performing skippers were having difficulty being able to influence the crew. For example, one skipper was unable to convince the crew on tactical decisions. The crew went as far as to take the skipper out of the decision-making loop.

Intuitiveness

Having the capacity to take decisions with limited information is important for building the confidence of the team in uncertain times or when the team lack experience. This element was more difficult to assess during the interviews. The best examples were situations when the communications systems had broken down and the crew would describe their skipper as being able to take decisions although they did not have all the information available. The higher-performing skippers seemed more able to take decisions in these circumstances.

Conscientiousness

This is very important for driving motivation. Those able to respect high personal standards and ensure their actions support their words will ensure discipline to drive performance and sustain team commitment. The teams with high-performing skippers were motivated by their skippers to uphold the values. By the end of the race it had become second nature to have respect for the values which had been agreed at the start of the race. 'Never step over a job', for example, meant everyone pulled their weight. Showing respect to other members of the team created a climate of mutual respect for one another.

A lower-performing skipper showing a lack of evidence of conscientiousness was poor at enforcing the values. He was punctual and always put in extra effort but did not enforce these values with the crew. Values for respect and recognition were not upheld and the values agreed at the outset were never reviewed. One legger was not even aware of the values and standards that had been set at the start of the race.

SUMMARY

Why were some skippers more successful than others in motivating their teams to stay ahead? Performance was achieved through the appropriate blend of personal, management and leadership attributes and skills. Analysis of data from the race produced some important findings for those wishing to understand the relationship between management, leadership and motivation introduced in Chapter 5.

More detailed analysis determined the attributes needed to drive high performance and enable people to give their best over a sustained period of time. This is achieved through focusing on performance supported by the right management systems and procedures, referred to as the X Factor. The attributes and skills that helped to inspire a team, through involvement, gaining buy-in to decisions and sustaining longer-term commitment, were referred to as the Y Factor. Inspiring leadership was achieved by utilising the X and Y Factors together.

LESSONS FROM THE RACE

As a leader today you need to:

1. understand your people and their particular needs and be able to maximise their potential and set goals that will motivate the whole team

2. ensure that goals are motivational, achievable and shared by the whole team

3. make work meaningful by explaining why people are doing things and how their work fits into the bigger picture

4. use the right leadership style, depending on the competence and commitment of the person and you will be more likely to achieve a motivated team

5. inspire leadership to give people a sense of direction through a clear vision, and to satisfy their need for belonging, achievement, recognition, self-esteem and a sense of control

6. adopt a positive attitude to your people and the team is more likely to achieve high performance

7. work on team cohesion. This means building a relationship with your people built on respect and trust

8. adopt an open style of leadership to encourage people to say how they are feeling

9. have fun and celebrate success – it is very important to sustain commitment

10. be aware that group norms and pressures ensure management of performance, supported by the right systems and procedures and the necessary preparation and planning

11. remember that in turbulent times inspiring leadership gives individuals the passion and energy needed to find new and better ways of doing things and builds emotional commitment to each other.

REFERENCES

Alderfer, C. P. (1969) 'A new theory of human needs', *Organisational Behaviour and Human Performance*, Vol. 4.

Blanchard, K., Zigarmi, P. and Zigarmi, D. (1985) *Leadership and the One Minute Manager*, Willow Books, Collins: London.

Emmerich, R. (2001) 'Motivating employees during tough times', *Business Credit*: New York, July/August, Vol. 103, Issue 7, pp. 10–11.

Hackman, J. R., Lawler, E. E. and Porter, L. W. (1977) *Perspectives on the Behaviour of Organisations*, McGraw Hill: New York.

Herzberg, F. (1968) *Work and the Nature of Man*, Staples Press: London.

Higgs, M. and Dulewicz, V. (1999) *Making Sense of Emotional Intelligence*, NFER-Nelson: Windsor.

Kennedy, K. (2001) 'Manager as motivator', *Executive Excellence*, June, Vol. 18, Issue 6, pp. 13–14.

Kotter, J. (1990) *A Force for Change*, Free Press: New York.

Locke, E. A. (1968) 'Towards a theory of task motivation and incentives', *Organizational Behaviour and Human Performance*, Vol. 3, pp. 157–189.

Maslow, A. H. (1987) *Motivation and Personality*, 3rd Edition, Harper and Row: London.

McClelland, D. C. (1961) *The Achieving Society*, Van Nostrand: New Jersey.

Murray, H. A. (1938) *Exploration in Personality*, Oxford University Press: New York.

Nadler, D. A. and Lawler, E. E. (1979) 'Motivation: a diagnostic approach', Chapter 5, pp. 216–229 in Steers, R. M. and Porter, L.W., *Motivation and Work Behaviour*, 2nd Edition, McGraw-Hill: New York.

Norgaard, M. (2001) 'Motivating people', *Executive Excellence*, June, Vol. 18, Issue 6.

Steers, R. M. and Porter, L. W. (1979) *Motivation and Work Behaviour*, 2nd Edition, McGraw-Hill: New York.

The Industrial Society (1999) 'Motivating employees', *Managing Best Practice*, 55, January.

Thomas, K. W. (2000) 'Motivation and how it works', *Training*: Minneapolis, October, Vol. 37, Issue 10, pp. 130–135.

Vroom, V. H. (1964) *Work and Motivation*, Wiley: New York.

STRESS AT WORK
British Airways

Even before the terrorist attacks in the US in 2001, market conditions were tough for airlines with the downturn in the US economy and the impact of foot and mouth disease in the UK. The events of September 11 were unprecedented and have required British Airways to make some tough business decisions. The need to support staff is always paramount, but in times of crisis it is even more important.

Support and advice

British Airways provides many systems and procedures to ensure its employees can find support and advice should they need it. Cabin crew can use Crew Care, a 24-hour confidential counselling service, run for cabin crew by cabin crew and funded by the airline. In addition, each crew member has access to a designated manager. For all employees and their families there is a confidential 24-hour support and information service called Helpdirect, run by an independent specialist company. In addition, managers must react to operational events that face the business. Immediately after the US attacks many staff were stranded away from home. Managers kept in touch and met them on their return to the UK.

Communication

Since September 11 the CEO and his directors meet weekly to review the business. Information is then cascaded to all staff using a variety of methods. Trade unions have regular face-to-face briefings and forums.

Strategic impact groups

Senior-level groups have been set up to look into the impact of September 11 and the actions the airline needs to take.

Headcount reductions

British Airways has been forced to look at headcount reductions but strives to achieve these on a voluntary basis, including unpaid leave and part-time work.

How do these measures relate to stress and what we have learned from the BT Global Challenge? The first point is that these measures aim to give people a sense of control. People feel they have more *personal control* when they feel they have accurate information (see communication) and involvement and control over their own destiny (see headcount reductions). Secondly, these measures aim to give people confidence that the *organisation is in control* through the clear communications and through the activities of the strategic impact groups, bringing together the top brains in the business to work together in a cross-functional manner.

As we will see in this chapter, control is a key element in helping to reduce stress. If people feel they have control this has been proven to enhance their well-being and reduce their stress.

7

STRESS MANAGEMENT AS AN ENABLER OF HIGH PERFORMANCE

Contributions to this chapter have been made
by the following Forum members:
Liz Straker and Peter Mulcahy, British Airways
John Metherell, Tesco Stores Ltd

INTRODUCTION

The negative impact of stress is well known. In the UK, the Health and Safety Executive (2001) reported that 6.5 million working days are lost through stress-related illness each year, costing employers around £370 million and society as a whole as much as £3.75 billion. In a survey for the IRS Employment Review, published in 1999, almost 90 per cent of the organisations questioned reported an increase in stress-related absence in the previous two years. Three-quarters also stated that stress had moved up the management agenda. Many other businesses have expressed concern for the mental well-being of their employees.

Effective stress management was identified during the BT Global Challenge race as a critical component of high performance. Too little stress and people become apathetic or bored and fail to perform; too much stress leads to similarly negative results. In these situations, stress can be viewed as disabling achievement. And yet what most people do not realise is that stress – if harnessed properly – can also have very positive effects, leading to high performance and thereby becoming an enabler.

The findings of this chapter are of particular relevance for leaders in organisations undergoing major change and for those dealing with the insecurity and uncertainties associated with such change. Leaders will also understand why stress is an issue today and learn about the nature of stress and its relationship with both positive and negative perform-ance. They will see how to recognise stress and the factors determining how it is experienced. The chapter will review causes of stress and tactics for effectively dealing with it – drawing on successful strategies from the race – to help leaders manage stress more effectively. It will conclude with a look at the relevance of emotional intelligence and stress.

WHY IS STRESS AN ISSUE FOR LEADERS TODAY?

Several recent trends contribute to the stress of leaders today. Many are now required to operate outside their 'comfort zone', where the demands of a particular situation do not match their skills and capa-bilities. Demands on people at work have also become much greater and a reasonable work/life balance is often impossible. This is discussed further in Chapter 8. Many UK leaders, for example, are working significantly more than the 37 hours a week specified by the EU Working Hours Directive. A number of organisational changes have put additional pressures on leaders.

What are the trends?

The changing organisational paradigm

Stress management must be set within the context of the changing organisational paradigm. The old style of organisation often had an autocratic, command-and-obey style, favouring a management approach in which the leader controlled others. Organisations have now become flatter and need to be more flexible to develop innovative solutions to complex issues. This requires shared leadership, shared control and greater self-awareness on the part of leaders to operate in a more open and involving way. Many leaders, however, still feel more comfortable with the old style of leadership. Even for those with a more modern approach, today's constantly evolving business environment often means a stressful working life.

The rate and scope of change

Globalisation and rapidly advancing technology have increased the rate and scope of change, bringing with it uncertainty and insecurity, as outlined in Chapter 2. These changes require leaders to learn new skills and ways of working. Constantly having to adapt to new circumstances brings added pressure for many managers.

Higher demands with fewer people

Leaner organisations have put greater demands on people to help them stay ahead or keep pace with the competition. Many leaders are responding to these increased demands by working longer hours, putting further pressure on themselves.

More cross-functional and cross-organisational working

This also adds strain as it requires leaders to have a greater breadth of understanding and to collaborate with a wide range of people outside their normal range of expertise.

WHAT IS STRESS?

To benefit from stress as an enabler of high performance, leaders must first understand its nature. In fact, the term 'stress' has become widely used only in the past few decades and rarely appeared in psychiatric and psychological literature before the end of the Second World War. Although early definitions focused on stress as an external force – thus seeing stress as pressure or as a reaction to pressure, either physiological or psychological – more recently the focus has switched to the interaction of the person with their environment.

Individuals go through a two-stage process when faced with a potentially stressful situation: primary appraisal, when they assess the relevance, significance and implications of the event, and secondary appraisal, when they assess what, if anything, can be done about the situation and their ability to cope. Stress is very personal, depending on the way an individual perceives a given situation.

The definition to be adopted for this book is interactional and was used by Cranwell-Ward (1990):

Stress can be defined as the physiological and psychological reaction that occurs when people perceive an imbalance between the level of demand placed upon them and their capability to meet that demand.

Three further elements (all of which can be both positive and negative) need to be explained to understand the exact meaning of the way stress is being defined and its relationship to performance:

1. Stressors – the factors which people report as causing stress. For example, excessive workload or being stimulated to meet a deadline.
2. Stress symptoms – the symptoms reported as a result of experiencing stressors, both physiological and psychological. For example, tiredness, irritability or feeling highly focused or energised.
3. Stress outcomes – the consequence of people experiencing stressors. For example, decreased work performance, withdrawal from others or exceptional results and creativity.

POSITIVE AND NEGATIVE STRESS AND THEIR RELATIONSHIP WITH HIGH PERFORMANCE

Stress, therefore, can enhance or detract from performance. Leaders experiencing positive stress at optimum levels of pressure can achieve optimal performance. This is the stimulating side of stress, sometimes referred to as 'stress arousal', which enables people to access hidden mental and physical abilities. When individuals experience positive stress they feel energised and focused and able to exert control over their situation.

When there is insufficient pressure, however, individuals can experience apathy or boredom. Similarly, if stress becomes excessive they may experience distress. The moment when stimulation becomes distress will vary from person to person and even for the same person from situation to situation. When individuals experience this negative stress, however, they may feel they have insufficient control and are unable to cope. This often has an adverse result on both the individual and the organisation. During the race, for example, high-performing skippers recognised the need for strategies to reduce excessive stress levels and sustain or reinvigorate performance.

Attaining high performance under pressure

Kriegal and Kriegal (1984), authors of *The C Zone – Peak Performance under Pressure*, identified a combination of skills and attitudes needed for leaders to attain high performance under any external pressure.

Attitudes – inner mental processes

Three key interrelated mental processes determine whether leaders can achieve high performance.

- confidence – stemming from self-belief, self-esteem and confidence in their ability to perform
- commitment – enjoying what they were doing, leading to total involvement
- control – being in control and focusing on those factors inside, and not outside, their control.

No one characteristic, however, is more important than the others. It is the synergy between the three that helps leaders achieve high performance. Under these circumstances stress is controlled and positive.

Competence

This requires a thorough knowledge of the job or task – in the case of the race, both sailing and leading others – and the ability to develop winning strategies and to make the best use of one's strengths.

The successful interplay between mental processes and skill makes the difference between success and failure – Figure 7.1 demonstrates the relationship between stress, pressure and performance. The difference between positive and negative stress is often small and managing stress is a delicate balancing act between too much pressure and not enough. Good stress management requires the use of appropriate strategies to maintain arousal at the right level to enable leaders and teams to operate at peak performance. Strategies used to manage this balance will be demonstrated later in this chapter, drawing on examples from the race and from business.

WHAT HAPPENS WHEN STRESS LEVELS ARE RAISED?

Leaders must quickly identify levels of stress, in both themselves and others, and if they are excessive or not high enough, take appropriate

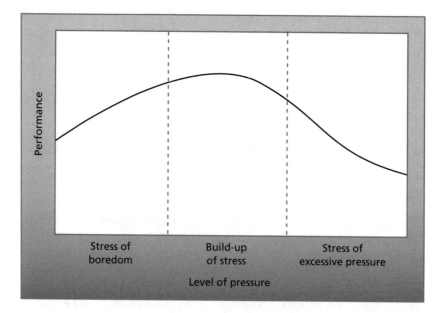

FIGURE 7.1 The relationship between pressure, performance and stress
(Adapted and reproduced from Melhuish, Dr A. (1978) *Executive Health*)

action. Often, when a person becomes excessively stressed, others notice the signs first. Stress manifests itself in a number of ways, but all, in fact, relate to the 'fight flight' response of Stone Age Man.

The 'fight flight' response

The alarm phase

Faced with a threatening situation, the body 'revs up for action', setting off a number of processes to enhance reaction, speed and physical power. Two separate areas of the brain, the hypothalamus and the pituitary gland, activate the stress reaction. Hormones from the pituitary gland then activate the glands which produce adrenalin and noradrenalin and corticoids, which in turn set off the chain of reactions listed below:

- Heart beat rises by 100 per cent.
- Airways to the lungs widen.
- Sugar is released from the liver for instant energy.
- Digestion stops so blood can carry energy to the muscles.
- The body begins to sweat to stop it overheating.
- The sympathetic nervous system is activated and sends messages to organs including the adrenal glands.
- Blood vessels supplying skin and intestines are constricted.
- Breathing speeds up to increase oxygen intake.
- Cholesterol is released from the liver for energy.
- Muscles tense ready for action.
- The immune system is inhibited.

The resistance phase

This chain of reactions happens very quickly and under normal circumstances the body gradually returns to normal. The smaller the event, the quicker this happens. However, in a challenging, dynamic environment the stress reaction is triggered again and the body remains in the aroused state. This can last for over a day, but in the alarm phase the end is always in sight. When the situation seems never-ending, or a series of events occurs, the body has to protect itself.

Managers and leaders can often maintain performance at a high level of activity for long periods of time. Sometimes this is referred to as the resistance phase or, more colloquially, 'life in the fast lane', when there is no time for relaxation from one situation to another. At this stage heavy demands are made on energy reserves, not normally available, and energy from adrenalin masks underlying fatigue and illness. As the pressure continues the person becomes both mentally and physically weaker. This can result in feeling depressed, a total lack of confidence and an inability to improve the situation. Warning signs of stress during the resistance phase are:

- irritability
- overreaction to minor problems
- altered sleep pattern
- outbursts of anger
- a feeling of being unable to escape
- loss of memory and concentration
- feeling out of control
- loss of confidence.

The exhaustion phase

Sometimes also described as 'burnout', when the mind and body grind to a halt. At this stage people feel mentally and physically exhausted and are less able to fight illness. Complete rest is needed to aid recovery. Energy reserves have been drained and a range of problems may occur, including:

- heart problems and high blood pressure
- increased levels of cholesterol and its associated problems
- digestive problems
- headaches and migraines
- greater susceptibility to illness and allergies
- less capacity to resist infection
- mistakes and accidents
- feeling unable to cope
- emotional shutdown except anger and frustration.

In what ways did the skippers exhibit stress?

Most of the skippers experienced excessive stress at some stage during the race. The ways in which they demonstrated negative stress included:

- performed badly or inconsistently
- became isolated and withdrawn
- became more prone to accidents
- were less communicative
- shouted at crew
- made bad decisions
- suffered impaired judgement
- were worried and agitated
- were irritable
- lost confidence
- made mistakes
- had attacks of insecurity
- suffered migraines
- smoked excessively
- were less sensitive towards others
- demonstrated excessive tiredness
- had relationship difficulties
- showed no sense of humour or fun.

The ways in which they demonstrated optimum stress included:

- highly focused
- energetic
- in control
- able to perform well
- good humoured
- calm
- enthusiastic
- 'in tune' with the yacht and the team
- performed consistently
- enjoyed the sailing.

Signs of negative stress can be summarised as:

- physical – tiredness, headaches, illness
- mental – inability to concentrate, loss of memory
- emotional – irritability, apathy, anger, helplessness
- behavioural – excessive smoking, withdrawal from people, hostile behaviour.

Meanwhile, positive stress leaves people feeling focused, energetic and in control.

WHAT ARE THE REASONS FOR PEOPLE REACTING POSITIVELY OR NEGATIVELY?

The research showed that the way skippers reacted to stressful situations could be analysed at three levels or 'worlds'. In each 'world' the reaction could be positive, accessing what is referred to as the skipper's 'bright side', or negative, accessing their 'dark side', depending on whether they were in a positive or negative frame of mind or emotional state.

> The three 'worlds' of the skipper include:
> 1. the inner 'world' – the skipper's thoughts and feelings, including emotional state and degree of self-control
> 2. the outer 'world' – the way the skipper projects himself in the outside world
> 3. the interactive 'world' – the way the skipper interacts with the team and affects the crew and shapes the culture of the yacht.

The inner world of the skipper

The inner world of the skipper developed from the interaction of three factors.

1. The skipper's competence

To be competent the skipper needed a good balance of sailing expertise and knowledge, an understanding of the weather patterns and navigation or, alternatively, someone who could brief them in this area. All the crews felt very confident with their skippers' sailing capability. However, as part of competence the skippers also had to develop winning strategies and tactics, make effective decisions and have sound leadership and people skills. In addition, they often had to take difficult navigation decisions with limited information, requiring intuitive behaviour.

> *I made a wrong tactical decision and it affected my confidence and I found myself taking panic decisions based on what the other yachts were doing.*

These navigational decisions had a great impact on the internal 'world' of the skippers by either enhancing or destroying their self-belief. If the decisions led to success, the 'bright side' of the internal 'world' was activated. If the decisions proved to be less successful, the dark 'side' was triggered.

2. Self-belief

If the skippers experienced positive self-belief they had confidence in their abilities, particularly to take the right decisions. As the race progressed some of the skippers lost their sense of self-belief. This impacted on the quality of their decision making and their ability to lead the team.

3. Commitment

If the skippers experienced positive commitment, they were enjoying what they were doing and were very involved. A number of the skippers, however, lost some of their commitment in ports of call because of conflicting demands, priorities and overload, which reduced their feeling of being in control. Similarly, if decisions were less successful, the skippers simply focused on arriving at the next port of call, no longer enjoying the journey.

When these three factors were positive the individuals felt a sense of well-being, in control of both themselves and the situation, and could therefore access their 'bright side'. In this context, stress acted as a stimulant to the skippers when they felt in control. If, however, competence, self-belief or commitment were missing, the skippers felt out of control of themselves and their situation, and experienced their 'dark side'. Skippers with good coping techniques were able to adopt the appropriate strategy to lower the stress levels, allowing themselves to perform and restoring self-belief.

For stress to act as an enabler of high performance the inner world also needs to be supported by a sense of purpose, a value set supporting performance and self-regulation. The 'bright' and 'dark' sides of the inner world are summarised in Figure 7.2.

The outer 'world' of the skipper

The inner world determined whether the skipper projected himself externally in a positive or negative way. In the positive outer world, the skippers shared control with their team. They also used appropriate skills and

> ' *When he is under pressure you can see him buzz.* '

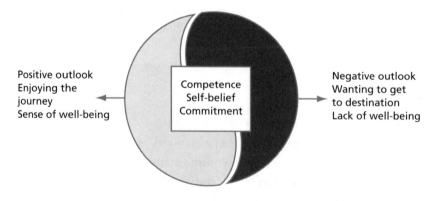

Positive outlook
Enjoying the journey
Sense of well-being

Competence
Self-belief
Commitment

Negative outlook
Wanting to get to destination
Lack of well-being

FIGURE 7.2 Inner world of the skipper

techniques and utilised their emotional intelligence potential to the full. This in turn gave the team members control of their own worlds and enabled them to perform well.

When the skippers projected this 'bright side' they came across as focused, consistent, energetic and with optimal stress levels. They demonstrated the ability to use emotional intelligence behaviours. This meant they were able to perform consistently under pressure, took account of the needs of the team when making decisions, and kept their emotions under control. The

> **' He doesn't respond well to setbacks, he screams and shouts and overreacts. '**

skippers were also prepared to show vulnerability: they admitted when they were uncertain about a decision or had made a mistake and shared leadership was evident.

When, however, the skippers projected their 'dark side' they were less consistent and focused, and stress levels tended to be too high or too low. They were less able to use their emotional intelligence behaviours. Consequently, they did not perform so well under pressure, were less likely to consider the needs of the team when making decisions, and had less control over their emotions. They were also less prepared to show their vulnerability. The 'bright' and 'dark sides' of the skippers are summarised in Figure 7.3.

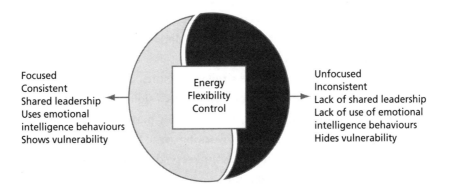

Focused	Unfocused
Consistent	Inconsistent
Shared leadership	Lack of shared leadership
Uses emotional intelligence behaviours	Lack of use of emotional intelligence behaviours
Shows vulnerability	Hides vulnerability

Energy
Flexibility
Control

FIGURE 7.3   Outer world of the skipper

The interactive world of the skipper with the team

Operating in the interactive world when the 'bright side' was accessed, the skipper had stress at the optimal level that enhances performance. The skipper and the team had belief in their capability to perform, and the skipper ensured that the team were in control and had accountability and responsibility. If the 'bright side' predominated, a positive performance culture developed. There was open communication and conflict was managed well.

> *He has the ability to keep everyone focused and relaxed, there is a no-blame culture, open management and a happy crew.*

When the 'dark side' prevailed, however, stress levels rose and the skipper became a source of stress for the team. The skipper and team lacked belief in their capability to perform well and the skipper had a more directive leadership style. Therefore, the team were not given responsibility and lacked control over the situation, which was stressful. Over a period of time, a negative culture developed where there was a lack of openness and trust, and poor conflict management. The team then became alienated from the skipper, although in one or two cases a positive culture persisted even when the skipper was alienated from the team. The 'bright side' and the 'dark side' of the interactive world are summarised in Figure 7.4.

> *It's like washing your car every day. If you keep having mud storms it's hard to keep going.*

Leaders in business today face similar pressures. Those working in a macho culture, where stress is often viewed as a sign of weakness, often keep their reactions well hidden, although they may suffer the negative effects quite badly. Others enjoy working in a fast-paced, changing environment and are able not only to keep stress at acceptable levels but also to thrive on its stimulation.

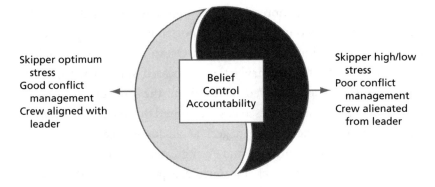

FIGURE 7.4   Skipper and team interaction – team dynamics

WHAT FACTORS CAUSE EXCESSIVE STRESS?

All the skippers faced similar pressures and all experienced excessive stress at certain stages in the race, including some quite traumatic incidents. However, there were different internal pressures which had an impact on the strategies which the skippers adopted to deal with stress. Similarly, business leaders need to be aware of their sources of stress, and those of others, to take preventative steps or use coping strategies to deal with the situation.

What comparisons, if any, can be drawn between causes of stress during the race and those experienced in business? Cooper and Palmer (2000), leading stress researchers, refers to six sources of stress at work which can all be related to the function of the skipper:

- factors intrinsic to the job
- role in the organisation
- relationships at work
- career development
- organisation structure and culture
- home–work interface.

Factors intrinsic to the job

The job itself

The job of a skipper has several inherent causes of stress, associated with both success and relative failure. For example, if they were performing especially well and out in front, skippers felt exhilarated sailing the yachts. They were more able to be highly focused, sail the yacht well, and felt 'pumped up'. They even reported enjoying the journey in the adverse conditions of the Southern Ocean and decision making, particularly in relation to navigation, appeared smoother. However, many sometimes experienced stress from the pressure to sustain outstanding performance. Tesco has recognised that having reached the No 1 position in the UK, managers at all levels face a new set of challenges to ensure continued and even greater levels of achievement.

Those skippers at the back, meanwhile, experienced the stress associated with poorer results. Their performance impacted negatively on their confidence and self-belief and they experienced high levels of stress. They appeared far less focused, experienced difficulty with decision making and could not wait to arrive at the next port of call. They derived much less satisfaction from the experience, and the task of motivating the crew and sustaining morale was much harder. This was discussed in Chapter 6.

Work overload/underload

Too much activity can be stressful, but as we mentioned above, so can too little. Cooper and Cooper (1988) was commissioned by *The Sunday Times* to draw up an index of the most stressful jobs. While some of the rankings might have changed since then, useful lessons can still be drawn from the findings. High on the list was the job of an airline pilot, partly because of the responsibility associated with the job, but also because of fluctuations in work pressure levels – compare, for example, the inactivity of a long-haul flight with the intense concentration of landing. Similarly, many of the crew on the race reported stress from boredom, particularly when they had very little to occupy them while sitting on the rail of the yacht for several hours to help the yacht sail faster. Many of the crew members also had some sailing experience, but the less successful skippers failed to utilise this expertise properly, again causing frustration and stress. In contrast the skippers themselves – particularly during the early part of the race – felt pressure from overload. In the business world, work overload was also top of the list of factors causing stress for managers in an IRS survey (*The Employment Health Bulletin*, 1999).

Working long hours

Working long hours is another potential cause of stress. Each of the yachts worked a watch system similar to a shift in organisations. The skippers had freedom to manage their own watch systems and it became apparent halfway through the race that some watch systems were working better than others, particularly in ensuring that skippers and crew had adequate sleep. One skipper, for example, spent 15 hours continuously at the helm, yet it is impossible to sustain high performance for this length of time on a task that requires intense concentration.

Similarly, Cooper reported that working beyond 40–50 hours a week results in time spent that is increasingly unproductive. Yet a survey conducted for the Institute of Management by Worrall and Cooper (2000) highlighted that 40 per cent of managers still work in excess of 50 hours a week.

Physical working conditions

This covers the design and layout of workspace as well as other environmental factors such as temperature and lighting. The cause of stress in this category will vary from job to job. In the race the physical conditions were, of course, stressful. In the Doldrums the yachts became extremely hot and there was very little wind. Conversely, in the extreme conditions of the Southern Ocean the conditions were wet, cold and the sea was potentially dangerous. In addition, the yachts were quite cramped and there was little privacy or means of escape from other people, sometimes for more than five weeks at a time.

Care, however, had been taken with the layout of the yachts, particularly the centre cabin and galley to allow for social contact and relaxation. Similarly in the business world, many leaders recognise that well-designed buildings and a comfortable environment stimulate staff and encourage well-being, for example, British Airways' corporate headquarters at Hounslow, Canon UK's at Reigate and Nationwide's in Swindon. These buildings all have pleasant surroundings and ample areas for meetings in a relaxed atmosphere with facilities for refreshments. Bayer Pharmaceuticals in Kyoto, Japan specially designed its gardens to be tranquil. Tesco is continually reviewing and refining the design, visual impact and layout of stores for simplicity of operation and work practices, for both customers and staff.

Role in the organisation

Role ambiguity

When roles are clearly defined and the expectations of individuals are clear and non-conflicting, stress can be kept to a minimum. All skippers were selected for their technical sailing ability and managerial competence. Many of the crew members, particularly the leggers, reported a lack of role clarity during the early part of the race when the skippers had not appreciated the importance of good briefing and integration with the rest of the crew. Successful skippers were more likely to redress this by spending time allocating and explaining roles, and quickly learned to trust their watch leaders. The less successful skippers were more likely to try to do too much and were then faced with conflicting demands of sailing the yacht, taking navigational decisions and managing the crew.

In business even successful senior managers often fail to communicate their vision and strategic direction to the rest of the organisation, or fail to delegate effectively. Tesco has invested a great deal of time and effort developing and communicating the core purpose, goals and values at all levels throughout the business.

Role conflict

The skippers probably faced the highest level of role conflict and higher stress levels on shore when they were faced with a range of conflicting expectations from the different stakeholders such as BT, the yacht sponsor, the Challenge Business, and friends and family. It left some feeling out of control and unable to fulfil their demanding schedules in port. In business, senior managers are often in a similar position, trying, for example, to reconcile demanding sales targets while staying strongly customer-focused.

Responsibility

While the skippers were all selected for their sailing expertise, the majority of the crew were novices. This clearly put great responsibility on the skippers for the safety of the yacht, particularly during such demanding legs as in the Southern Ocean from Sydney to Cape Town. Cooper has emphasised the high level of stress associated with responsibility for people. One skipper, for example, voiced out loud the pressure he felt knowing that he was responsible for the safety of his crew, particularly after hearing of a traumatic experience on another yacht. This feeling was shared by all the other skippers at this time. In business today such concerns can weigh heavily on senior managers who are forced to keep costs to a minimum but at the same time consider the welfare of their staff.

Relationships

Most research has associated relationships with people as a potential source of stress. During the race 18 people were required to live in very close quarters with little opportunity for personal space. Most yacht crews handled this aspect well. The successful skippers spent time with the crew – sometimes on a one-to-one basis – to keep on top of issues and give support when necessary. The less successful skippers failed to build relationships in this way and some leggers reported feelings of isolation and alienation.

The skipper's leadership style was another critical factor. Successful skippers adopted an appropriate style which helped crews to feel involved and supported. Those skippers who used the directive style extensively and inappropriately caused their crew stress. Effective managers in business recognise the importance of investing the necessary time and energy to establish strong emotional bonds with their staff and clients.

Career development

The race represented an important part of career development for skippers. The need to perform well in the race was therefore an important stressor for some of them. After the stopover in Sydney, some were already thinking of the next steps in their careers, while at the same time needing to stay focused on the race. The crew had a whole range of career issues and life changes before them and for many it meant managing the transition either back to an existing career or making a fresh start. Fear of failure was probably an issue for some, either in terms of the race or in managing a life transition.

In most business sectors today the pace of change means that employees have constantly to adapt to change. In career terms, this means that people have constantly to reskill. In the face of competition many organisations are involved in mergers and acquisitions to gain economies of scale which can result in redundancy for some staff. This provides some people with the opportunity for a career change either within the organisation or outside.

Organisation structure and culture

The way organisations are structured and the prevailing culture can be a source of stress. In particular it can affect the extent to which people feel a sense of involvement and participation in decision making. The resulting control is vital for the sense of well-being of employees. This worked at two levels in the race.

1. Challenge Business

The skippers were employed by the Challenge Business and were also subject to rulings by the International Race Jury when incidents occurred and the yachts were seen to contravene international race regulations. Skippers who were involved in such decisions had the potential to suffer stress. The successful skippers, however, adopted a positive approach and helped the crew put unpopular decisions behind them. The individual sponsors also put the skippers under pressure, and when issues arose that affected the skippers, the Challenge Business and BT, as the overall sponsors of the race, could not always involve them in decision making. This sometimes made the skippers feel frustrated.

In organisations today there are further levels of complexity. Managers at Tesco increasingly work in natural/cross-functional teams and may have a greater variety of structures to work within with less definite reporting relationships.

2. The yachts

On the yachts the skippers led with appointed watch leaders and the styles adopted varied from yacht to yacht and during different legs of the race. Successful skippers retained a flexibility of style and tended to involve others, particularly in navigation decisions, while the less successful skippers retained a much more directive style. In some situations a fear culture prevailed, raising the crew's stress levels.

Home–work interface

Stress at work can affect home life and home responsibilities and these issues can impact on performance. The home–work interface is also critical for achieving a good work/life balance. Prior to the start of the race the skippers had to be totally focused on preparing the yachts. Several of the skippers were married and four had young children. Although the wives and partners gave considerable support and came out to the ports of call, several skippers still struggled with their racing responsibilities and family commitments. The wife of one skipper had a baby during the race, which put considerable pressure on the skipper concerned, and although he was able to be with her when the baby was born, he experienced a lot of pressure both before and after the birth. One skipper, who was single, felt he had an advantage over those with children, as during ports of call, for example, he was able to stay more focused on the race.

Skippers needed to be sensitive to the work/life balance during the race and in ports of call. Several crew members experienced personal problems with friends and family, and time spent in ports of call was very precious for the crew to help maintain relationships. The skippers who were well organised, planned the yacht preparation to allow the crew to have the maximum amount of time with family and friends and for relaxation and enjoyment.

In business today family-friendly policies are becoming far more important, addressing flexible working, maternity and paternity leave and job-sharing. However, leaders with greater responsibility often have less opportunity to reduce their hours and still struggle to manage the home/work interface. This is discussed further in Chapter 8.

WHAT WERE THE SPECIFIC CAUSES OF STRESS DURING THE RACE?

Many causes of stress were identified during the interviews and these are summarised in Tables 7.1, 7.2 and 7.3.

TABLE 7.1   On-board stress for skippers

Outer world of skippers	Inner world of skippers
• Job itself – analysis of charts, routing decisions, managing relationships • Race performance – position tables • Communication • Expectations of others, crew, sponsors • Lack of goal alignment of stakeholders • Physical conditions – wet, cold or hot • Managing emotional stress of others • Traumatic incidents – collisions, accidents, illnesses	• High level of responsibility, life/death situation • Pressure of success • Stimulation from performing well • Expectations of self • Physically demanding • Managing relationships • Pressure of failure • Working long hours/managing the work/life balance

TABLE 7.2   Onshore stress for skippers

Outer world of skippers	Inner world of skippers
• Managing the work/life balance • Managing expectations of stakeholders • Lack of time for preparation • Corporate entertaining	• Meeting deadlines for the race start • Issues of control • Family and friends • Managing career and life after the race

TABLE 7.3   Causes of stress for crew which skippers had to manage

- Conflict with the crew
- Lack of clarity of roles and responsibilities
- On-board culture and climate
- Getting in late for a port of call
- People not pulling their weight
- Lack of one-to-one communication
- Skipper taking irrational decisions
- Skipper himself
- Feeling of isolation especially for the leggers/integrating leggers

- Personal problems
- Boredom
- Fear of making mistakes
- Lack of involvement and consultation
- Physical tiredness
- Handling fear of potential situation
- Expectations from the race

Specific issues for skippers

1. Having an appropriate purpose

One skipper started the race viewing it more as an adventure to sail round the world. This caused conflict with some of the crew who had signed up to race. It caused the skipper great stress and he resigned after the first leg.

2. An issue about control

One skipper had delegated successfully to his team. They had reached the stage where they could perform very well without any intervention from the skipper, who then experienced a loss of confidence, feeling he was no longer needed. Performance on the yacht dropped, but a meeting resolved the situation and the crew were able to achieve high performance again.

3. Beliefs about performance – 'I am expected to win this race'

One skipper experienced great pressure from his yacht sponsor to win the race. This put him in a stressful position where he found it more difficult to perform. During the second leg the skipper had a meeting with the crew and they reassessed their goals in a more realistic way, thus reducing this pressure.

4. Now that I have shown I can perform, I have to win the race

Having won a leg, one skipper then felt under terrific pressure from the crew, family and friends, as well as himself, to win. He felt the crew expected to be out in front and found the pressure affected his performance adversely.

5. I must improve my performance

The skippers lower in the fleet felt under enormous pressure to do better. Some were reluctant to tell the crew when a result was bad. The skippers felt the crew blamed them for the poorer performance. This put them under pressure when they were making navigational decisions.

6. If I win it brings a new set of responsibilities

Certain skippers had difficulty in sustaining a winning position. One skipper felt that while he wanted to be the winning skipper, there was also a downside, such as having to undertake media interviews.

7. Styles of leadership

All leaders have a preferred style of leadership and support. Styles different from their own are often more difficult to execute. One skipper, for example, felt his relaxed style was not the right one, especially when the crew members had paid to be in a competitive race. Similarly, another skipper was aware his style could be rather autocratic. Although he tried hard to employ different styles, this took him outside his 'comfort zone' and the pressure built up. After receiving feedback, another skipper knew his style was unacceptable. He tried to change his approach but the pressure was too great to sustain a less preferred style.

8. The job itself – working outside the competence zone

Some of the skippers found the navigational decisions very difficult. This was particularly relevant once they had made one or two poor decisions impacting on performance. Subsequent decision making was even more difficult because they had lost confidence and sometimes felt they had lost the respect of the crew.

WHAT STRATEGIES WERE USED TO ENABLE HIGH PERFORMANCE?

A detailed analysis showed that all the skippers experienced stress at some time, and all demonstrated situations when they handled it well and other situations when they handled it less well. Those who managed it well were aware of the need to recognise stress and deal with it. It was vital that the skippers managed their own stress levels effectively as the mood and state of the skipper had, of course, a major impact on the crew and overall performance and stress levels.

> *' He didn't mean to do it, he felt under so much pressure that he couldn't control himself. '*

Skippers at the back of the fleet experienced intense pressure as they tried to improve their position. In several cases their confidence and self-belief took a hammering, and the skippers themselves became a source of stress for the crews. The high performers, however, tended to use strategies that restored stress levels to the optimum.

To ensure stress acts as an enabler of high performance, leaders need to have strategies in place. They should ensure stress is sustained at the appropriate level to keep physical, mental and emotional states in balance. Once stress is no longer at the optimum level, coping strategies are needed to restore the balance. The strategies adopted during the race will be described in terms of the inner and outer worlds of the skipper and the team dynamics and culture described earlier in the chapter. These strategies will be supplemented with advice to help leaders manage stress more effectively.

The inner world of the skipper

The skippers used three main types of strategy to help them maintain or restore self-control and self-confidence.

1. A clearly identified purpose

This purpose is driven from within, is visionary and gives a sense of direction beyond the immediate goal. In terms of stress, it helped the skippers to be mentally focused. For example, skippers wanting the team to perform at the highest level encouraged the crew to look continuously for ways to raise their level of performance.

2. Self-regulation

Discipline is necessary to enforce appropriate regimes of behaviour. This includes following a suitable diet, ensuring adequate rest and sleep, exercise and a balanced lifestyle. These are the major elements of physical well-being and an essential strategy for preventing excessive stress; alternatively, they can be used to cope with stress. Most of the skippers struggled with self-regulation at some stage during the race, although the higher-performing skippers quickly recognised its importance and took steps to ensure they were physically and mentally fit.

Rest and sleep

The higher-performing skippers were better at ensuring they had adequate rest and sleep, particularly as the race progressed. They took the view that, to work effectively and make the right decisions, they must ensure they slept well. They delegated responsibility to their crew while they slept and also established guidelines to ensure they were woken up in an emergency. Some lower performers, however, insisted on rigorous control – for example, that they be woken to supervise every sail change or decision to change course. Unsurprisingly, they then dozed at the chart table, or in the main cabin, and regularly complained of tiredness

> ‘ *I haven't had much sleep and I have so much responsibility.* ’

Appropriate diet

A nutritious and balanced diet is an essential element of preventative stress management, and menus were carefully planned prior to the race. Some of the yachts made adjustments at ports of call to make the variety of food more interesting. Plenty of good food was also motivational. At least one yacht had persistent food-related problems, either due to a shortage or a bland diet. Similarly, leaders who experience high stress levels could do much to remedy the situation by following the advice given by nutritionists:

- Eat plenty of fresh fruit and vegetables and low-fat options.
- Limit alcohol consumption. A small amount of alcohol is fine, larger quantities lead to health problems including anxiety, insomnia and depression.
- Drink approximately two litres of still water a day to ensure working at peak performance under pressure. Dehydration leads to tiredness and a dramatic reduction in effectiveness. (At least one crew suffered the effects of dehydration that had a negative impact on their performance.)
- Limit caffeine as this simulates the stress reaction and therefore increases stress levels.

Exercise

Exercise is one of the best ways both to relieve and to build resistance to excessive stress. Provided the heart rate is raised, the excessive adrenalin in the body will be used up. This allows the body to relax in between stressful situations. In addition, endorphins are produced which make people feel good and act as a natural sedative.

Most of the skippers were physically fit and had an exercise regime prior to the race. Some undertook heavy physical duties during the race to reduce stress levels and two of the skippers organised exercise programmes for the crews during very calm conditions to ensure fitness levels were maintained. Leaders who follow regular exercise programmes are also more likely to maintain optimal stress levels.

Work–life balance

Working excessively is a known killer in Japan. Referred to as *karoshi* – death through overwork – people often work long hours, fail to take holidays and in extreme cases work themselves to death. A balance between work and leisure is essential as rest allows the body to recharge after a period of intense activity and performance suffers without an opportunity to relax. In the early stages of the race, many of the skippers had difficulty managing this balance and keeping stress at optimal levels.

Most suffered from a lack of sleep which impacted on their physical, mental and emotional well-being. Those able to maintain a more balanced lifestyle were less likely to experience excessive stress.

3. Mental techniques

Strategies are needed to ensure mental control. Some skippers had techniques to be used in difficult situations.

'What if' scenarios

One skipper, concerned about the dangers of the Southern Ocean after one of the yachts was hit by a freak wave, spent time reflecting in his bunk. He developed strategies in the event of life-threatening scenarios such as man overboard, for example. This helped him feel more confident and prepared for difficulties.

Visualisation techniques

Several skippers visualised situations they would have to lead. They used this technique and it helped them to stay in control of situations when they arose. These approaches either helped them to remain positive or they could be used when they experienced the 'darker side' of their inner 'world'.

Positive thinking

Some skippers used self-talk approaches or spoke with a respected crew member to help change negative thoughts – which in turn determine feelings – into the positive, thus switching from the 'dark' to the 'bright' side. When teams work in close physical proximity, negative feelings are transmitted very quickly, leading ultimately to low morale and decreased performance.

The outer world of the skipper

These strategies impacted on the way the skippers projected themselves to the outside world.

1. Clear focus on goals

The higher performers sustained their focus most of the time. If it was lost they quickly took corrective action. The focus reinforced the feeling of being in control. One high-performing skipper, for example, would clarify the goals at a daily lunchtime meeting attended by all the crew.

2. Remaining unemotional under pressure

One skipper performed really well under pressure. Thirty-six hours before the end of one leg his yacht was in eighth position. The skipper was still adamant the race plan was the right one and persisted with his strategy, although there was pressure to change it. He didn't share his feelings with the crew, nor did he let his emotions and thoughts get in the way of what he believed was the right course of action. 'You haven't got a clue what he is thinking,' one crew member said. The skipper remained emotionally resilient and the strategy paid off when the yacht finished the leg in fourth position.

Lower-performing skippers, however, showed their emotions in difficult situations. For example, when one crew were required to undertake a difficult sail change quickly, the skipper would shout at crew members or be critical if the sail change was not handled smoothly.

3. Ensuring thorough preparation and planning to reduce pressure

Several of the skippers who achieved high performance were meticulous about the preparation of the yacht before each leg of the race. In Wellington, the skipper of one yacht drew up a list of jobs, including about 250 items, which all had to be completed prior to the race restart.

‘ *Preparation is everything.* ’ The skipper wanted no excuse. This approach helped him feel in control, in the knowledge that once these jobs were completed, the yacht could perform at maximum potential and there was less likelihood of experiencing equipment failure. This increased his confidence in the yacht and its likely performance.

Another skipper, on the other hand, lost ground because of insufficient planning. He had underestimated the complexity of the situation. Racing up the River Plate to the finish line, he chose a course where the current turned out to be very strong. Stress levels were unacceptably high and the yacht was overtaken by another yacht that had taken a course where the current was less fierce.

Team dynamics – interaction between the skipper and the team

Whether the inner and outer worlds of the skipper were positive or negative had a major impact on interaction with the crew, team dynamics and culture. The skippers adopted several strategies to ensure the team dynamics were positive.

1. Staying calm and using the right leadership styles for the situation

On one occasion a yacht needed to make a very quick and difficult sail change and the crew had got into difficulties. The skipper did not raise his voice once, unlike some of his fellow skippers in similar situations, and just helped haul the sail down very quickly. Afterwards, however, the skipper said: 'You very nearly messed this up and this is why…' Then, using a coaching style of leadership, he explained what should have happened. One of the crew members also explained that the skipper never talked down to people or shouted orders, remaining calm under pressure and always consistent.

2. Focusing attention on the task rather than worrying about pressures from the environment

Shortly after one yacht had been severely damaged in the Southern Ocean, one skipper briefed his crew on the importance of racing the yacht in storm conditions. The skipper emphasised the need to observe safety standards but made the crew focus on what they had to do to sail the yacht rather than constantly worrying about the stormy weather conditions. The crew enjoyed the experience of racing in the Southern Ocean and it thus turned a negative situation into a positive one. Finally, they were so focused on sailing the yacht that the adverse weather conditions assumed less importance.

Leaders need to adopt a similar strategy during times of uncertainty and insecurity. Worrying about the future is very stressful because it is beyond people's control. It is much better to live in the present and focus on those factors one *is* able to control.

3. Handling fear prior to the event

Planning for difficult situations is imperative. Most of the crews were nervous about rounding Cape Horn. In the previous race one of the skippers had told his crew the rounding was 'nothing to worry about'. The crew had faced horrendous conditions in this area of sea, and a volunteer had attacked one of the skippers with a knife because he had not been straight with the crew and had not dealt with their fear.

Unsurprisingly, many of the skippers learned the lessons from the previous BT Global Challenge race. Many now tried to calm feelings of anxiety by discussing the Cape Horn situation well in advance. The crews also shared their feelings with each other and, once they had realised they all felt the same way, were able to offer mutual support. The skippers drew up special plans for dealing with this part of the race, further building the crews' confidence and helping them cope with the situation.

> ' *The crew understood about the fears of others and were able to support one another.* '

Leaders can make use of this strategy when they are aware of anxiety within their team. New situations or activities, such as giving a presentation or negotiating an important piece of business, can often raise stress levels.

4. Recognising the importance of open communication

To deal with stressful unresolved conflicts and potential relationship problems, a number of the skippers adopted measures to ensure channels of communication remained open between the different members of the yacht. For example, on one yacht there was a Sunday service which not only had hymns, prayers and Bible readings but also acted as a forum for the crew to discuss any issues that had occurred during the week.

The 'kangaroo court' was another type of meeting that brought issues into the open in a lighthearted way. During this mock-up court, the skipper took on the role of the judge and a crew member was prosecutor, with the rest of the crew in attendance. After the 'case' was made against him, the accused was brought before the judge who gave his judgement and administered punishment if necessary. One crew member, for example, came before the court and was given the 'whingeing badge'.

Those yachts that had no such mechanism for discussing issues tended to have a higher level of conflict, issues festered and stress levels rose. In business, leaders must be prepared to address conflict and confront issues when they arise. Differences of opinion can also lead to healthy conflict. This is discussed fully in Chapter 10.

5. Showing vulnerability

Higher-performing skippers were also prepared to admit mistakes, discuss issues when they did not know the answers, do the mundane tasks when necessary and share how they felt with the crew. Those who adopted this approach were also more likely to give their crew responsibility and accountability. In return, the skippers were trusted and respected by their team and were more likely to receive support when it was needed.

Other skippers worked hard to try to hide their inadequacies and were less likely to admit to mistakes. The crew, however, were aware of these weaknesses and mistakes and the skippers lost their trust and respect. In one or two cases the skippers became quite isolated and alienated from their crew.

6. Developing an appropriate culture and climate

The higher-performing skippers all developed a performance culture. This is described as part of culture, Chapter 13. This helped to keep stress at the optimum level as the culture was more supportive and focused and gave importance to dealing with issues and learning from mistakes.

7. Providing support and one-to-one communication following stressful incidents

Most of the skippers experienced stressful incidents. The worst incident happened shortly after the fleet left Sydney. A yacht was hit by a freak wave, one of its crew lost a finger and another was severely injured. After this traumatic event the skipper recognised the need to talk to the individuals involved separately. After the latter incident, external counselling was offered at the next port of call. Leaders need to recognise when situations are beyond their capability and seek outside help to deal with the stress of others or their own stress.

THE RELATIONSHIP BETWEEN STRESS MANAGEMENT AND EMOTIONAL INTELLIGENCE

Stress management and emotional intelligence are inextricably linked. The skippers who used stress as an enabler were able to enhance performance by using their emotional intelligence potential to the full. Analysis of behaviour exhibited by these skippers demonstrated a higher level of emotional intelligence behaviours. In contrast, those who were stressed became swamped by their emotions and the behaviour observed or reported by these skippers showed emotional intelligence behaviours deteriorating and performance suffering as the race progressed.

The emotional intelligence behaviours were rated high, medium or low based on the judgements drawn from the data collected from the interviews. The following emotional intelligence behaviours were seen to be the most important for skippers utilising stress as an enabler.

Self-awareness

Self-awareness is perhaps the most important dimension for stress management. The higher-performing skippers tended to use a high level of emotional control. By contrast, skippers performing less well were described as irritable, moody or showed vindictive behaviour through loss of control and seemed less aware of their impact on others. Those skippers demonstrating high self-awareness were better able to judge when it was appropriate to take control of a situation and times when this control would be resented. It was reported that one skipper would come on deck and give directions to make changes, even though the crew were sailing the yacht well. This directive style was not well received by the crew, particularly when subsequently the directions had to be reversed.

Emotional resilience

Emotional resilience had a great impact on race performance. Higher-performing skippers demonstrated high emotional resilience by performing consistently well, even under pressure, and one crew member commented on the highly consistent performance of his skipper. These skippers also handled setbacks very well. By contrast, some lower-performing skippers became less focused and performed less well. For example, one skipper did not like to be disturbed when under pressure or in intense situations and told people to shut up or get out of his way.

Motivation

Motivation determines the extent to which the skippers were focused on goals. All the higher-performing skippers had a clear focus that was also shared by the crews. In contrast, the lower-performing skippers took much longer to define their goals and were much less focused. This was a source of stress for the skippers and crew. One skipper resigned because of a conflict of long-term goals for the race, which was causing great stress for himself and the crew.

Interpersonal sensitivity

Skippers able to keep stress at the appropriate level regularly set aside time to listen to the crew and based decision making on these consultations. The skippers of yachts performing less well spent less time listening to the crew and were less likely to be sensitive to their needs, particularly the crews' need to feel in control of their situation and be involved with decision making. Several of these skippers, however, made changes, giving their crews greater responsibility and accountability as the race progressed.

Conscientiousness

The skippers achieving high performance tended to have consistency in terms of what they said and what they did. They upheld the values of the yacht and were prepared to take corrective action if people did not observe the values. In contrast, certain skippers on yachts performing less well were not so consistent. For example, a couple of skippers showed a lack of respect for people, a core value of those yachts, by failing to listen to them and being rude or dismissive. Others failed to maintain standards so that tidiness and cleanliness became an issue. One skipper reprimanded the crew for having food on the chart table. The crew resented this as the skipper regularly left food on the chart table himself. All these situations generated additional stress.

SUMMARY

As the race clearly demonstrates, stress levels can make the difference between success and failure. In today's turbulent business environment, many leaders are required to work outside their 'comfort zones' and those able to recognise quickly the signs of excessive stress and use appropriate coping strategies are able to use stress as an enabler of performance. Conversely, others, like the less successful skippers, fail to deal with stress properly and their performance suffers. Analysis of the research findings showed that the skippers reacted to stress at three levels, referred to as 'worlds'. In each of these worlds the skippers had a positive or negative reaction to stress depending on their mental and emotional state and their level of self-control. A range of strategies for keeping stress at the optimal level was discussed. Some strategies kept stress at the appropriate levels, others helped the skippers deal with excessive stress.

LESSONS FROM THE RACE

As a leader today you need to:

1. remember, optimal stress is more likely to be achieved when you feel a sense of well-being and self-control

2. be aware that you will experience excessive stress when you feel out of control

3. realise when you experience optimum stress you are more likely to be focused and energetic and to share leadership and control with others

4. utilise the positive energy of stress to enhance performance

5. avoid excessive calm and too relaxed an atmosphere which will detract from performance

6. encourage yourself and your people to be highly focused on the task during stressful times

7. prepare carefully in advance of situations

8. use flexibility of leadership style

9. stay in control

10. create a no-blame culture, a good work/life balance and inject humour.

REFERENCES

Cooper, C. L. and Cooper, R. D. (1988) *Living with Stress*, Penguin Books: Harmondsworth.

Cooper, C. L. and Palmer, S. (2000) *Conquer your Stress*, Institute of Personnel and Development: London.

Cranwell-Ward, J. (1990) *Thriving on Stress*, Routledge: London.

Employee Health Bulletin (1999) 11 October, Stress at Work Survey.

Health and Safety Executive (2001) *Tackling Work Related Stress, A manager's guide to improving and maintaining employee health and well-being*, Health and Safety Executive: London.

Kriegal, R. J. and Kriegal, M. H. (1984) *The C Zone-Peak Performance Under Pressure*, Anchor Press/Doubleday: New York.

Melhuish, Dr A. (1978) *Executive Health*, Business Books: London.

Worrall, L. and Cooper, C. (2000) *The Quality of Working Life*, Institute of Management: London.

WORK/LIFE AT WORK
Nationwide Building Society

In 2001 Nationwide was ranked joint first in the 'Graduates Guide to Work/Life Balance Employers' and the society's approach to work/life balance also contributed to it being placed in *The Sunday Times* 'Top 50 employers' in 2001.

Nationwide is an interesting example of a company committed to an inclusive employment environment that attracts and retains employees across the demographic spectrum. It recognises the business benefits of encouraging employees to balance work and home life and has introduced a wide range of policies, practices and procedures to support this. At Nationwide, work/life policies are 'owned' by line managers throughout the business rather than being enforced by the personnel department. The society makes every effort to understand how its employees feel and to balance their needs with the needs of the business and its members. There are Intranet sites on Flexible Working, Homeworking, Parents at Work and Work/Life Balance, giving information on leave policies, childcare, how to manage a flexible team, as well as tips on how to achieve a work/life balance and real-life case studies. A wide range of flexible working options exist, including part-time, term-time, job share, annualised hours, flexi-time, home-working and compressed working week.

Nationwide believes that its attention to the work/life issue, as well as its commitment to equal opportunities, has given the society:

- access to a wider recruitment pool which gets the best person for the job
- a flexible, multi-skilled workforce
- a diverse workforce that better reflects its customer base, helps it to understand customer needs and develop business solutions to meet market needs
- the opportunity to demonstrate that it values the contribution of all employees which in turn improves commitment, motivation, morale, productivity, reduces stress and absenteeism and improves customer satisfaction.

In a survey in 2000, 77 per cent of employees responded favourably to the statement '*I am satisfied Nationwide provides me with the opportunities to balance working arrangements with personal life*'.

Finally, Nationwide believes that a work/life balance is:

- good for employees
- good for teams
- good for business!

8

WORK/LIFE BALANCE –
THE WAR FOR TIME

Contributions to this chapter were made
by the following Forum member:
Carol Whitaker, The NEC Group

INTRODUCTION

By the end of the 20th century many people were working exceedingly
long hours and there was little time for any form of private life. The
balance between work and a
private life had become dis-

' To neglect the social side is
really at your peril, things
often start to fester. '

torted. Charles Handy (1995)
said that profit came from
half the people working twice
as hard for three times the
money. The term 'work/life balance' arose when individuals and organisations realised that the pace could not last.

Today's workplace is mainly one of 'presenteeism', where visibility
counts for everything and 70-hour weeks are common. The burden on
employees has become onerous as employers trim and restructure in
pursuit of global advantage. The work/life balance has consequently
become distorted as workers subscribe to the company's fiercely competitive culture. However, closer scrutiny of the relationship between
work/life balance and productivity is beginning to see the emergence of
new patterns, with both employers and employees recognising that long
hours and one-dimensional lives have little correlation with sustained

success. In an environment where competition for talent is huge, attrition is costing billions and mergers and acquisitions are daily headline news, balancing the demands of an employee's work and home life is imperative. As a result, improved work/life balance has become a major business issue.

Nowhere has this been a more difficult challenge than on the yachts in the BT Global Challenge race where work and life were necessarily intertwined since there was no escape. Productive teams make for faster yachts so crews, guided by their skippers, were forced to come up with their own ways of bringing a life balance into the workplace.

> ❛ *As an adult this is the first time that I have not been able to walk away from work.* ❜

This chapter will help the leader understand why the work/life balance is an issue today, the environment that has led to it becoming an issue and its relationship with performance. Lessons will be drawn from the BT Global Challenge, and it will explore the relevance of emotional intelligence when dealing with the issues of work/life balance in the workplace.

THE ISSUE OF WORK/LIFE BALANCE

Work/life balance has become a business issue as a result of equal opportunities for women in the workplace and later family-friendly policies. Both the US and Northern Europe have led the way. Changes in family structure, particularly the demise of the male as the sole breadwinner, as well as changes in technology and demographics, have made it increasingly clear that work/life balance is also a bottom-line business issue. At the same time business organisations are expecting more of their employees. The environment is so competitive that there is a huge pressure for high performance within organisations.

Balancing work demands with enough time and energy for other parts of people's lives is a growing concern for everybody in today's pressurised workplace. The cost of family and community breakdown is not only devastating for those involved but has an impact on people's working lives and companies' economic competitiveness. Many people are living the majority of their lives at the office in a state of bad health and high stress.

REPERCUSSIONS OF WORK/LIFE IMBALANCE

The next generation are expecting different things from work. Graduates today are more demanding in wanting to be able to balance work and life. A study from the Leadership Institute of Southern California (Conger, 2000) compared Generation X (see Chapter 3) with the Baby Boomers (1943–1964). The research found four Generation X traits that have implications for today's workplace and leadership in the future:

- the need for balance between work and private life
- the need for mobility
- total fluency with information technology
- a strong need for a workplace that provides a community.

The more work intrudes on people's lives, the less time there is for a healthy lifestyle. Long hours preclude exercise, relaxation and fun. Adrenalin that has accumulated through the working day is not released, causing interrupted sleep patterns, exhaustion and stress. Energy drops. The immune system becomes less efficient, leading to illness. With mental and physical fitness closely linked, the impact on business is obvious.

However much people believe they can separate their work life from home life, the two are intrinsically linked. Available energy is a daily commodity. Mellott (2000) calls it an 'Energy Pie'. One pie has to last the whole day. There are no bakers to issue a second pie on the way home from work. How

> **❝ Avoid situations that waste energy on trivial issues. ❞**

that pie is cut and used is a matter of personal choice, but many people realise that large pieces of their energy pie are being squandered and there is little left for the things that are really important in their lives. It is often only when relationships have broken down irretrievably that people realise that there was nothing in the pie left for that relationship.

In the early legs a couple of skippers admitted to getting the balance wrong. One of the podium skippers started out with too strong a focus on performance, expecting total commitment and dedication. He realised this could not be maintained without injecting an element of fun. When things were going well 'extras' were not required, but when they were not, the skipper realised the crew needed them. He injected light relief on leg 2, introducing a completely different atmosphere above and below decks. When the crew were on deck they had to be totally focused on making the yacht go as fast as possible; down below they were able to read and relax. Another skipper, having done well on leg 1, increased the pressure to maintain that position and again focused solely on performance. He was heavyhanded. The crew became very unhappy, felt the skipper was too intense and the fun element that had been so important to them and was stated in the goals had disappeared. The crew started to get snappy with each other, arguments flared and the team spirit was lost. Their position at the end of leg 2 was much lower than leg 1. As a result of both of these teams addressing the issue and bringing balance back into their lives, their performance improved and both yachts achieved podium positions.

On the yachts it was very often newcomers, or leggers, who spotted the lack of balance in the crews. One crew member who joined the yacht in Buenos Aires instantly saw the lack of fun on the boat and took on the job of entertainment. On another yacht, a legger joined in Wellington and found that there was not enough balance and that the skipper was suffering as a result of it. This legger took it upon himself to provide humour and fun.

What is required is cultural change. In a nation characterised by a 'long hours culture' this type of shift will only be driven by leaders who see the changing drivers of value in their business. The tone these leaders set and their own behaviour are key indicators of their core beliefs.

Ed Smith, Partner, PricewaterhouseCoopers and
National Work-Life Forum consortium chair

EMERGING TRENDS IN WORK/LIFE PATTERNS

To laugh often and much; to win the respect of intelligent people and the affection of children; to earn the appreciation of honest critics and to endure the betrayal of false friends; to appreciate beauty; to find the best in others; to leave the world a bit better whether by a healthy child, a garden patch, or a redeemed social condition; to know that even one life has breathed easier because you lived; this is to have success.

Ralph Waldo Emerson (Handy, 1997)

Mori (1999) carried out a poll among today's 30-year-olds and found one in five said they were so concerned about the lack of balance in their lives they would accept a cut in pay to have more free time. This balance ranked higher than the quality of their boss and the opportunity of promotion. The National Work-Life Forum was set up in the UK in 1999. It believes that aligning personal values with those in the workplace and feeling more in charge of life will be pivotal personal success factors.

As today's working life becomes less tolerable, people are beginning to ask what they really want from life. Large salaries, big bonuses and excessively long hours no longer appear to fulfil most people. Success is beginning to mean more than financial reward. Leadership is no longer about position, it is a state of mind. People are rethinking their priorities and redefining what success and fulfilment mean to them. They are analysing their inner purpose in order to decide whether their current direction is leading towards that purpose. Inner conflict often occurs when work and inner purpose are not aligned.

> *' Live for the moment.*
> *Find contentment.*
> *Look after the environment. '*

Individual skippers defined success in several ways. Although wealth was not an issue in this race as there was no prize money, some wanted fame and position. Others were looking for adventure. One skipper made it clear from the start that his goal was the achievement of something much bigger than the race. Winning was not part of the goal. He wanted to give 'life prizes', to share with the crew a real life experience. He wanted the crew to look for their own purpose, to reflect on their lives and to be able to build something together after the race.

ACHIEVING WORK/LIFE BALANCE

In order to achieve balance in life, facets of both work and life have to be individually balanced and fulfilling. The responsibility lies with both the individual and the organisation.

Personal life balance

Personal life is the responsibility of the individual. No matter how many policies an organisation may adopt, it is up to the individual to achieve work/life balance. Sharp (2001) argues that different aspects of our life make us what we are and that we frequently become overfocused

' Having a physical break gives people a mental break as well. '

on just one area, typically work, to the detriment of others. He believes there are several areas in people's lives that need a healthy balance:

- physical health
- family
- friends
- spiritual
- recreation, hobbies, holidays
- financial
- work
- emotional literacy
- mental health.

Each of these areas requires regular and consistent attention. They need to become second nature because they are the sole responsibility of the individual. Investment in self is the only way to effective performance.

This requires self-regulation and discipline. For many people, work has 'won the war' for time and these vital areas are being neglected. In a recent survey, 76 per cent of senior women questioned had sacrificed personal activities in the majority of these areas in the war for time.

Physical health

Gyms have many members, most of them absent. Although most people are aware that exercise gives energy, they are lacking the drive and energy to take the exercise. Most of the crews set out to build the team physically before the race. There was a real desire to keep fit in mind and body and every opportunity was taken to go running to relieve pressure and take time to think. This was hard to sustain for the whole race and many crews failed to keep their fitness programmes going. However, some teams had fitness sessions on deck on the calmer legs that helped them both physically and mentally, especially when boredom was creeping in.

Sleep deprivation was a big issue on the race, especially for the skippers. It was essential for them to regulate themselves. Some saw the importance of training crew members early on so that they could take responsibility for the running of the yacht and give the skipper a break. Several skippers achieved this by introducing a separate watch system for themselves with their navigator, or with watch leaders, so that they could all benefit from sleep. Others had to be told by their crews that they were lacking sleep. In most cases of sleep deprivation, emotional resilience fell and this affected performance. In a business environment it is very easy to forget that hours worked does not equal efficiency.

Nutrition was critical for the crew members and the yachts spent a great deal of time researching the best possible diet. Most appointed a food person, or team, to learn about nutrition and to source the best food. Although the majority of the food was freeze-dried, the nutritional content and quantity had to be carefully calculated. Although there was a recommended supplier of freeze-dried food, some teams used companies in France and New Zealand to source their food. The imagination of the appointed food specialist was put to the test in an endeavour to make the food exciting. Fresh and tinned items were used to enhance supplies and also for celebrations. Most yachts baked fresh bread each day and some baked cakes to celebrate birthdays. Some squirrelled away treats to be brought out when the mood was low or when food stocks were low. A couple of the legs lasted longer than predicted and rationing had to be introduced. On occasion, the quantity of food was miscalculated and the crew were reduced to practically no food by the time they reached the port of call.

The quantity of fast food restaurants and takeaways in the world today is an indication of the pace of people's lives. Many people are too busy to eat properly and exist on unhealthy snacks and instant food.

Family, friends and the community

I am of the opinion that my life belongs to the whole community and as long as I live it is my privilege to do for it whatever I can.

George Bernard Shaw 1856–1950

As the blur between work and home life becomes greater, so the need for support increases. Families need to be considered and a holistic approach to employees taken. Some societies deal with this better than others. In Japan, employment would never happen without consideration being given to housing and family support. Other societies have no interest in the private lives of their employees. Today there is often little time for social interaction outside of work. Friends are made at work, relationships start there and the only friends outside of work are those who are email-friendly. Family and friends see little or nothing of each other as work demands ever increasing amounts of time.

Local communities are suffering as more and more people leave their community to go to work each day. Communities can thrive only when there is commitment to them. They require the time, energy and talent that are tied up in the workplace. There are many people who would like to be involved in this kind of voluntary work who are too committed to the workplace.

The larger BT Global Challenge yacht community was made up of all the people who were involved in some way with the race. Many family and friends travelled to the ports of call, where friendships were established across the whole fleet and support teams. One skipper realised, by being in the race, just how important his family was to him.

❛ The race is for ten months, your family is for ever. ❜

On the yachts the support network proved invaluable. Families and friends were utilised in many different ways. They helped to prepare the yachts before they left, they gave support in the ports of call and provided a close support network for each other while the yachts were at sea.

The crews developed their own support system during the race. When a rogue wave seriously injured two of VERITAS' crew members as they headed towards the Southern Ocean, the first response they received to their call for help was from the skipper of Quadstone. When it was obvious that Olympic would have to put on its engine in order to reach La Rochelle before the start of the final leg, several other yachts volunteered to help with the preparation of the yacht to have it ready for the restart. The sign-off from a crew volunteer's email was more evidence of the total support: 'Say a little prayer for Olympic, that they get in before the next leg starts.' Olympic helped out Quadstone by doing some of their corporate sailing for them following the accident between Save the Children and Quadstone.

Olympic, Logica and Compaq joined together to hold a party to raise funds for one of the crew members who was suffering from cancer. There was a huge turnout for the event, showing the degree of mutual support within the fleet, and more than £8,000 was raised.

The yachts were asked to help with the publicity of Red Nose Day. They were filmed all together before the start of the Wellington to Sydney leg with Red Noses on their bows (see Plate 8). The crew of Save the Children held up a large board with the pledge phone numbers. The film was later broadcast on television.

Several yacht sponsors found that the family support network was a vital ingredient in the success of their campaigns. Logica realised early on the necessity of balancing the needs of team development with the need for family time. In order to find a way round this pull on time they decided to run two workshops side by side, one for the crew and one for the families. At the end of the day the two groups joined together and discussed each other's learning. They discussed their different concerns about life on and off the yacht.

The families expressed:

- fear for the physical safety of their loved ones
- anxieties about whether their relationship was strong enough to cope with the long separations
- jealousy around potential new relationships on board, both platonic and otherwise
- concern about coping alone with family responsibilities
- bitterness towards the sponsor for 'taking the crew member' away from them.

The crew felt:

- guilt about leaving loved ones behind to achieve a personal ambition
- concern about partner's potential infidelity
- concern about family members who were ailing or in ill health
- fear about how they would cope if things happened 'back home'.

This was a powerful session and was a realisation for Logica that in business where an executive's family is overlooked this can have a direct impact on the success of the executive and so the business. A demanding, time-consuming job can cause resentment, jealously, anger and frustration with partners. This leads to conflict in the home and this in turn is bound to have a detrimental effect on any executive's performance. Psychologically, patterns in our home lives are recreated in our work lives. Happy people are productive people and relationships are such an integral element of our overall happiness that it is worthwhile considering the business benefits of paying more attention to families.

Logica then set up a chat room for the family members and once the company started to integrate with the families, thoughts, ideas and suggestions began to flow. The sponsor was surprised at the positive effect the families had on the sponsorship exploitation programme. They contributed a great many useful ideas and practical advice and knowledge. Their understanding of the crew and their motivations provided a valuable resource to the yacht management team throughout the race. The sponsors believe that, though family-friendly policies are still in relative infancy in business, the results from the work they did with their yacht crew and their families indicates it is an area where much more work can be done. They believe that it will have a positive effect on the financial success of the business.

Larry Quinn, a member of Logica's executive committee, joined the yacht for the executive leg from Wellington to Sydney. His report as a legger on board Logica is given below.

LAUGHING ALL THE WAY ACROSS THE TASMAN SEA

As a keen cruising sailor who owns and sails his own boat, Larry had a good deal of experience on the water but little of ocean racing. He joined the Logica crew with some trepidation, fearing negative or positive 'special' treatment because he had some sailing experience and was also a senior manager within the sponsoring company. But having attended the initial team-building programme created by Logica with VisionWorks, where the crew worked together learning how to communicate effectively and to take responsibility for their relationships, Larry found that the crew, having already sailed halfway round the world together, were able to be authentically themselves. This, in turn, allowed Larry to observe the team dynamics from a different perspective – that of not being 'the boss'.

'I took the opportunity to watch the crew members and how they interacted with one another and it underlined for me the fact that some people just aren't comfortable with certain roles or responsibilities, and as a consequence they have little impact in their positions. The team's success or disappointment hinges around the ability of the leaders. I watched as crew members "failed to hear" a watch leader when asked to do things. Sometimes having authority isn't a comfortable situation for people and it leads to ineffectiveness. It reminds me that not everyone thinks the way I do and sees the world the way I do and that I need to go back to my desk and just check the levels of comfort around what I am asking for from my team.'

In fact, Larry had cause to question his communication skills during the lead-up to the race. 'I was so totally focused on the race, my sail training and ensuring that I gave my best during my leg of the race that I effectively shut out not only my colleagues but my family too, for nearly a month. I assumed that everyone saw the race and my participation in it as I did. But, of course, they didn't. I learned a huge lesson in the importance of taking time out to involve my family and colleagues and to explain my perspective and to listen to theirs. My concerns were around doing my personal best in participating in what, for me, was the pinnacle of my sailing experience. I felt like the lad pulled off the local park being asked to go and play for Liverpool Football Club. I wanted to do well both for me and for Logica. My colleagues had concerns about how they were to manage while I was out of the office and my family had concerns for my personal safety. I failed to see their perspective.

'Having email facilities on the yacht did allow me to make some amends. I am told that I can communicate well by email and being in regular contact with my wife and our three children did give them some comfort. As a family we are used to me being away on business and in total I was only physically absent for two-and-a-half weeks. My family came to Sydney to cheer Logica home and the support of the other families and friends helped them enormously.

'Through the work that had been undertaken prior to the race start with family members, which had then been built upon throughout the race, my family found a much appreciated under-standing and informal "support group" with whom they found some solace and also had a lot of fun. This project had the fami-lies at the heart of it from well before the race started. Their involvement has given us both valuable feedback on how we ran the overall programme and has provided those onshore with a network of contacts with whom they could share some of the worry and also the logistics of travel and accommodation. It has worked well and gives us in the business something to consider in how we look after our key people.'

Paradoxically, in his working life Larry is very mindful of maintaining a good work/life balance. He is always very conscious of the needs of his wife and children, both because the better the relationship he has at home the more effective he can be at work and because he recognises that total focus on work isn't a good thing. It can reduce creativity and energy levels. Larry also has the ability to switch off, which he found very useful when sailing with so many people in such a relatively confined space.

'I never felt claustrophobic on the yacht. I have an ability to create my own "sanctuary space". I use it at work and it helps me stop and get a better perspective when things are getting to me. I kept a diary of my emotions while I sailed the Wellington to Sydney leg and I think that it helped, but oddly I haven't looked at it since.

'As I was at sea for a very short leg I never really felt the need to confide in anyone about any personal issues, although I was forever asking questions about the running of the yacht, but the atmosphere on board Logica was certainly conducive to doing so had the need arisen. Any issue that needed to be resolved was brought out into the open as it arose and dealt with honestly. There was a great sense of openness and understanding on board. This was, I believe, created by our team training, carried out over several sessions, prior to the race start and in ports of call. Everyone worked together in a remarkably cohesive way and although I was sailing with amateurs I never once felt any risk to my personal safety. We all had to rely on the work of the team and everyone had total confidence in the team.

'The crew comprised such a disparate group of people from all age groups and walks of life – we had a ballet dancer, a policeman and a gynaecologist on our yacht – and yet everyone worked together effectively. Our teambuilding sessions had allowed people to recognise and to be themselves. Everyone was pretty comfortable being authentically who they were and so we didn't experience any huge character changes when we reached stopovers.'

The crews' commitment to the community at large was by way of Save the Children, the official charity for the race. The target for this race was to raise £300 000 for children round the world. The target was reached before the start date. A new target of £500 000 was quickly established. Crew members raised as much as £25 000 each towards the charity. At the prize-giving ball in London at the end of the race an auction was held which brought the final amount raised overall to £1 million. It was a remarkable achievement.

Mike Aaronson, Director General, Save the Children (UK), commented at the ball: 'The fundraising smashed through the initial target before the race even started and has gone on to raise so much more than we expected. As the official race charity, Save the Children has been very fortunate to have had the support of The Challenge Business, BT, sponsors and crews of the race. It has been a truly international effort, with money raised in countries as far afield as Canada, Australia, Argentina, New Zealand and the UK. The funds raised represent a huge contribution to Save the Children's work, helping to give some of the world's most disadvantaged children a better start in life.'

Several crew members visited a Save the Children funded project in Cape Town during their stopover there. The report from Rona Cant, a crew volunteer on Save the Children, is given below.

'For us it was a day of investigation, for them one of celebrations. The project we visited in Cape Town was the John Parma School in Nyanga Township where Save the Children works with RAPCAN (Resources Aimed at the Prevention of Child Abuse and Neglect).

'The teachers, in traditional dress, greeted us. With us was a representative from each crew, some of the sponsors' representatives and the film crew. Walking behind the drum majorettes we passed houses made of corrugated iron or planks of wood and black refuse sacks, the better ones made of breeze-block with corrugated iron roofs (some areas policed by gun-carrying soldiers). The townsfolk came out to watch, wave and cheer. The sheer strength of our welcome combined with the abject poverty these people live in moved all of us deeply. We had to help them.

'Touring overcrowded classrooms, we were met by cheeky, smiling faces, so pleased to see us (and smile for the cameras – they had never seen a photograph of themselves so we have sent copies). When the choir sang it was incredible, they could have been adults.

'At a RAPCAN workshop the children, aged 6–7, were asked to draw something bad. The pictures were of murder, rape, sodomy and beatings, part of their everyday life. They were congratulated on recognising that these were wrong. Sodomy was explicitly explained to them, confirming that they should tell someone they trust if it was happening to them.

'After a special lunch the children danced for us, with ex-pupils dancing in tribal dress. School fees are R20 per annum (£2) but 80 per cent cannot afford them. Most of the money is spent on repairing windows, broken daily by outsiders. On the coach, R2000 was collected for files for the 1000 children, which was handed to the principal when we returned to the school ten days later.

'BT, impressed by the film of the choir, invited the children to sing at the prize-giving, where we raised £800 for drums (which they hired for music lessons). This I handed to overjoyed teachers just before the choir sang at the Blessing of the Waves (see Plate 2). Further money raised by Serco's employees was directed to pay for grilles for the windows.

'It was very humbling to be associated with people so happy despite their living conditions, but it was good to help them in some way, albeit so small. As our yacht left for the start line, the choir sang their own farewell to us. It brought a lump to my throat.'

Spiritual

The spiritual dimension means different things to different people. It is a private one, but an important one for many people. It is the source of inspiration and relates to core values. Taking time to draw on what life is all about brings renewal, refreshment and the ability to put life back into perspective for most people. With so much uncertainty in the world, many people are looking for an inner peace. When personal and global disaster strike, more and more people are finding solace in churches of all denominations.

Within the yacht fleet, some crew members found meditation a way of finding space and tranquillity. Others gained strength from sitting on the rail and contemplating the sea. Several crew members found great value in taking time to stand back and reflect. For most, the pace of life at work had always prevented it and reflection, or meditation, was something they now felt was important and they wanted to continue after the race. One yacht had a special place where people who wanted quiet time for thinking, or for being emotional, were allowed to sit. The degree of respect for this was illustrated when one person sat there uninterrupted for two days.

The skipper of Olympic held Sunday services each week for the spiritual needs of the group. This took the form of hymns, readings and prayers and involved everyone. It became the highlight of the week and whatever the weather they sang together on deck with great gusto. Some of the crew members wrote home to ask for hymn requests from family and friends.

Recreation, hobbies, holidays

For many people today any form of recreation or hobby has been forfeited for work. Even holiday entitlement is not taken up. It was very important that the crews were able to have time to relax and most yachts allowed reading and listening to music down below. On some of the calmer legs, music, reading and writing were permitted on deck. Stopovers were a large part of the overall race and most crew members wanted to see as much as they could of the different countries during their time in ports of call. This had to be factored in around yacht maintenance. The crews returned fresh and rested and ready to tackle the next leg.

Emotional literacy

Morris (2001) argues that by studying emotional intelligence, individuals can regain the passion they had for their work and for their private life; they can regain the energy and drive they once had to do the things they want to do; they can regain the confidence, enthusiasm and delight in whatever they do. The skippers were assessed on their emotional intelligence at the start of the race but as it was an element in the research study being undertaken, no development work was done with them during the race.

Mental health

Many people spend so much of their day at work that there is no energy left for the many mental challenges. Books lie unread, new interests are not found, friendships flounder and there is certainly no time for standing back.

The value given to books, CDs, etc. varied on each of the yachts. Those who were strongly focused on performance tended to limit anything that would detract from such focus and add undue weight. Others felt that the crew's morale was key to performance and so encouraged external mental stimulation. One skipper felt it was very important to strike the right balance between weight and morale. He considered music to be an important element in enhancing the mood of the crew. Time and thought were put into deciding the CDs that should be taken on each leg.

On one yacht the reading, and more importantly the sharing, of books was encouraged. This led to literary discussions on board and one crew member, who had never been a reader, was converted. The majority of those taking part in the race wrote journals, some of which are being converted into books. On another yacht poetry writing became a fascination and the skipper of Spirit of Hong Kong held an art competition for the crew. Quizzes and games were features during the longer legs of the race. Several skippers read poetry and the stories of Shackleton to stimulate and motivate their crews.

In summary, bringing balance into one's life is a personal choice and it is made much harder by the ever demanding work environment. It requires discipline and self-regulation to get it in order, with an established sense of purpose, specific goals and objective and effective channels of communication. It requires even more discipline to leave work and the office at the appropriate time.

THE BARRIERS TO WORK/LIFE BALANCE

There are a number of barriers that prevent people from being able to balance their lives:

- Working long hours may have become a habit – what used to be a nine-to-five job has become a five-to-nine way of life. Presenteeism has become a norm and some organisations expect their employees to be working all hours.
- Many people have a materialistic style of living that they would find hard to forego. However much they may dream, or even talk, of a balanced lifestyle, the reality is that their financial commitments will hinder the balance.
- Technology has made global communication quick and efficient. Emails and mobile phones allow for 24 × 7 working anywhere in the world. However useful, any attempt at a balanced life is immediately threatened. There is no hiding place. Mobile phones ring constantly on trains, in restaurants, even on the beach. Lack of respect for global time zones and different days of rest causes even more intrusion into people's lives.
- Many people have become so addicted to the workplace that their home life is totally out of control. Domestic arrangements are neglected. Home finance, personal administration, gardens and houses all require attention. Relationships at home may be more complicated and less rewarding than those at work. Recognition may be greater at work. The lure to stay at work becomes strong and the end result is that homes that used to be lived in are now houses that are slept in.
- Flexible working brings its own problems. A 2001 Reach BT Flexible Working Survey carried out in the financial sector showed that although the industry is keen to change the way it works, many businesses still have serious concerns about ingrained conservative management attitudes. The major barriers found were:
  - organisational culture and management attitudes   77%
  - reduced communication with colleagues/managers   70%

- loss of visibility at work   61%
- loss of access to centralised corporate resources
  and information sharing   56%
- Technology, although a great asset to work/life balance, can also be the barrier to it. Email is omnipresent and brings with it a suggestion of urgency. An AT&T study found that half those on holiday call into work or check their emails. On some yachts it became a distraction and crew members were sneaking down to access their mail when on watch. On the shorter legs, which were intense sprints, some skippers banned email for the duration of the leg. The crews had to make important decisions as to whether or not they wanted personal information going on and off the boat. Some wanted to know if there was a family crisis; others felt that there was nothing they could do about it so it was better not to know.

WORK BALANCE INITIATIVES

Beliefs form the foundations of the business culture; they dictate what is sacred, what is sanctioned and what is taboo. By demonstrating their own personal commitment to and achievement of a balanced lifestyle, these leaders are by their very behaviour sanctioning consistent behaviour among others in the organisation. Only then will employees feel empowered to attain a true balance between work and life

Ed Smith, PricewaterhouseCoopers

Work balance can be greatly enhanced by the policies that organisations put into place to enable a flexibility of working. There are many different initiatives to help with the work/life issue. UK government initiatives include paternity leave as well as longer maternity leave. Tony Blair launched the Employers for Work-Life Balance (EWLB) in March 2000 and it was extended for a second year. This is a 22-strong group working closely with the Department for Education and Employment to promote flexible working practices. Companies are looking at flexible working, the use of technology and introducing family-friendly policies. These initiatives will succeed only if there is a culture to support them. There is no point in talking about flexibility if there is a culture that breeds workaholics.

Retaining employees

The real source of wealth today is the sum of the knowledge of an organisation's employees. The market value of a business is partly assessed on its intelligence quotient. Knowledgeable people are the most valuable asset a company can have and keeping that asset is becoming increasingly difficult.

One of the most important elements of the work/life balance is that work should be enjoyable. Successful organisations aim to ensure that they are creating the right environment where people are happy and fulfilled and want to stay. This requires looking at the work environment, the flexibility and the culture.

Deloitte & Touche believes that employees should be viewed as volunteers who put in time because they believe in the purpose of the organisation. They know that these volunteers go home every night and come back in the morning only if they want to. The crew members were not only volunteers but paying guests. The skippers had to find ways to create the right environment that would prevent people wanting to leave.

Paying employees

Evidence has shown that if salaries are seen as competitive, they are not a significant factor in retention. However, it is how compensation is evaluated that makes the difference. If people skills are part of the assessment process, there is a far greater chance that the environment is one of caring where people really do matter.

Steve Hasson (2001) believes that you have to cherish people and revere their talent to value them as individuals and genuinely care. Likewise if compensation can allow employees to share in the profits of the company there is a feeling of inclusion. On the yachts each crew volunteer had paid to be part of the Challenge. It was even more important that they were made to feel included and looked after. They wanted the reward of having done the best job they possibly could and to know that their personal and team goals were aligned and achieved. They were prepared to go along with the risk if they could share the reward.

Satisfying employees

If people feel that they are growing in their jobs and they are still being stretched, the likelihood of leaving is diminished. If they know where their contribution fits into the whole picture and feel theirs is a valued contribution, they are more likely to stay. There needs to be optimism.

' You can sail better if you have the whole picture, if you know what's happening. '

There needs to be creativity and empowerment where pro-activity is encouraged.

People naturally want to learn. A culture where the development of vital skills and behaviours is encouraged will again prevent people walking. No matter how many benefits a company is prepared to lavish on its employees, without a challenging work environment people will feel unfulfilled and will have wanderlust. Jack Welch, former CEO of General Electric, believes that: 'A learning company is a high-spirited, endlessly curious enterprise that roams the globe finding and nurturing the best people and cultivating in them an insatiable appetite to find that better way every day.'

Many crew volunteers had signed up because they wanted to learn to sail. On some yachts they were never given the opportunity to learn and they felt unfulfilled. On other yachts the learning culture encouraged cross-functional working, coaching sessions, both from the skipper and fellow crew members. Towards the end of the race everyone was beginning to think beyond the race. Several skippers made a point of finding out what the crew members wanted to achieve and used the long leg from Cape Town to La Rochelle to achieve this. The skippers who satisfied their crews were those who brought genuine passion into the job.

Managing employees

People's relationship with their boss greatly influences job satisfaction. The example of their boss determines their perception as to the overall culture of the company. No matter what policies are in place, if the immediate boss is not representative of them, they will have no impact. Leaders must be positive role models and must set an example of self-discipline. Leaders must live the values and share the vision of the company. They must encourage the growth and success of others and they must manage the business. If their management style encourages work/life balance, they must be the first to show it.

Value sets had been agreed by most of the yacht teams before the race began. Where the skipper lived up to these values, they became a way of life. Work and life were balanced so that the crew members could have time with their families in ports of call. However, some skippers lost the respect of their crew if they failed to live up to these values. Some found the pressure of the job so great they had little time to relax. The crews found pressure in trying to balance the needs of their friends and families with the needs of yacht maintenance.

At PWC we are transforming our business to ensure that we continue to attract people with the skills and talent that we need to deliver excellent client service. By demonstrating a personal commitment to achieve a balanced lifestyle and a diverse workforce, our leaders can help our people to feel a connection between policies/programmes and daily work/life, which reflects our mission to be a terrific place to work.

Ed Smith, PricewaterhouseCoopers

Ultimately people need to know that they are cared for as individuals in all aspects of their lives, from health to their future and their fulfilment.

Flexibility

Retaining the best talent in an organisation requires accommodating different needs. There is untapped resource in women who leave to have children but don't return and disabled people who cannot work a full day. There are also many people who have realised that climbing the promotion ladder may not be the way to fulfilment. If business intelligence is the greatest asset a company can have then employers will have to offer more flexible ways of working if they are to retain their talented employees. It is estimated that only 1 in 10 UK companies allows flexible working.

Companies like BT, PricewaterhouseCoopers and FedEx have all converted to flexible working. BT, in its brochure on its new 'lifestyle-friendly' policy, includes a stark health warning about the dangers of 'presenteeism', its effect on family, staff and the community. John Steel, BT Group Personnel Director, spoke at the Diversity and Work-Life Forum at the beginning of 2001. He made the following points:

- Work/life balance is important to the future success and sustainable development of business.
- If employers are to attract, retain and motivate top-quality employees they need to respond innovatively and pro-actively to the pressures that they are dealing with in achieving a balance between work and personal life.
- Work is what we do, not somewhere we go.
- Flexibility of work location and attendance is hugely inclusive, opening opportunities to women, carers and people with disabilities that may otherwise be inaccessible to them.
- Employers must create an environment that recognises the importance of life outside of work.
- BT's technology must be used to make human connections and liberate, not devour, personal time.
- The potential to transfer skills and knowledge between business and community is huge.

BT sponsors both the Employers for Work/Life Balance web site and the National Work/Life Forum web site. The company initiated a project entitled 'Freedom to Work' which incorporated a trial offering individuals the ability to design the attendance patterns which would help them to rebalance their personal and professional lives. It found increased loyalty and increased team performance. By establishing a culture that promotes inclusivity and embraces work/life balance it has reduced absenteeism and employee turnover and achieved significant savings in recruitment and training costs alone. The company has 93 per cent return rate following maternity leave.

The NEC Group in the UK has increased the number of part-time workers by a factor of eight in three years. Many staff who had been on maternity leave have been able to return to work on a part-time basis.

One nursery in the City of London is now charging £15 a minute for every minute parents are late in picking up their children. There is no better way to ensure that work is finished on time.

On the yachts several different ideas were used to increase a flexibility of working to ensure effective personal performance. On one yacht the skipper introduced 'The Big Sleep', giving people 12 hours off once a week. This proved to be morale boosting and meant they were far better able to cope. Others introduced a system where they missed a watch every week. Other skippers showed flexibility by allowing those who were really in need to have extra time off. One of the podium skippers banned books on the early legs as he felt the need for sleep was paramount and that reading could detract from it. The skipper felt that the crew were not experienced enough to be aware of this need. By the latter stages of the race they were allowed books as the skipper felt they were able to regulate their sleep patterns. Another skipper made it known to the crew that if they let themselves 'go' the whole team would suffer and that self-regulation was a key factor in the success of the race.

> **' Having flexibility gives people freedom to work more effectively. '**

Maintenance and yacht preparation had to be done in each port of call. On some yachts this went very smoothly, with flexible working provided the job was done. Work was usually done efficiently and effectively in a short time. On other yachts friction erupted when inflexibility demanded rigid work patterns, often

> **' Outcome orientated leadership is great. '**

when there was not enough work to occupy all crew members. 'Presenteeism' was required; output was not taken into consideration. This resulted in low motivation, poor performance and longer working. These issues have to be carefully managed if flexibility is to provide the positive outcome desired.

Ford has introduced a 'Total Leadership for the New Economy' that operates in three domains – work, home and community. 'Total' leaders take advantage of the connections. They believe achieving work/life balance brings competitive advantage. Hence it's quite acceptable to take care of a personal issue in the middle of the afternoon; if the results are there, it doesn't matter.

Flexibility is required if effective work/life balance is to be achieved. Leaders today should seek to introduce systems that look for output rather than method of achievement.

Technology

The sheer sophistication of technology today has aided and abetted work/life balance. Employees who are adopting a flexible working pattern that allows them to work at home, in their own time, are greatly aided by the facilities on offer. With a laptop, a mobile phone and Internet access, distance working can be every bit as productive as travelling to the office. For parents with young children, it allows freedom to be part of the children's day, part of their school activities and still a part of the organisation for which they work. Virtual teams can operate globally without so much need to travel.

Technology allowed several crew members to keep their businesses going while at sea. One crew volunteer clinched a large deal while deep in the Southern Ocean. His client had no idea he was out of the office.

‘ *The world is only as large as the dome on the back of the boat.* ’

Technology also allows families to keep in touch. With more families spread globally and with more business travel, mobile phones and email provide an instant link across the world. The technology on the yachts was so much more sophisticated on this race than that of four years before. The race web site provided families with six-hourly updates of yacht positions and a plethora of journals written by crew members to keep them informed. They were often better informed than the crews themselves. The capability was there to allow daily access to family and friends through email. Different systems were set up to allow fair access for everyone.

> ❛ *We were able to hold hands across the Web.* ❜

Technology also provided an amazing link-up for many crew members:

- The skipper of Olympic was able to take his vows as a godfather. With a monitor placed by the font in the church the vicar was able to incorporate the skipper into the christening service (see Plate 12).
- Pam Taylor, a crew member on Compaq, was able to see her granddaughter soon after she was born, and the girlfriend of one of the injured crew on VERITAS was able to have daily contact while he was in hospital in Melbourne.
- On Christmas Day the crew of TeamspirIT organised a rendition of 'The Twelve Days of Christmas' in which all the twelve crews got together over the airwaves and sang a verse each.

Work facilities

Many organisations are being innovative in their attempts to improve work/life balance:

- The NEC Group has introduced a Holiday Club for school-age children during the long holidays. It also has a 35-workplace nursery which is open all day. It has been highly successful in retaining its middle-level managers as a result.
- BT has a comprehensive range of childcare options, from nursery care to out-of-school support.
- Asda, as a result of its work/life policies of job sharing, study leave and shift swapping schemes, has seen improved levels of motivation, customer service, labour turnover and absenteeism.

- Xerox has introduced flexible working patterns, location-independent working, enhanced maternity benefits and has built and retained workforce diversity, has strong leverage in the recruitment market and benefited from the commitment and loyalty of its employees.
- Looking after the elderly is becoming as great an issue as looking after children. In the US more and more people are taking time off to look after elderly relatives and some have stopped work altogether. Peugeot in Coventry in the UK now runs a day-care centre for the elderly.

Celebrations at work

Many leaders today are aware of the motivational boost that celebrations can give. Recognition at the end of a project, when a contract has been won or when achievements, however small, have been made will boost the morale of the team.

Jack Welch, former CEO of General Electric, believes that business has to be fun. 'We found every reason in the world to celebrate. We could break out a keg of beer if we won a £200 order. We found every reason we could to party.'

The skippers and crews also believed that their race had to be fun, but they had to make decisions about the amount of celebrating they did at sea. To take any luxuries meant adding extra weight to the yacht. Some agreed that celebrations should be kept for ports of call and others had celebrations but with few extras.

The crew of Compaq agreed to celebrate Christmas early in great style in Buenos Aires before they set sail and kept 25 December as a normal working day at sea. The LG FLATRON crew who were keen to celebrate on the day but wanted no extra weight decided to make one Christmas present each out of anything they could find on the boat. There were some ingenious presents, from necklaces made out of 'bits' to hand-embroidered caps. Others celebrated in style, believing that team morale was more important than the miles covered on the day. They brought fresh food and gifts. Very often the skipper cooked the meal. Some crew members tried to take surprise presents on board for the team before leaving Buenos Aires. Although some skippers saw this happening, they chose to ignore it. Others put a stop to it and this caused a huge drop in morale.

Birthdays were celebrated with many varied presents. The crew of one yacht gave inflatable toys that were fun, but light; some crews had miniature bottles of spirit; others kept a large bottle of spirits and issued tots on special occasions. Some baked cakes. One yacht celebrated their first snows in the Southern Ocean by declaring a 'public holiday'. This gave them an excuse to have freshly brewed coffee. Coffee mornings were also held on Sundays and latterly on Wednesday as well.

Olympic decided to boost the crew's morale when they were stuck in the Doldrums on the run up to La Rochelle. They got over their frustration by blocking the drainage holes in the cockpit and filling it with water. The team had their own ready-made 'hot tub' – using shampoo to create a Jacuzzi effect (see Plate 14).

Many parties were held on board and any excuse was acceptable. The crew of VERITAS held a party for the 'worst race schedule', celebrating their worst six-hour log in the race. Another crew had a '007' party. All the yachts made 'crossing the line' a large celebration. Those who had never crossed the equator were christened with well-fermented, foul-smelling slops.

Bringing life to work – company towns

Recognising that work is becoming home for many people has led to a new company culture where the best aspects of home are taken and incorporated into the workplace. *FORTUNE* magazine identified the three traits that make a great place to work as:

- a sense of purpose
- inspiring leadership
- knockout facilities.

A new breed of town is springing up with everything from banks to hairdressers, food stores to fitness centres, dry cleaners to nail salons. These are not, strictly speaking, towns but company parks. Everything is provided so that the overworked employee can handle personal matters during the working day. These towns allow people time to get away while still there and give balance without them having to leave.

Microsoft has its UK headquarters on a sprawling campus in Reading, Berkshire. It has a great environment, restaurant, gym, parklands and a company shop. There is an 'anarchy zone' where workers can 'chill out', watch MTV, play pool and talk to the tropical fish.

The yachts had to provide the crews with everything they needed and they became so much part of their lives that for some it was difficult to leave at the end of the race.

The barriers to company towns

> *Work can become all sparkly and glittery and home seems kind of empty and colourless.*
>
> Useem

The danger in these places according to Useem (2000) is that a cult develops which separates from the community; work becomes life to the exclusion of all else. 'Anytime you sacrifice who you are for what you do, you've given up too much of yourself.'

THE RELATIONSHIP BETWEEN WORK/LIFE BALANCE AND EMOTIONAL INTELLIGENCE

The emotional intelligence behaviours were rated high, medium and low based on judgements drawn from the data collected from the interviews. The following emotional intelligence behaviours were seen to be the most important for skippers managing work/life balance.

Self-awareness

Work/life balance and self-awareness are closely linked. The ability to recognise and manage feelings is often related to the degree of stress and tiredness involved. If there is an imbalance in work and life, adverse stress and over-tiredness are often the outcome. The ability to control feelings diminishes.

Some skippers were able to help their crews balance their lives by being aware of the need to balance their own. Self-regulation was necessary to ensure that sleep, food and exercise allowed for the best emotional control. Some skippers achieved this by setting up a watch system with their navigator or watch leaders to enable them to get adequate sleep. Sleep deprivation was often the cause of loss of control and irrational behaviour.

Emotional resilience

By having a balanced life the skippers were able to use their emotions to enhance their performance. They were able to balance the needs of the situation with the needs and concerns of the individuals. Those who were under a lot of stress and had not taken time to relax found it difficult to perform consistently. As the race progressed and on the longer legs the skippers became more tired, their emotional resilience was less in evidence.

Motivation

The race lasted for ten months and it was essential that the skippers maintained the team morale for that length of time. Balancing the short-term goals and the long-term goals was important and many of the skippers put in goals that could be celebrated. One skipper gave each of the waypoints the name of one of the crew so that they felt special on the day it was reached. Their drive and energy had great impact on the amount of fun that the crew had. They created 'A Great Place To Be' and a feeling of a job worth doing.

Interpersonal sensitivity

The team's work/life balance was enhanced when the skippers were able to utilise their interpersonal sensitivity. The skippers who understood the crews' need for space and time off were able to come up with agreed workable solutions. By making decisions around personal needs, people felt recognised and they were able to manage conflict more effectively.

Conscientiousness

A culture of work/life balance was encouraged when the skippers addressed the balance in their own lives. There were some skippers who were unable to get the balance right in ports of call and made it very difficult for crew members to feel relaxed about taking time to be with their families. There were skippers who were strict with their teams about the amount of sleep they required their crew to have, but who would doze at the chart table themselves.

SUMMARY

The skippers who were able to balance their lives and the lives of their crews enhanced performance through the motivation and morale of the team. Their yachts saw fewer disputes, a greater element of fun and a motivation that led to competitive advantage. The ability to balance work and life is critical to the sustained success of a company. If employees have balance in their lives, absenteeism will be reduced, attrition will fall and organisations will become 'A Great Place To Be'.

LESSONS FROM THE RACE

As a leader today you need to:

1. inspire purpose in your team

2. help your team to realise their potential

3. be a positive role model for work/life balance

4. appreciate that others have a personal life

5. build in flexibility to your culture and endorse it

6. involve the families

7. value output, not attendance

8. give as much attention to your personal relationships as you do to your working relationships

9. take time for all the aspects in your life:
   - physical
   - family, friends, community
   - spiritual
   - recreation
   - emotional literacy
   - mental
10. inspire others to do the same.

REFERENCES

Conger, J. (2000) in Owen, H., *In Search of Leaders*, Wiley: Chichester. *Strategy for Business*, Booz, Allen and Hamilton: USA.

Handy, C. (1995) *Beyond Certainty*, Hutchinson: London.

Handy, C. (1997) *The Hungry Spirit*, Random House: London.

Hasson, S. (2001) Employers for Work-Life Balance web site.

Mellott, R. (2000) *Stress Skills for Turbulent Times*, CareerTrack: Milton Keynes.

Mori and WFD, 1999 in Owen, H. (2000) *In Search of Leaders*, Wiley: Chichester.

Morris, E. (2001) 'Turned on', *People Performance*, April 20.

Owen, H. (2000) *In Search of Leaders*, Wiley: Chichester.

Sharp, P. (2001) *Nurturing Emotional Literacy*, David Fulton Publishers: London.

Useem, J. (2000) 'Welcome to the New Company', *FORTUNE*, January 10, pp. 44–50.

COMMUNICATION AT WORK
Nuffield Hospitals

In early 2001, in the face of constant change through growth and acquisition, Nuffield Hospitals embarked upon a values-led approach to managing the business.

Having spent 18 months defining and understanding the use, benefits and impact of such an approach, the Corporate Policy Group (CPG) shared this with over 200 senior managers at the annual conference. The CPG understood that embedding the core values would impact on processes throughout the business, have significant communications implications and require a change of their own behaviour as role models. To assist the understanding of the senior managers and to get their buy-in, the CPG ran a series of role-playing exercises and encouraged their feedback.

Actions agreed among the CPG were shared with the senior managers as an example of openness and living the values. This demonstrated their commitment and signalled change within the organisation. To ensure the business was aligned with its values, a series of reviews were identified:

- operational processes
- reward policy and process
- induction process
- appraisal process.

It was recognised that the CPG should review its own communications behaviours as leaders and role models for core values. They decided:

1. Their visibility should be raised within the hospitals and corporate office.
2. They should be more accessible to staff at all levels in the organisation and encourage their direct reports similarly.
3. They should instigate a process which encouraged feedback on their leadership and communications styles from all levels in the organisation.
4. They should review the processes for disseminating information 'owned' by them within the organisation.
5. They should review the processes for communications between them and the rest of the organisation.

Some of the actions were small but significant and were implemented immediately. Other actions were longer-term projects. Recognising that people need both operational and routine information as well as contextual information to do their jobs effectively, the CPG agreed to review their information disseminating processes and their role and responsibility in providing big-picture information.

In reviewing their own communications processes and behaviours, the CPG showed a commitment to role model leadership and values within Nuffield Hospitals.

9

MANAGING AND INSPIRING TEAM COMMUNICATIONS

**Contributions to this chapter were made
by the following Forum members:**
Jacqui Land, Nuffield Hospitals,
Ian Rudland, Vail Williams

INTRODUCTION

This chapter sets out to look at the subject of managing team communications and the impact of good and bad communications on performance. It will explore the issues a leader will need to address in order to drive performance and inspire commitment, support and loyalty among team members. It will highlight the importance of communications in creating 'A Great Place To Be'.

In the first instance, the chapter will explore the ease and speed of today's communications and the volume of information that individuals are bombarded with in their daily lives. Attention will be given to the pitfalls of communication in a busy and turbulent world where the real meaning or impact of a message can easily be lost. With a focus on performance, the chapter will review the different purposes of communication within a team and the results a leader can achieve from each. The direction of communication will also be assessed. Are we communicating up to the leader, down to the team or, in an environment of shared leadership, are we communicating across the team?

The chapter will use a two-part communications model focused on task dimension and relationship dimension. This will explore the systems through which information can be exchanged and the appropriate attributes, skills and behaviours a leader needs to deliver this information effectively and shape the behaviour of others.

Focusing on the BT Global Challenge race skippers and their teams, examples will be drawn to highlight the importance of communications. The illustrations will feature some fun and memorable methods as well as the inspiring behaviours used by the skippers to build a committed and high-performing team. The chapter will conclude with a look at the relationship between emotional intelligence and communications plus a summary of lessons from the race.

THE E-WORLD

It is little wonder that leaders are facing a communications dilemma. Never before have there been so many channels of communication available to them and never before has it been so easy to communicate with others than now, with the growing electronic network.

As the speed of business transactions increases, expectations are changing. More and more, the sender of an email expects a reply within a few hours. Globalisation is extending working hours. No longer can leaders, who utilise the tools of mobile telephone and email, expect to leave their work behind them at the end of a working day. As individuals choose to work 'virtually' to give themselves more flexibility in their working hours, more people are finding themselves accessible 24 × 7.

Today, technology offers leaders the opportunity to:

- access a wealth of information through the Internet and the World Wide Web round the clock
- compose emails on a laptop and send them off any time day or night, reaching their intended recipient anywhere around the world in minutes
- leave voicemail or send text messages to mobile telephones without having to speak to anyone
- conduct meetings with overseas colleagues or clients via audio or video conferencing, eliminating the time spent travelling

- hold conversations with virtual team members in electronic chat rooms and use forums to post messages and share information to keep everyone up to date
- locate the latest client information through the Intranet and organise appointments online in colleagues' diaries.

For a leader this makes communication so much easier. At any time and from anywhere, it is possible to stay in touch using a computer and mobile telephone. Ironically, however, this digital age of connectivity has increased the complexity of communications and reduced the need for human contact.

REMEMBERING THE HUMAN FACTOR

In a virtual world, communication is in danger of neglecting the human factor or the physical contact that is an essential element of communication. Anecdotal evidence compiled over 20 years by Edward M. Hallowell (1999), a psychiatrist and researcher, together with a growing body of scientific research shows that a deficit of the human 'moment' damages a person's emotional health.

Physiologically, people need others around them to reduce the levels of stress hormones in the blood. Without human contact people's primitive instincts can start to get the better of them and feelings of loneliness, depression, paranoia and self-doubt start to invade their minds.

Being in the presence of others gives rise to feelings of empathy and stimulates the brain to release hormones that promote trust and bonding, an important aspect for team development. Bonding hormones are at suppressed levels when people are physically separated, which explains why it is often easier to deal harshly with someone via email than it is face to face.

While e-technology allows us to communicate without the necessity for human contact, leaders need to recognise the physical reactions e-communication can evoke and address this appropriately. Additionally, leaders must recognise that when communicating by e-technology, the possibility of misinterpretation of the tone or the meaning of a message is much higher. Emails tend to be written in a more abbreviated form than a letter and less time is spent in phrasing words. As a result, an email can appear sharp and abrupt and can often be misinterpreted. A person's feelings may be hurt. Worry and self-doubt may creep in and the level of performance may suffer as a result.

E-technology removes the cues that are there in physical meetings. The intonation of the voice, facial expression or body language is missed and the real energy created by two people when they physically meet is simply not released.

While there are many reasons why human contact is important, the reality is that we are living in an ever-advancing technological world. The evolution of the e-world will continue, offering us even more valuable time-saving tools and opportunities in the future. As Sir Peter Bonfield, former CEO of BT, stated: 'The communications industry is growing and will continue to grow, whatever the short-term fluctuations in the market sentiment. Communications are the lifeblood of the 21st century economy. Technology changes rapidly, which opens up all sorts of opportunities.'

For leaders in this new economy it is therefore important to strike the balance between communicating via technology and the personal approach.

> Leaders today must:
> - understand the physiological effects associated with limited human contact
> - consider the purpose of the message being conveyed and select an appropriate medium
> - assess the possible impact of the message on the recipient
> - carefully construct the style and tone of the message.

Remembering the human factor will help leaders to select the most appropriate method of effectively and sensitively communicating.

Creating a sense of commitment

Leaders today aspire to creating high-performance teams and the focus of organisations is on gaining employee commitment to the company's success. The key to both lies in creating an environment where everyone is involved and where openness is paramount. While employees need to be informed of the strategy and business plans of the organisation, they also need to feel a sense of responsibility, be encouraged to express their ideas, opinions and thoughts, be involved in decisions and made accountable for outcomes.

Sharing leadership, building trust and respect and creating openness are key to creating this type of environment, but without appropriate communication this cannot be achieved. Knowing what to communicate and the processes through which to do this is an essential management skill, but being able to understand the impact of one's own behaviour on the delivery and receipt of communications will make the difference.

One of the greatest skills of a leader today is being able to inspire and manage two-way communications. Communicating to inform and educate is important for team buy-in. Sharing best practice and previous successes to achieve competitive advantage is critical. However, having the ability to inspire others through an open and involving style is paramount to achieving shared leadership and leading a committed and successful team.

IDENTIFYING THE PURPOSE OF COMMUNICATION

There are many different reasons for a leader to communicate with their team and in each case the leader will be trying to elicit a particular response within the individuals, as outlined below:

- **inform** – to keep the team up to date
- **share/exchange** – to identify best practices and processes or to educate through coaching and training
- **inspire** – to encourage others to perform
- **gain commitment** – to involve others in decision making
- **enhance culture** – to acquire information to make changes.

The desired outcome of this communication is summarised in Table 9.1.

TABLE 9.1 The purpose and desired outcome of communication

Purpose of communication	Desired outcome
To inform	
Keep the team up to date	Gain support and trust
	Reduce stress
To share/exchange	
Identify best practices and processes	Improve continually
	Share learning
	Generate creativity
Educate through coaching and training	Develop individuals
	Build self-belief
	Create knowledge
To inspire	
Encourage others to perform	Motivate individuals
	Fulfil purpose
	Achieve goals
To gain commitment	
Involve others in decision making	Receive loyalty
	Get buy-in
	Share leadership
	Live values
To enhance culture	
Acquire information to make changes	Create openness
	Resolve conflict
	Optimise resources
	Improve relationships

IDENTIFYING THE DIRECTION OF COMMUNICATION

For a leader to communicate truly with a team it is essential that communication is two-way. Too often, leaders use the downward direction of communication and believe that they are communicating well. Real communication needs to be multi-directional and the leader needs to encourage team members to feed upwards as well as across the team itself.

The high-performing skippers utilised and encouraged all directions of communication, creating an open, learning environment. These successful skippers were seen as part of the team and buy-in was obtained before a decision was taken, leading to a sense of shared responsibility and enhanced performance.

Downward communication

The most common form of communication used by all the skippers was group briefings. These were held in advance of each leg of the race to outline the strategy and, on most yachts, the skipper would hold a daily briefing to set out the tactics and weather forecast and update the crew on performance in the last 24 hours.

On yachts where coaching was evident, skippers spent time throughout the race developing the skills of the individuals in key areas such as helming and trimming sails.

Upward communication

Although not as common as the group briefings, many skippers held team reviews at the end of each leg to address any interpersonal issues affecting the working environment on the yacht. Some skippers had individual debriefs with every crew member in each of the ports of call. These allowed crew confidentially to raise issues around the behaviour or style of the skipper's leadership. Other teams had an appointed person who represented the crew's views, feeding them back to the skipper.

While it was important that these reviews did not become griping sessions, the impact of this upward communication was seen to have a significant impact on the development of the skipper's emotional intelligence behaviours and leadership style.

Horizontal communication

On the higher-performing yachts, shared learning and continual improvement was evident. The skipper and crew would hold end-of-leg debriefs where knowledge and best practices would be shared across the two watches to refine systems, tasks and roles. On these yachts, watch leaders would also instigate reviews at the end of each sail change and information would be passed between crew members at every watch handover.

Communicating 'with' the crew as opposed to 'to' the crew was seen to have some very powerful results. A survey undertaken on Norwich Union, midway through the race, allowed the crew to share their real feelings, concerns and ideas for change. Through open discussion, the crew addressed a number of festering issues and headed off into the Southern Ocean with renewed vigour and focus, surpassing previous performance and finishing second in the leg.

In the workplace, as in the race, involving team members enhances the psychological contract. Greater involvement leads to commitment that generates flexibility, creativity and success. In the race, the teams were motivated by performance success in the legs; in the workplace, results are reflected mostly in bonuses, profit sharing or employee share-ownership schemes.

IDENTIFYING THE PROCESSES OF COMMUNICATION

Having identified why communication, whether upwards, downwards or horizontal, is important, the chapter will now focus on how to manage communications through relevant processes and inspire communications through appropriate behaviour. This will be defined as the task dimension and the relationship dimension.

The task dimension will explore the management systems and processes put in place by the skippers through which information could be exchanged. The relationship dimension will explore the skippers' behaviour and ability to communicate effectively and shape the behaviour of the team. The chapter will look at the task/relationship model, as shown in Figure 9.1, by breaking this down into two parts: prior to the race and during the race. Examples from the race will be used, working through the five purposes of communication identified in Table 9.1.

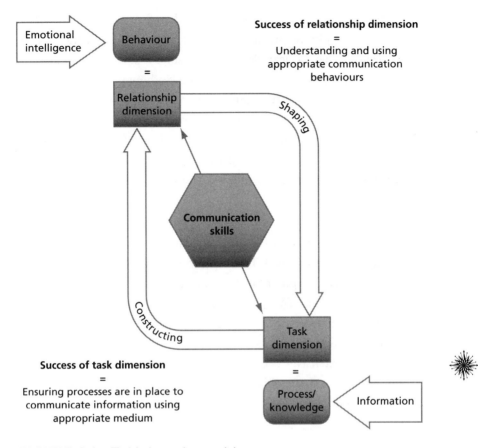

FIGURE 9.1 Task/relationship model

USING TOOLS TO COMMUNICATE PRIOR TO THE RACE

Between the announcement of the team on 8 January 2000 and the start of the race on 10 September, there were very few occasions when the skippers were able to gather together their entire team of 27 in one place. Many crew members scattered around the world were working right up until late August, trying desperately to raise their berth fee. Spirit of Hong Kong had the most international crew, with members from seven countries. Remarkably, one crew sailed together for the first time on day one of the race.

Communication before the race was therefore critical. The teams needed to get to know one another and learn more about their yacht. They needed to have a clear idea of specialist tasks and be able to develop key aspects of the project, such as food and clothing programmes.

Many leaders today direct teams that are scattered around the world. As in business, a number of media were available to the skippers to help them manage communications with their virtual team. In the initial teambuilding and race preparation stage, skippers chose to use different media to communicate with their team for specific purposes.

Email

Email was a primary tool for communication for all yacht teams and was used to inform crew. While 5 per cent of crew members had no direct access to a computer, they found ways to keep up to date by visiting Internet cafes. This encouraged some of the less technically minded crew members to learn how to use new technologies.

Email provided the teams with a speedy means of communicating and was used extensively. Some teams used it for circulating key documents, for sharing the skipper's weekly round-up of activities and preparing agendas for teleconference meetings.

Telephone

Some skippers encouraged team members to telephone one another using a rota system. This ensured every team member spoke to at least one other every week. One skipper believed a telephone call was worth 100 emails and ensured he spoke to every crew member at least once every ten days to forge a personal relationship.

Teleconferencing

Teleconferencing was a popular communication tool for some teams which held weekly or bi-weekly conference calls with an agenda. The meeting would be chaired by the skipper and minutes would be taken.

Internet conferencing

Internet conferencing was used by one team who had a deaf crew member. They found the ability to use voice and text of great benefit in keeping this crew member involved.

Newsletter/mail

A few yacht teams prepared and mailed out monthly newsletters to the team and their supporters. One skipper used mail to send motivational tools to his team at specific intervals.

Teambuilding sessions and meetings

All teams had an initial teambuilding session where goals and values were addressed. Some teams held follow-up sessions to address specific interpersonal issues where conflict had arisen. For yachts with a large proportion of team members located in the UK, it was much easier to hold meetings to review progress. However, most teams had some form of meeting where crew working on specific projects could get together to progress work.

Training sails

Specific sail training sessions were also held on small and large yachts where the skippers focused on coaching the teams in sail trim and performance-related techniques.

Web site

BT provided each team with a secure web site with access passwords for each individual team member. This collaborative workspace offered a number of facilities through which the team could communicate:

- Diary – used to inform crew of forthcoming meetings and training sessions and to enhance relationships through highlighting team birthdays.
- Forum – used primarily for sharing knowledge and learning on key issues. A crew member would instigate a topic and others would add to the thread of the discussion. It was also used to collate responses from all crew on a topic. This system proved to be far less cumbersome than using email that could elicit up to 27 separate emails.

- Hot documents – used as a form of online reference library where teams could post and file important documents and images in an orderly manner for future reference. Teams used this facility to share notes from specialist training courses and to inspire each other with fun photographs from teambuilding or sail training events.
- Chat – used mainly as a social tool for crew members to chat and banter online and enhance relationships. This was also a key tool for crew members in different countries who could log on at low cost and have one-to-one chats with team members. Often seeing the words proved easier than hearing them in a telephone conversation. Some teams had predetermined times when team members would go online and 'chat' to whoever else logged in.
- Links – used as a reference page where crew members could share useful URLs.
- Contacts – used as an online address book which was accessible to all team members and enhanced relationships.

Some yacht teams used the collaborative working site purely as a bulletin board to inform one another of events and deal with logistical issues. Others used the site to share tips and shortcuts and to inspire other team members to get involved with project work. The site was also used to gain commitment by involving everyone in brainstorming new ideas and by promoting discussion to reach a team decision on a specific topic. The chat areas were predominantly used to enhance relationships through social interaction.

USING BEHAVIOUR TO COMMUNICATE PRIOR TO THE RACE

Gain support and trust through information exchange

In the early stages of the project it was critical for the skippers to build the trust and support of their team members. Leading a 'virtual' team of 27, it was essential that the lines of communication were kept open and the team felt well informed. One skipper accused of being slow to respond to emails took time out to describe in detail one of his average 12-hour working days. It was then that the crew members realised just how busy the skipper was and why responses sometimes seemed slower or less focused than might be anticipated.

As the project progressed and the yachts were launched and handed over to the skippers, the focus shifted from the team to the yacht. Skippers spent several weeks in the boat yard, away from their computers, and found it harder to keep in touch with their team. Lack of regular communication led to feelings of isolation and concern about what lay ahead. Some crew members needed a lot of reassurance from their skippers. Several skippers had to take time out and drive long distances to meet crew members who were showing less commitment or even doubts about whether they should or could undertake the race.

Share best practice to continually improve

As the team started to develop, individuals' confidence and self-belief grew and there was more of a willingness to share knowledge and to learn from one another.

Some skippers took time to put together quite comprehensive guidelines on aspects of food, clothing and health. Sub teams were formed that took on responsibility for researching these subjects, pooling their knowledge and devising a suitable programme for the race.

Exchange knowledge to develop individuals

Crew members were identified for specialist courses where they would be coached in aspects of sail trim, engine maintenance or yacht photography. Some would prepare a precise document to share this technical knowledge with other team members using diagrams or explanations. Others would give briefings and share best practice at the next team training session.

In relation to the collaborative web site, it was noted that team members were open to sharing their technical knowledge and educating others. One skipper who was having difficulty in using the technology showed his vulnerability in noting on the web site that he had posted a document more by accident than good practice. A crew member immediately responded with a step-by-step guide. A crew member on Spirit of Hong Kong wrote a basic user guide with visual images and screen shots for fellow team members who were struggling with the technology. Others took time to coach their team mates on either a one-to-one basis or in a small group when they met at a training session.

Inspire others to perform in pursuit of the goal

All the skippers were seen to be highly motivated and driven to achieving their own personal vision, and early on it was key that they were able to share their vision with their team. The skipper of LG FLATRON encouraged his crew to visualise themselves as winners of The Princess Royal Trophy. They produced a computer-generated picture of their yacht crossing the finish line in first place with the team proudly brandishing the trophy.

Understanding what motivated the individuals within their team was important to many skippers. Using motivational questionnaires they were able to determine who was driven by achievement, who needed power and influence and who needed a high level of interaction with others to keep them motivated. Identifying these motivators made it easier for the skipper when allocating roles and encouraging team members to perform. A watch leader would need to take tough decisions in difficult conditions and would not always be liked for his actions. It was far better to select someone who enjoyed the sense of responsibility and could handle the fact that they were not going to be liked by everyone all of the time.

There was a direct correlation between the level of team activities on the collaborative web site and the level of skipper activity. Where the skipper openly encouraged the team to use the tool or actively used the facilities for communicating with the team, team activity was much higher.

Gain commitment to agreed values

All twelve skippers held a teambuilding session within the first two months of the project in order to identify a strategy and goal. They orchestrated sessions where the teams could openly debate and agree overall team goals.

Values were equally important and the crews agreed standards by which they wanted to live and work. Living in the restricted space of the yacht, the skippers knew it would be the interpersonal issues that would have the greatest impact on the cohesiveness of the team. Skippers facilitated open sessions to define a set of 'rules' to which they were all committed.

One skipper, whose team had agreed to be pushed to the limits, felt it was prudent to build in a safety valve to allow the crew to tell him if they thought they were being pushed too hard. The crew did this after the qualifying sail when they felt the skipper's expectations of their abilities was too high.

Bridging the gap between expectations and actuality was important for many skippers as they were dealing with crew members whose perception of what it took to win was often unrealistic. The skipper of Logica used anecdotes and stories from previous races to illustrate and reinforce the importance and need for a set of agreed values.

Team image was important to many of the teams and their dress code became a symbol of their solidarity and togetherness. Crews sported their team colours and logos proudly as it communicated their message of unity and professionalism.

Enhance the culture by improving relationships

The skippers went to great efforts in the early stages of the project to develop a good relationship with their individual crew members and create a trusting and open environment. While many telephoned their crew on a regular basis for a chat, others took time to physically visit their crews. The skipper of Save the Children visited his crew in their place of work, while the Isle of Man skipper stayed as a guest in crew members' homes. Seeing someone in their own environment and being part of their family life was a good way to break down the barriers and really get to know individuals.

Humour was also a good medium for breaking down barriers, especially in the areas of diversity, nationality and sexism. Teams developed their own vocabulary and in-jokes that created a feeling of togetherness and familiarity and a sense of trust and belonging to the 'in' crowd. However, humour proved a double-edged sword. While some skippers used it effectively to lift spirits, others proved inept in their timing and delivery, causing offence to crew members and a general deflation of morale. It was, in some situations, a dangerous tool if used inappropriately.

Most of the skippers started group debriefs following the qualifying sail in July. Issues of conflict and ambiguity over individual roles had arisen on many yachts and these feelings and concerns needed to be aired and addressed at this early stage. A couple of skippers chose one-to-one debriefs to address these issues privately. As the race progressed, these yacht teams showed a less open culture. They were seen to espouse a blame culture, were less trusting of each other and less cohesive than other teams.

The collaborative web site was a powerful tool for some of the social interaction of foreign team members. The French crew member on Spirit of Hong Kong felt the tool had significantly enhanced his relationship and particularly the depth of information shared with particular crew members. The feeling was mutual: 'I feel that I know more about my French team mate, having corresponded on all sorts of topics through the web site, than I do about my team mates that I have actually physically spent time with.'

The skipper of BP promoted an 'open door' policy and would go online at the same time each week to be available to chat to any crew who wished to log in. This skipper offered one-to-one online chats for those crew members who wanted a private word. This created an openness that led to a very close-knit team whose trust and support for each other grew stronger throughout the race.

It was interesting to note that the human contact made a difference to the level of communication between crew members using technology. Where teams physically met for a team meeting or training session, there was a significant increase in the level of activity on the collaborative web site.

9. *Skipper gets crew buy-in*
Norwich Union skipper Neil Murray discusses the tactical options with his team

10. *Skipper leads his team through crisis following horrific accident*
VERITAS skipper Will Carnegie and his crew confront their fears of returning to the Southern Ocean

11. *Teamworking to achieve optimal performance*
Quadstone crew keeping a close eye on the trim of the sails

12. *Satellite communications allows godfather to take his vows*
BT's advanced equipment links Olympic Group skipper, Manley
Hopkinson, with Portsmouth Cathedral in a live video link-up

13. *Teamwork and team spirit are essential on and off the yachts*
TeamSpirIT crew work on the sails before setting off round the world

14. *Easing the frustration of the notorious Doldrums*
Olympic crew cool off in their makeshift pool

15. *Meticulous timing and planning pays off*
   LG FLATRON powers up The Solent on her winning tack

16. *Holding aloft the ultimate prize*
   After ten months of hard racing, LG FLATRON skipper Conrad
   Humphreys and his team claim The Princess Royal Trophy as the overall
   winner

USING TOOLS TO COMMUNICATE DURING THE RACE

The advances in satellite technology during the four years between races gave rise to an increasing number of methods of communication from ship to shore. For some skippers this provided access to a wealth of information that had a direct impact on their performance. For others, new technologies provided vital access to emergency assistance in times of crisis.

Inmarsat C

Inmarsat C technology is a reliable analogue system of transmitting data via satellite. Although over 12 years old, this reliable system of text messaging to and from the yacht was used for all official race communications, e.g. messages to the fleet and daily text weather forecasts. In the event of an incident, it was the primary channel of communication. During the race, yachts were polled automatically by Inmarsat C every six hours and more frequently when required, such as towards the end of a leg. Race headquarters processed the positions and released these to the whole fleet and to the public through the race web site.

Inmarsat B

This satellite system allows high-speed digital communications at 64k bits per second and gave the teams access to the Internet and World Wide Web. Access to the Internet had an enormous impact on the ethos of the race, with friends, family and supporters able to 'share' the experience of the race from home, something that had not been possible in the 1996/7 race. Each yacht was given a weekly Internet allowance of 60 minutes, limited by the expense of the satellite link and the amount of diesel that the yachts could carry to power the generator to run the Inmarsat B.

Through Inmarsat B technology, the skippers and crews had a number of means of communicating:

- Email – some 98 000 emails were sent to and from the crews during the course of the race. Many of these were journals giving accounts of life on board that were sent via race headquarters and released to the web site. Others were private email messages sent directly to loved ones.

- World Wide Web – access to the World Wide Web gave the skippers the ability to draw down the latest weather and sea current information from publicly available web sites. With the limit on time, some skippers monitored this carefully, allocating a specific number of minutes per day to ensure they had the latest and most accurate information on which to base decisions.

- Photographs – approximately 6000 photographs were sent from the yachts allowing others to share in the conditions and life on board. The ability to forward photography from the yacht had greater advantages when technical issues needed to be resolved. A photograph of the watermaker pump on Isle of Man helped race organisers identify the problem and re-order spares for arrival in port. Another showing the cooker problem on Compaq was resolved while at sea.

- Video – newsworthy footage of between three and five minutes was forwarded from each yacht each week for use by local television stations and for mounting on the web site. Compaq edited footage for a corporate advertising campaign shown over the Christmas period. A total of 19 hours of video footage was captured for use in the supporting BT Global Challenge documentaries and post-race videos.

Marine Mobiq

The prime usage of the satellite telephone was for the duty yacht to report the positions and safety of the fleet after 'chat shows'. Media interviews were also conducted with live links into local radio stations to give 'life at sea' reports. Additionally, the crews used the telephone to speak to their families – the human contact that email did not provide.

The most crucial use of the satellite telephone followed the accident on board VERITAS in the Bass Strait. With two seriously injured crew members, the skipper was able to connect directly to the Flying Doctor in Australia who was able to advise on appropriate emergency treatment. Further detail follows.

VERITAS hit by freak wave in the Bass Strait

Challenge yacht VERITAS, skippered by Will Carnegie, was sailing through the Bass Strait when the yacht was hit by a freak 40 ft wave. Two core crew members were severely injured. In the same incident the communications dome critical for Inmarsat B digital communications was washed overboard. After assessing the injuries, Carnegie made emergency contact with Race Headquarters in Southampton. Using the satellite telephone, Marine Mobiq, he was able to speak to the Race Officer, brief him on the incident and seek medical assistance.

Options were assessed for an evacuation airlift but it was agreed it was best to proceed to Eden, 95 miles away, on the South East coast of mainland Australia. Carnegie maintained constant contact with Australia's Royal Flying Doctor service and Race Headquarters to ensure proper treatment was administered. Speaking to Carnegie via satellite telephone, medics were able to advise on how to stabilise the injured crew members.

Meanwhile, the Race Officer contacted key crisis team members, including race organisers, core media team and sponsors, to ensure effective response to all stakeholders, including next of kin and media. He then arranged for a radio interview link up with Carnegie over the satellite telephone.

VERITAS arrived in Eden after 11 hours and transferred the injured crew members to waiting emergency services personnel. Carnegie and crew regrouped before heading back out to rejoin the race.

Single side band radio

A long-range radio communications system for voice communication yacht to yacht was used for the twice daily fleet 'chat shows', hosted by the appointed duty yacht. All yachts tuned to a specified frequency at a predetermined time and when called by the duty skipper would confirm their position and daily news.

Communications with home

The numerous and sophisticated methods of technology available to the yacht teams ensured a constant stream of communication from and to the yachts and email was seen to be a real motivating tool, energising crew members who received news from home. Back on shore, families were kept well informed and also felt that they were part of the team, 'sharing' the experience on a daily basis. Partners were better able to understand what their loved ones were going through and the rebonding time was reduced when crew members met their partners again in the ports of call.

However, while communication technologies made it possible for some crew to leave families, for others it created problems. The ability to send and receive email from the yachts raised expectations, and families came to expect regular contact. When the yachts were outside the satellite range or tough conditions prevented the use of the communications equipment, emotions on shore ran high.

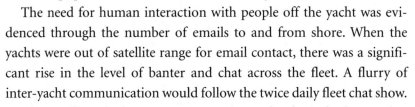

The need for human interaction with people off the yacht was evidenced through the number of emails to and from shore. When the yachts were out of satellite range for email contact, there was a significant rise in the level of banter and chat across the fleet. A flurry of inter-yacht communication would follow the twice daily fleet chat show.

The satellite telephone was an amazing technological advance that allowed crew to hear the voice of their partners many thousands of miles away. However, the lack of privacy on the yacht made conversations artificial and stilted. This often prevented crew members from having the more personal conversations they and their loved ones really wanted.

USING BEHAVIOUR TO COMMUNICATE DURING THE RACE

While the skippers had some of the most advanced technologies for communication with the outside world, their main method of internal communication with their team was through basic human contact.

Both on board and ashore, the skippers were communicating face to face. Many put in regular systems for pre-leg briefings, on-board task briefs and debriefs and post-leg reviews.

What really mattered to the development and performance of these teams was how the skipper utilised his leadership attributes, skills and emotional intelligence behaviours to keep the team informed, involved and motivated. The following section addresses the relationship dimension of communications. It will explore this dimension using examples of the skipper's behaviour and its impact on the crew and performance.

Reduce stress through information exchange

Keeping the crew up to date with the race positions within the fleet, their performance over the last few hours and the oncoming weather was important for many reasons. On the one hand it encouraged greater effort in terms of improving or enhancing performance. On the other hand it ensured that crew could

> **❛ People will gossip if there is insufficient communication. ❜**

physically and mentally prepare for the oncoming weather, reducing levels of stress and fear about the unknown.

The higher-performing skippers held daily briefings for these reasons. Others would sometimes slip several days without an update, leaving crews uninformed about performance and therefore unmotivated. This also left the crew unprepared for any nasty conditions that were coming which often led to rumour and provoked uncertainty and fear.

> **❛ Keep the harmony and keep team morale up. Make sure crew is happy and well briefed. ❜**

Getting the balance right was important. The crew on one yacht got fed up repeatedly asking their skipper for more information. At the end of every leg they would repeat the request for more information on the next leg. However, even if the skipper started the leg with all good intentions, the information updates would tail off as the leg progressed.

The crew of another yacht had the opposite problem; their skipper insisted on a briefing every six hours. While it ensured the crew were kept in the picture, the crew felt overloaded by the detailed information and asked the skipper to reduce this to one briefing per day.

Some skippers preferred not to share bad news and when the position reports did not look good, they would hide these from the crew. This had a negative impact on the team as it was obvious that the news wasn't good but they were never quite sure just how bad it really was.

The skipper of VERITAS was very aware that the first storm they encountered after their horrific accident in the Bass Strait would create fear among the crew. In advance of the first forecast storm, he called a crew briefing and openly discussed what they were likely to face. He set out exactly how they were going to prepare and how they would carry out any tasks such as changing sails or putting in reefs. This helped to dispel fear and evoked a sense of collaboration.

> **‘ You have to deal with the “now” and fear disappears. ’**

Share learning to enhance performance

The higher-performing skippers had a philosophy of continuous improvement and actively encouraged the sharing of information and best practice across the watches. These skippers were keen that crew members identified new or better methods of changing sails. Not only would this speed up the sail change process and minimise the time that the yacht was not travelling at optimum speed, it also reduced the time that the crew were exposed to high levels of danger up on the fore deck.

Some skippers also encouraged continual development and learning among the crew. They would take time out to coach and develop the helming and trimming skills of crew members, allowing non-specialist crew members to learn a new role.

Several higher-performing skippers encouraged good communications between the watches at the watch changeover. One crew realised to their peril – and with the loss of many miles – that the communications among the sleepy offwatch crew had not been good and there was confusion over the instruments being used.

The skippers of the podium yachts put huge emphasis on information exchange and in turn created a communication culture on board. On LG FLATRON the crew appointed a watch member to stay up for an extra hour after the watch handover.

One skipper was keen for the growth and development of individual crew members and set up a system where crew members rotated through key roles, spending a specified amount of time on each.

Inspire others to perform better

Keeping the team motivated and focused on the agreed goals and values was hard but proved to be the key to success. For those performance-focused skippers it was something that was required to ensure the crew ate, slept and breathed their agreed team goal.

The skipper of BP focused the crew on their overall goal and leg objectives in every daily briefing. As the team had agreed the goals at the outset it was easier for the skipper to keep reminding them of what they had said they wanted to achieve. One less performance-focused skipper never reviewed or referred to the original goals. At one point midway through the race, the crew even felt compelled to ask him whether they were racing or just getting through to the end.

When the conditions deteriorated in the Southern Ocean and the crews were wet, cold and exhausted for weeks at a time, it was important that the skippers could inspire their crews well. The Compaq skipper kept up the crew morale by telling a story from past experience or reading a passage from Shackleton's expeditions to inspire his team.

When things went dramatically wrong for one yacht that fell from top three to bottom three, the skipper took time to address the team. Holding a strong sense of belief, the skipper turned to his crew and said, 'Dig deep, work together to work it through and we will succeed – we're good enough to get away with it'.

> *' He underestimates the impact he has on other people. '*

The Sunday service held by the Olympic Group skipper served the

> **' People need recognition. '**

purpose of inspiring his team, as well as catering for their spiritual needs. The sight of their surroundings, the poignant words of the prayers and the singing uplifted spirits and inspired the team to fulfil their purpose.

Some skippers realised the importance of recognition; by praising the crew after a particularly tough sail change or acknowledging their efforts in gaining more miles, they engendered a passion within the crew to work even harder. Other skippers rallied the team in a different manner, giving powerful inspirational speeches at significant times.

One team were totally uninspired by their skipper. Having built them up to believe they were doing well, the skipper would dash their

> **' It is important to go through things carefully with the team, so that they know what is expected of them. '**

spirit with one single phrase or inappropriate comment. The crew's resilience diminished. Their self-belief and confidence had been crushed and by the end of the race they had lost the will to perform.

Gain commitment by sharing leadership

Involving the team in decision making paid off for several skippers when the outcome of the decision later proved to be wrong. The skipper of Norwich Union realised early on in the race that given their performance, they would be unable to attain their goal to win the tro-

> **' Leadership only works if you have respect. '**

phy. Calling a briefing, the skipper discussed the situation with the crew and identified the need to refocus

and redefine their goal. The team were understandably disappointed and dejected, but in articulating the reality of the situation and involving the crew in the revision of the goals, the skipper was able to rally them and retain their commitment and loyalty.

It was clear that getting crew involved in decision making and sharing leadership was beneficial. One podium skipper never made a decision without ensuring the crew understood what was going on and were privy to his thought processes in weighing up the options.

A middle-performing skipper didn't communicate the value of weight distribution and failed to get his crew to use their body weight to the team's advantage. As a result they were overtaken by another yacht in very close proximity to the finish line and lost a valuable race position.

‘ People want direction as well as communication. ’

The lack of explanation when a job was not well done was the source of great irritation on one yacht. Sometimes the skipper would pass no comment on a job but would then get upset when the job was done in exactly the same manner the next time.

‘ Good communication minimalises marginalisation. ’

One middle-performing skipper clearly did not wish to encourage ideas and views from his crew and took the approach 'I know best'. He kept the crew well informed but would 'tell' them rather than 'ask' when decisions had to be made. Not open to ideas, he would shoot down any suggestions. Team members were soon uncomfortable with this behaviour and as the race progressed tended not to offer ideas or input. The result on performance was devastating. Rather than wake the skipper to suggest a need to alter course or change a sail, the team would sail for hours in the wrong direction or at a slower speed, sacrificing any chances they had of a good race finish.

Enhance culture by creating openness

Interpersonal relationships were seen to have a huge effect on the atmosphere on the yachts and indeed the subsequent performance of the team. Some skippers were very aware of the potential damage caused by unresolved or festering issues and were proactive in addressing these situations.

Olympic Group's skipper was concerned about enhancing crew relationships and avoiding any possible division of crew through the two-watch system. He was aware that there were very few times when all crew members were together at any one time. To overcome this he introduced a watch system where crew members with comparative skills would swap across watches. The following day another pair would swap and the system of rotation would continue throughout the leg, adding a new team dynamic every day.

> ' *Getting it on the table is essential for winning.* '

The skipper of Logica encouraged openness among his crew. In their post-leg debriefs, crew were encouraged to talk about their feelings relating to any incidents in the leg. Because the skipper openly shared his feelings and admitted his mistakes, the crew were able to do the same and grew much closer. The skipper created an environment where crew would constantly feed back to one another, openly addressing irritating habits that could otherwise have festered.

> ' *Say what you mean and hear what is said.* '

Openness can be achieved only if the skipper creates the right environment. On one lower-performing yacht the lines of communication were rigid. Any upward or downward communication came through the watch leaders. While the skipper would be asked a question by a crew member, he would instruct the watch leader to answer.

IDENTIFYING THE PITFALLS TO COMMUNICATING

The manner in which messages are delivered has a significant impact on the understanding, interpretation and actions of the recipient. Many of the skippers understood these pitfalls and created fun and memorable ways in which to communicate.

Presenting a message

Making a message memorable and delivering it in a powerful way is a skill. For the skippers of these race yachts facing life-threatening conditions it was important that messages were not only memorable but were understood, agreed and that everyone knew the task they had to deliver. Anecdotes and stories from previous races gave skippers powerful illustrations of specific messages that really embedded in crew minds.

Skippers used humour in a number of situations. When faced with a long period of concentrated racing in tough and often frightening conditions, for instance, it was sometimes important to lighten the atmosphere. At other times it reduced the risk of conflict, and in light, slow conditions where there were long periods of inactivity it was good to inject some humorous activities to overcome boredom. The balance between appropriate and inappropriate humour was fine and it was important that the skippers avoided the sarcastic and flippant remarks that could hijack the message.

Several skippers used visual aids to reinforce messages. Using white-boards and markers it was often helpful for skippers to draw a picture to explain the movement of a complex weather system or set out the steps of a procedure for a difficult sailing manoeuvre. Visualisation was used by the Compaq skipper, who encouraged his crew to use their minds to imagine a particular scenario and work through a procedure as to how they might cope.

Establishing eye contact with individuals when addressing them specifically encourages a greater level of concentration on the message being conveyed. In the midst of a severe storm in the Southern Ocean, the skipper of Olympic Group was faced with a crew member almost paralysed by fear. This crew member had a key role to play in an essential operation. Calling him by name, the skipper established clear eye contact and successfully talked him step by step through the operation.

Seeking confirmation

Skippers soon realised it was not enough to brief the crews and expect them to understand and deliver. Remembering these were amateur crew members with little or no previous sailing knowledge, skippers needed to be sure that the actions required were those that were taken. Getting a crew member to summarise and repeat a procedure to the rest of the crew was a good way to clarify that the message had been understood correctly.

Encouraging disagreement

Agreeing with the skipper was not always the right solution and skippers realised it was wrong to assume that everyone agreed just because no one challenged them. Knowing their experience far outweighed that of the crew at the outset, some skippers selected specific individuals to actively challenge their decisions and thought processes. By doing this it ensured that ideas were exchanged and built on and conflict was used positively for the greater good of the team.

Nominating explicitly

One skipper found an aversion among the crew to the more mundane jobs such as pumping the bilges and making the tea. While he would advise the crew of the need for a job to be done, he would not explicitly nominate anyone to do it. The result was these jobs were left unaddressed for hours and the yacht sailed slower with the excess weight of water in the bilge. Or, it was the same conscientious crew members who always ended up doing the jobs. When communicating the need for a job to be done, it was clear that there needed to be a clearly nominated person and a timeframe in which it had to be completed.

Behaving consistently

Skippers who were consistent in their behaviour and communicated regularly created an environment in which crew members trusted and respected them and wanted to prove themselves. Where the mood and behaviour of the skipper was unpredictable, crew members were reticent in trying out new ways of working and often found that their performance dipped through fear of performing badly and receiving a sharp rebuke. When briefings were erratic, crew involvement in decision making was irregular, and identical procedures were sometimes accepted and other times rejected; crews felt uneasy, confused and disrespected. Crew members needed to have a clearly defined framework in which they could work.

THE RELATIONSHIP BETWEEN COMMUNICATIONS AND EMOTIONAL INTELLIGENCE

The emotional intelligence behaviours were rated high, medium and low based on judgements drawn from the data from the interviews. The following emotional intelligence behaviours were seen to be the most important for the skippers managing and inspiring communications.

Self-awareness

Awareness of the impact of their own behaviour on the team was critical for some skippers who in the early stages of the race were unable to deal with setbacks. Equipment and sail breakages or loss of mileage or a position in the race schedule would give rise to emotions that would trigger inappropriate behaviour such as shouting and swearing at the crew.

One skipper took to his bunk for several days following a tactical mistake which cost the team many miles and several places. This skipper later realised his total lack of self-awareness when he realised the impact his action had had on his team. With no review of what had gone wrong and no understanding of how they might try to recover, the crew had become dejected, sat on deck with hoods pulled up and avoided conversation with one another.

Having the ability to recognise feelings is the first step in developing self-awareness. Being able to control them takes longer to learn. One skipper whose self-awareness developed considerably throughout the race got to the first stage and then communicated this to the crew. Whenever he was feeling under pressure and knew that he might find it hard to control his feelings he would warn the crew, saying, 'I may be roasting you today, but don't take it personally'.

Emotional resilience

Upward feedback to skippers helped them to understand the importance of utilising emotional intelligence behaviours. This was seen to enhance their ability to lead successfully and drive performance from the crew.

At the end of leg 1, one skipper was given feedback from his crew regarding his lack of communication and a lack of openness. The team felt this highly competitive skipper was obsessed with things going right all the time. When things were not going so well they became uptight, less open and did not share the bad news. As a result of this feedback, the skipper utilised his emotional resilience. He accepted the criticism and changed his behaviour to perform consistently in good and bad times. This skipper subsequently went on to lead the team to a podium position.

Motivation

Being highly motivated skippers, it was necessary to transfer this motivation to the crew who had varied and differing reasons for undertaking the race. Using inspiring words and behaviours was critical, and many of the skippers showed their motivation through their continual energy and drive, tweaking sails and tuning processes to achieve results.

Putting a positive spin on a situation to encourage crew members was something many skippers did well. There was, however, a very fine line between being optimistic and being unrealistic. Skippers who tended to be unrealistic found this behaviour had a negative effect on crew morale. One skipper told his crew at the beginning of each leg that this time they could win. The team had never achieved a top three finish and felt daunted by the goal and despondent when they never achieved it.

Interpersonal sensitivity

Getting the crew involved in decision making proved to be important for the success of several skippers, particularly when the decision proved wrong. The higher-performing skippers who took time to explain to the crew a particular scenario and set out the possible solutions found that the crew considered it a shared decision and the responsibility for the outcome was also shared.

Some skippers admitted they didn't have the answers to every decision and instead turned the problem over to the crew. Being open to the ideas and inputs from the crew often gave rise to some of the best solutions.

Influence

Having the ability to persuade others to change their viewpoint was clearly seen to have an impact on the performance of many yachts. One skipper who had not taken a tough stance on crew roles and allowed crew members to have a go at whatever they wanted continually achieved poor leg results. Halfway through the race, the skipper addressed the crew and set out the reasons why they should select only the best person to undertake each job. With the crew's agreement, the team undertook the next leg focusing on getting the best performance from each person. The result was a dramatic improvement in their leg position.

Conscientiousness

Gaining and retaining respect was key for the skippers in this long race that encountered some of the worst conditions on the planet. Skippers who truly meant what they said and matched their words with actions managed to retain the commitment of their crew and ultimately achieved higher performance from their teams.

Goals that had been set at the outset were often far harder to achieve than the crew had envisaged. One skipper regained the respect of his crew by reviewing and revising the original goal. Another skipper appeared to be leading in 'textbook' style. What he said sounded 'perfect'. However, his behaviour did not match these words. Genuine sincerity was not there. Midway through the race, this crew had seen through his words and, while agreeing with the skipper outwardly, they would disregard his requests and do what they thought was right.

SUMMARY

Communicating effectively and appropriately is extremely powerful. Leaders need to remember that people have feelings. They should consider carefully the impact of their behaviour and the message that this conveys to others. Using communications effectively, a leader needs to create an environment where team members are respected, genuinely involved and valued.

The higher-performing skippers ensured their crew were well informed and understood the decisions that were being taken. This reduced fear and stress. They made their crews feel involved and responsible by seeking and valuing their contributions. This generated commitment and a focus on performance. By involving the crew, the skippers built respect and the team trusted the skipper's judgement. Knowing the skipper valued contributions, the crew looked for new and better ways of doing things and continually improved their performance. There was a cohesiveness and supportiveness among these teams. Information and best practice was shared to enhance individual and team performance and to achieve competitive gain.

The higher-performing skippers were able to motivate their crew through their actions. These skippers focused continually on the performance of the yacht and were constantly striving to gain an extra mile. They used words that gave encouragement and demonstrated a belief in their team. These skippers used humour to address conflict and improve the relationships and atmosphere on board.

LESSONS FROM THE RACE

As a leader today you need to:

1. remember people have feelings

2. keep your team informed

3. share learning and best practice with your team

4. coach individuals to build their self-belief and enhance their performance

5. encourage team members to fulfil their personal ambitions and inspire them to achieve agreed goals

6. involve your team in decision making and share responsibility

7. acquire information to optimise your management of resources

8. understand the feelings of individual team members and use this to resolve any issues and improve team culture.

REFERENCES

Buggy, C. (2000) 'Are you really listening?' *Professional Manager*, July, Vol. 9, No. 4, pp. 20–22.

Clark, Dr C. (1999) 'Effective briefings are as easy as 1,2,3', *Professional Manager*, May, Vol. 8, No. 3, pp. 32–33.

Clark, Dr. C. (1999) *How to Give Effective Business Briefings*, Kogan Page: London.

Ettorre, B. (1997) 'The unvarnished truth', *Management Review*, pp. 54–57.

Green, T. and Knippen, J. (1999) *Breaking the Barrier to Upward Communication*, Quorum Books: Westport Conn.

Hallowell, E. M. (1999) 'The human moment at work', *Harvard Business Review*, January/February, Vol. 77, No. 1, pp. 58–66.

MacDonald, J. and Tanner, S. (1998) *Successful Communication at Work in a Week*, Hodder and Stoughton: London.

McCormack, M. (1999) 'Reality check' – the illusion of communication', *www.ftmastering.com*.

No author (2000) 'Towards commercial consciousness raising, *IRS Employment Trends*, 718, pp. 12–16.

Sandford, I. (1999) 'The vital ingredients of communicating change', *ER Consultants*, Issue 3, pp. 23–25.

CONFLICT AT WORK
Conflict management during mergers and acquisitions

A study of several mergers and acquisitions provides leaders with some useful lessons for effective conflict management. In one recent merger, task forces were set up to focus on different areas to understand differing practices and share ideas. All the organisations involved in the merger were represented. This helped the people discuss conflicting processes and ideas constructively, find a way forward and incorporate best practice. Making decisions that harmonised benefits across the organisations was a key aim but difficult to achieve, with perceived fairness being a key issue.

A senior executive involved in one merger said that one reason for its success was that clear accountability for success of key aspects of the merger was assigned. This reduced the potential for ambiguity and for blame being unfairly directed at those who were not responsible, in the event of any problems. A merger process needs to be transparent to ensure that it is a fair process.

At times of mergers people will have concerns, as in any change management intiative in business. It is essential that all parties are given the opportunity to express benefits and concerns. It helps to warn people managing the merger of potential conflict and enable them to avoid conflict or confront issues as they arise. This also serves to deepen relationships and understanding and therefore brings much-needed cohesiveness early on.

The number of stakeholders in mergers and acquisitions gives rise to different objectives and needs which will sometimes conflict. Successful mergers and acquisitions need to be driven through common work on business goals. At the same time the range of stakeholders needs to be managed very sensitively, through a long period of consultation, in order to understand and satisfy different demands.

In summary, in managing a merger potential conflict needs to be anticipated and addressed early on and on a continuous basis. Involvement and understanding the needs of all the different parties, ensuring a transparent process and being clear about accountability and the way forward play a key part. A positive attitude towards channelling differences to produce something even better than the predecessor organisations is also important. Finally, driving mergers and acquisitions through a focus on common business goals helps the integration process and the management of conflict.

10

EFFECTIVE CONFLICT MANAGEMENT

Conflict management is at the heart of leadership. I have learnt over the years in consulting and executive roles that conflict avoidance was the trademark of weak managers, who were incapable of leading change and often ended up with an uncontrollable crisis on their hands. The art of putting differences of opinion and aspiration on the table and leveraging them to achieve prompt decisions is a common skill of great business leaders.

Philippe Masson, Global Leader of the Strategic Consulting
Profession for Cap Gemini Ernst & Young

**Contributions to this chapter were made
by the following Forum member:**
Karen Gervais, Cap Gemini Ernst & Young

INTRODUCTION

There is little doubt that bad conflict management can lead to poor performance and a loss of creativity within an organisation. Managing conflict is an increasingly important concern for business leaders, but many still struggle with a task that is complicated by a constantly evolving global business environment. Today's manager, for example, must often communicate with colleagues or team members at a physical distance and contend with cultural differences. Given the negative connotations surrounding conflict, the approach of most organisations has been to prevent, avoid or even try to ignore it.

Much of the literature on the subject has also focused on conflict's negative consequences, and yet, like stress, conflict can have a very positive impact if harnessed correctly. Indeed, in some circumstances it should even be encouraged. The results of the BT Global Challenge race demonstrated the importance of effective conflict management for today's leader: the higher-performing yachts all managed conflict well, and two of the high-performing yachts laid down formal conflict management procedures. The lower performers, however, either managed conflict badly or avoided it altogether.

This chapter explains the concept of conflict by outlining its importance today and explaining the link between conflict and leadership for inspiring high performance. Causes of conflict and ways of dealing with it are discussed, drawing on experience from the race. By comparing the more and less successful yachts, lessons for business leaders on positive approaches to conflict management are also offered.

WHAT IS CONFLICT?

This chapter focuses on interpersonal conflict – the conflict that arises between individuals and groups – and does not address the 'internal conflict' an individual can experience. Conflict can be defined as: 'Differences in goals, views, values, beliefs and behaviours between people that disrupt harmony/flow' (K. Gervais).

The opposite of conflict is congruence, where differences may still exist but flow/harmony is complete and uninterrupted. Conflict and congruence are represented in Figure 10.1.

Is conflict positive or negative?

Conflict can be both positive and negative, depending on how it is viewed and managed by the leader. If conflict is managed well and relates to differences of opinion in a factual decision-making process, it can be positive and the energy arising from the conflict can be channelled in a positive way – for example, situations when the leader asks for the views of the crew. If, however, conflict is managed badly, for

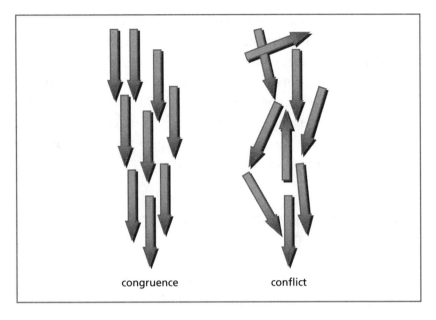

congruence   conflict

FIGURE 10.1   Representation of conflict and congruence

(Reproduced with permission from K. Gervais)

example when the leader fails to take account of the views of the team or avoids conflict, then it will be negative. When conflict relates to interpersonal differences, however, it is generally negative, although there can sometimes be a positive outcome if it is resolved well.

Do people vary in their attitude to conflict?

Until recently in the business world the word conflict had a predominantly negative connotation and was often viewed as something best avoided if possible; dealing with it was likely to be an unpleasant experience. People, however, do vary in their attitude to conflict, based on a number of factors such as experiences in childhood or cultural background. For example:

- Those brought up in a family where conflict was openly addressed and dealt with constructively are more likely to feel comfortable confronting situations and less likely to fear – and hence avoid – conflict.

- Those brought up in a family where conflict was avoided or viewed as destructive may be more likely to think of conflict as negative and best avoided.
- People also vary in the importance they attach to harmony and/or wanting to be liked by others. Those who like to operate in a harmonious environment could view conflict as a threat. Alternatively they could strive harder to resolve conflict in order to restore harmony. Cultural differences may also play a part.

CONFLICT MANAGEMENT IN TODAY'S ENVIRONMENT

Understanding and dealing with conflict is especially important when one considers today's organisation in terms of infrastructure and environment. The following factors have an impact on conflict management.

Organisation structure

Today's organisations are larger and flatter than in the past. More organisations are adopting matrix structures and there is greater reliance on teams and empowerment and less on hierarchy and a command-and-control management style. The need for greater collaboration between people means the scope for conflict is therefore higher.

The pace of change is fast

Organisations that thrive are those able to adapt quickly and innovate smartly in today's rapidly moving business environment. Conflict that helps broaden perspective and results in generating new and different ideas is critical. However, conflict which impedes such creativity can have a very negative impact on performance.

Diversity

With increasing globalisation and changing demographics, cultural diversity is increasing. Diversity can significantly enhance performance through encompassing a wider range of ideas and approaches. It can also create conflict, particularly from misunderstanding the use of humour and different value sets. Managing it well is key to realising the benefits.

Growing importance of employee satisfaction

Employee satisfaction is a key concern for employers at a time when talented people are scarce and greater demands are being put on people to become geographically mobile and learn new skills. High levels of unresolved conflict impact adversely on morale. At the same time, creating opportunity for involvement and buy-in, likely to involve openly addressing conflict, is critical for gaining employee commitment.

Increased reliance on technology and remote working

The possibility of misinterpretation through the use of new technologies also implies greater scope for conflict. Much of what we interpret from others depends on body language and voice intonation. Email, though, can easily be misinterpreted as there are, of course, no such non-verbal cues. Alternatively, lack of non-verbal cues could encourage more focus on the facts.

CONFLICT AND ITS RELATIONSHIP WITH HIGH PERFORMANCE

For today's leader, inspiring competitive advantage means taking a hard look at conflict management. Eisenhardt *et al.* (1997) identify a number of ways in which conflict impacts on high performance:

- By channelling energy, commitment and ideas it helps to build understanding and respect for differences.
- By allowing the expression of different views and opinions, people gain a greater understanding of, for example, possible options available before taking a decision.
- Using conflict as a stimulant, leaders and their teams maintain effectiveness and remain actively engaged.

- Creating a climate which encourages openness and confrontation improves team morale and subsequently performance.
- Positive conflict involving active debate allows teams to consider all the issues and generate significantly different alternatives.

Amason *et al.* (1995), having conducted a series of interviews in various organisations, found that the way organisational teams managed conflict was central to their effectiveness. Successful teams used conflict to their advantage, allowing it to stimulate discussion and creative thinking. The less successful teams, however, did a poor job of managing and resolving their differences. They found conflict a burden and something best avoided.

In addition, Hultman (1998) stresses the importance of shared values to increase the potential for harmony within a team and decrease interpersonal tension. When team members have different core values and beliefs, they experience friction and tension. Crawley (1996) also states that when unresolved differences exist within a team, it leads to defensiveness, lack of creativity and under-achievement. Sound management of these factors was also central to the success of high-performing skippers in the BT Global Challenge race.

WHAT ARE THE TYPES AND CAUSES OF CONFLICT?

Understanding different types of conflict and their underlying causes is key to effective conflict management. During the race there was plenty of scope for conflict within each of the competing teams, with 18 people from diverse backgrounds living together in a confined space and under extreme conditions for weeks at a time.

Conflict can be categorised in a number of ways based on causes.

Cognitive and affective conflict

The categorisation of Amason *et al.* (1995) was based on two types of conflict:

- Cognitive conflict (C-type conflict) – this occurs through cognitive issue-related disagreements and is a natural part of a properly functioning team. When teams have a discussion prior to decision making they bring together different ideas, information and perspectives. C-type conflict occurs as team members analyse and reconcile their differences. The process of debate encourages the questioning of assumptions and this process is key to the team's ability to reach high-quality decisions, empowering them through an understanding of the issues, options and rationale behind the decision. The process also ensures buy-in from the team and commitment when the decision is implemented. This type of conflict is positive and improves overall team performance.

- Affective conflict (A-type conflict) – this is based on personal, individually related issues and is negative because it undermines team cohesion and blocks the possibility of reaching consensus in a decision-making situation. It fosters cynicism, mistrust and avoidance, thereby inhibiting open communication and team integration. When A-type conflict occurs within a team, members become mistrustful or apathetic towards one another, the decision-making process becomes less open and commitment suffers because team members cease to understand decisions taken and the reasons why they are required to take certain actions. A-type conflict tends to focus on anger, usually directed at specific individuals.

Task, process and relationship conflict

Jehn (1997) built on the work of Amason *et al.* by adding a third category: process conflict. This relates to the way that the task is executed and includes role assignation and how much responsibility different people should get. This form of conflict seems detrimental to performance – when teams disagree about task allocation, for example, they are also unable to perform effectively. Three categories of conflict have been used to describe conflict situations on the yachts. There appeared to be a huge variation in the apparent causes and no two situations were exactly alike, but deeper analysis did unveil some clear distinctions.

CAUSES OF CONFLICT

Analysis of conflict situations during the race showed at least seven causes of conflict:

1. unclear goals, roles and allocation of roles
2. a lack of fairness
3. different values, views and opinions and different standards of performance
4. a mismatch between people's perception of situations and the reality
5. assumptions made by people which were not checked out with others
6. a lack of crew involvement in decision making
7. individual insensitivity to the needs of others.

THE NATURE OF CONFLICT WITH NEGATIVE EXAMPLES

Three categories of conflict have been chosen as the best to differentiate between the types of conflict experienced during the race and are shown in Figure 10.2. The three categories are similar to those outlined above by Jehn. The same categories are useful to describe conflict in business life.

The 'what' category

Conflict arises when there is disagreement about:

- what the goals are
- what tasks have to be done
- decisions on the way forward.

In this category, lack of communication and involvement can lead to conflict. For example, at one stage a yacht had to reach a port of call quickly to be in time for the start of the next leg and therefore remain in the race. Some of the crew wanted to start up the engine to ensure

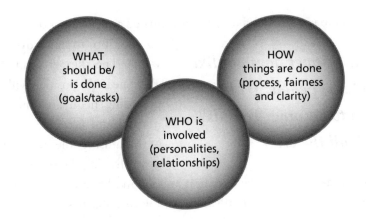

FIGURE 10.2 Categories of conflict

(Reproduced with permission from K. Gervais)

' *Our team did not define the team goal clearly at the start of the race. We are still struggling as we have no clear direction to focus on.* '

they arrived in time, while others wanted to take the risk by continuing to proceed just with the sails. The crux of the issue was essentially a disagreement about the team's goals: those wanting to put the engine on were motivated by the primary goal of continued participation in the race; those sailing around the world without mechanical help wished to remain with the sail.

The 'how' category

Conflict arises when there is disagreement about:

- how the goals are to be identified
- how tasks should be carried out
- how clearly and fairly things are dealt with.

Clarity of roles and responsibilities and perceived fairness are important in avoiding conflict. This was illustrated during the race by a situation that arose on the deck of one yacht in very stormy seas. A crew member, designated to helm, was turned away by the skipper after coming up to take over his watch. The skipper wanted to alternate in the position with the preceding helm and thus the normal and accepted method of organising the watch was upset, leaving the second helm confused and rejected. For the first and second helm there was ambiguity and, for the second at least, a feeling of unfairness – a potential conflict situation.

> ‘ *The skipper does not like to blame people. He has tried to become "friends" with all the crew.* ’

The 'who' category

This category embraces conflict which involves:

- personal differences
- relationships.

This category stems from diversity in terms of personal values, behavioural traits and personality types. Conflict arises when there is a lack of awareness, understanding or consideration of the differences between individuals. For example one crew member did not pull his weight. He had 30 per cent more sleep than anyone else and also slept on deck. In the end no one wanted to be on the same watch.

> ‘ *Some people cause more problems than others; it is in their nature.* ’

Conflicts can, of course, have their root in various elements spread across the different categories, especially over a certain period of time. For example, on the second Southern Ocean leg one skipper spent most of his time dealing with personality issues concerning certain crew members. What started as process issues related to procedures on the yacht quickly became deeply personal and moved into the 'who' category. This again reinforces the view that conflict should not be allowed to go unresolved for too long as it often becomes personal and disruptive.

Examples of positive conflict

The three-type categorisation above is also useful when it comes to exploring examples of positive conflict.

The 'what' category

On the yachts there were clear examples of conflict over what needed to be achieved in a certain situation and the best way to do it – for example, choosing the yacht's routing. Debate often led to an increasing number of ideas being offered and considered, and the result was more creative, informed solutions and greater buy-in from the crew. This type of well-managed 'what' conflict motivated the crew through involvement and the knowledge that the decision was likely to be more effective. It also increased commitment to the decision.

> *‘ There were poor routing decisions being taken on our yacht. This led to conflict within the team. ’*

The 'how' category

Although often negative, conflicts of the 'how' type could occasionally be beneficial when they led to identifying weaknesses in methods or more open discussion about goals and tasks. Confusion over sail changes on one yacht, for example, led to more efficient methods being agreed, and in this instance effective conflict management was critical, steering the issue swiftly towards a task debate and away from a possible relationship tension.

> *‘ Seeking the views and opinions of the crew – this is simply the culture of the yacht, it happens as a matter of course. ’*

The 'who' category

This type of conflict rarely had a positive impact in the race. The only exception was when the relationship issue masked or existed as a result of a 'what' or 'why' type issue and could be clearly and quickly brought back to this focus. For example, arguments over personal standards of tidiness below deck occurred frequently on some yachts. In one incident it quickly became apparent that individuals had different understandings of the rules for drying wet kit. Some yachts had a designated area for drying wet gear but crew members sometimes put their wet gear elsewhere, upsetting others.

Redirecting the conflict to the real cause prevented any real relationship harm and could be viewed as having a positive effect as the rules were made clearer as a consequence. While 'what' type conflict, however, can be actively encouraged as a positive, it would be a risk to encourage 'who' type conflict in the uncertain hope of some spin-off benefit! Again the key is the resolution and management of the conflict.

> *' Sailing the boat is easy – it's just the people on board who are the problem. '*

The causes of conflict and its impact on the yachts give a useful framework for understanding the nature of conflict. The race also gives some excellent insights into styles and strategies for managing conflict well in the business world and ways of preventing negative conflict.

STYLES OF CONFLICT MANAGEMENT – THE DIFFERENCES BETWEEN THE HIGHER AND LOWER PERFORMERS

How did the higher-performing skippers approach conflict?

> *' The difference between conflict being managed well and badly is accepting it exists rather than ignoring it. '*

The skippers, like many typical leaders, had a natural dislike of conflict. However, the higher-performing skippers recognised the importance of conflict management even before the race had started and made plans to minimise it.

1. The higher performers were more likely to recognise the importance of directly addressing conflict and not allowing it to fester.

On one yacht there were different rules for the use of email – one watch could use it during a watch, another could not. This resulted in conflict between the two watches and, after discussion with the two watch leaders, the skipper made a decision on the use of email and later advised the whole crew on his reasons, thereby diffusing the conflict situation.

2. **Another high-performing skipper was described as being proactive and able to quickly 'nip conflict in the bud'.**

   While observing a sail change, for example, he heard the watch leader yell instructions at the person in charge on the fore deck. The fore deck person disagreed with the watch leader's instructions and yelled back that he was going to follow his own initiative. Before tempers could flare, however, the skipper had intervened, saying the sail changer was in charge at that particular moment and not the watch leader.

3. **One higher-performing skipper addressed conflict by acting as a mediator.**

   This is a popular technique in conflict management. The skipper listened to two crew members who had clashed and calmed both down. The skipper then made a decision on the conflict and finally resolved it at the port of call.

4. **The higher-performing skippers all kept a distance from the crew and were therefore able to take a detached standpoint on such occasions.**

   They had a hierarchy in place and day-to-day issues were handled by either the watch leaders or the crew members themselves. The skippers only became involved in the bigger issues or matters involving the whole crew.

5. **All higher-performing skippers had 'sensing' as a competency.**
   This allowed them to read the emotional atmosphere of the yacht better and diffuse potentially difficult situations quickly.

6. **All the higher-performing skippers had a strong set of shared values with their crew which had been discussed and adopted prior to the race.**

   The skippers upheld these values and the higher-performing ones also ensured all crew members 'pulled their weight', emphasising such value statements as 'never step over a job'. This minimised any conflict related to an individual crew member's performance.

How did the lower-performing skippers approach conflict?

> *It was the avoidance of difficult interpersonal issues and lack of openness and honesty… that led to the festering of problems and to poor performance throughout the race.*

The lower performers had fewer processes in place to help them manage conflict. The pressure of lower performance also seemed to add to the level of conflict on most of the lower-performing yachts. In the end several of the lower-performing skippers became the source of conflict themselves.

1. **The lower performers either avoided conflict or allowed it to fester.**
   One lower-performing skipper had an interpersonal issue with a crew member on leg 1 which remained an issue for most of the race. The skipper wanted to be liked by others and had real difficulty handling conflict, adopting the conciliatory phrase, 'leave it on the wave behind', to try to persuade crew members to forget any grudges. Previously, the approach was to discuss an issue, learn from it and then move on, leaving any bad feeling behind; the new ethos may well be seen as a convenient manner for ignoring unpleasant issues!

   The same skipper also had an issue with a watch leader who lacked the competence for the role. Although the lack of expertise contributed to poor performance, the skipper was reluctant to deal with the issue and replace the watch leader.

2. **One lower-performing skipper, especially when challenged, had a bullying, condescending or sarcastic manner.**
   This style choked the crew's involvement and initiative and they finally took over some decision making and excluded the skipper.

3. **The lower performers were also poorer at active listening.**
   Active listening is a critical skill for ensuring the needs of the team

are met. On one yacht the crew complained that the skipper was never prepared to listen to their ideas, resulting in lack of buy-in to the skipper's decisions.

4. **Some of the lower performers did not create enough 'distance' between themselves and the crew.**

   There was a lack of distance between the skipper and their crew, either because they became 'one of the lads' or because they failed to command respect through their own sub-standard behaviour. Dealing with difficult issues, especially interpersonal issues, was therefore not easy because some were too 'close' to the problem or they failed to command the necessary respect when unpopular decisions had to be taken.

5. **The lower performers also had less strong value sets and failed to lead by example.**

   For example, a lower performing skipper on one yacht not only failed to uphold the values of cleanliness, tidiness and hygiene and was the worst culprit, but added to the conflict by reprimanding the crew when they failed to uphold the values.

WHAT STRATEGIES WERE ADOPTED FOR SUCCESSFUL CONFLICT MANAGEMENT?

' If conflict management is to be successful it needs to be nipped in the bud early on. Deal with sources and deal with it firmly. '

What methods, for example, differentiated the higher-performing skippers from their lower-performing colleagues?

The 'what' category

1. **Shared and stated goals.**

   The crews of the higher-performing yachts had common goals. These goals were discussed and agreed before the outset of the race. For example, one crew agreed their goal was to race well, be real contenders for winning and be consistent in their performance and not to try to win at all costs (which might drive different behaviours). Importantly, goals were also regularly revisited – and sometimes modified – to ensure they remained realistic. One crew, whose goal had been to win the race, realised part way around that this would not be possible. Instead, they reworked their goal after discussion.

Several of the lower-performing yachts were still experiencing conflict related to goals halfway around the world, such as a conflict between 'are we here to race or is this just an adventure and a cruise?' The higher performers, however, gained agreement much sooner.

2. **Bringing attention back to the bigger picture.**

    What was the best solution in helping to achieve the goal? This was either the overall goal for the race or a shorter-term goal for a particular part of the race. Having the whole team set and then buy into a goal was important. It meant a common point of reference was the context for putting issues into perspective and helped move attention from issue to solution quickly. It also resulted in a more motivated team who were prepared to go that extra (nautical) mile to perform well.

3. **Realignment of goals.**

    Where there were individual differences in desired goals, these were discussed with a view to understanding them and/or exploring how they could be met or realigned. Contrast this with the team mentioned earlier who were unable to resolve the conflict satisfactorily about whether to turn on the engine or continue with just the sails because they were split in terms of their primary goal. Such a conflict halfway around the world did not, of course, help team morale or performance. Individuals are also likely to have other personal goals in addition to the, hopefully shared, corporate goals. Understanding these and helping ensure they are met and aligned to the bigger goals can avoid conflict later on.

4. **Actively encourage a degree of conflict to ensure issues were debated.**

    This results in more creative solutions and more informed decisions. One of the leggers from a high-performing yacht said:

'With 18 minds on the problem, someone will come up with a good idea. The skipper must be in a better position if he allows that and he does.' All decisions about the 'what' factor need not be discussed or arrived at by consensus (on a yacht in the Southern Ocean in the face of an 80ft wave, with the skipper at the helm, it would hardly be the moment to start challenging a recent navigation decision). The higher-performing teams were more likely to open up the dialogue and take different perspectives into account.

The 'how' category

1. **Using the wide-ranging knowledge and experience within the crew.**
It was very important to identify expertise within the team and not to assume the crew had no experience to offer or need not be consulted. The skippers' success in embracing conflict of the 'how' nature depended heavily on open, constructive debate in which crew members were collaborative rather than competitive. It also depended on timely commitment to outcomes and not allowing conflict to fester. Skippers on the lower-performing yachts did not have conflict resolution mechanisms in place and as a result lost valuable knowledge and ideas.

2. **Mechanisms for communicating and sharing knowledge in place.**
Skippers of the higher-performing yachts typically had more mechanisms in place for communicating and sharing knowledge within the team, such as daily morning briefings. They did much to ensure clarity with the crew, whether about goals, decisions or processes. The lower-performing skippers, however, were not so good at having such mechanisms in place, particularly towards the end of the race.

3. **Clear rules and standards of performance agreed early on and enforced helped avoid conflict.**
It was stated at the outset on one yacht that parties were allowed only below deck, leaving little room for ambiguity. On at least two of the best-placed yachts there were also rules for how conflict would be addressed if it arose. In some cases, however, rules were

fluid or not apparent at all. In many of the lower-performing yachts, rules were not applied in a consistent and fair manner or there was less clarity regarding standards of performance and discipline was lax.

4. **Clarity about an individual's role and ensuring roles were well executed.**

   Skippers needed to properly define the scope and accountability of each position, a process that extended beyond the more obvious roles of watch leader to food monitor and heads (toilet) cleaner. Some of the roles were also rotated to avoid tedium and here proper handovers and briefings were important. When roles were poorly executed, the lower-performing skippers found these issues more difficult to deal with.

The 'who' category

1. **Focus on solutions rather than blame.**

   The skippers who managed well in the last category – where conflict is caused by personal differences – were also encouraging and understanding in difficult situations, refusing to blame individuals when things went wrong. Many of the lower-performing skippers, however, perpetuated a blame culture, despite having agreed a shared value of avoiding this at the outset.

2. **Striking a balance between acknowledging the emotions involved in a particular dispute and the pure facts.**

   To focus purely on the content of the disagreement – without acknowledging the emotions involved – can result in ugly monsters resurfacing later on even if agreement and peace have seemingly been restored.

Whatever the cause of the conflict, an individual must believe that conflict can be resolved. Jehn (1997) terms this 'resolution potential'. If skippers had and conveyed this belief, for example, then there was a willingness to divert energies and a greater likelihood of successfully resolving issues.

THE RELATIONSHIP BETWEEN CONFLICT MANAGEMENT AND EMOTIONAL INTELLIGENCE

Emotional intelligence is an important factor in managing conflict. The emotional intelligence behaviours were ranked high, medium or low, based on the judgements drawn from the data collected from the interviews. The following emotional intelligence behaviours were seen to be most important for skippers managing all types of conflict.

Self-awareness

The higher-performing skippers with high self-awareness recognised the impact that their behaviour had on others and shared their feelings more readily. This built the support and respect of the crew who valued their openness. They were less likely to be misunderstood or do things that would have a negative effect on their team members.

The lower-performing skippers were far less prepared to discuss their feelings with crew members. One or two found difficulty controlling their emotions when they faced difficult situations and were not always aware of the impact they were having on their crew.

Emotional resilience

Skippers able to perform well under pressure were at an advantage as this was a time when conflict could occur. For example, during the Southern Ocean leg one skipper had to mediate between two people when a situation got out of hand in a stressful situation. The lower-performing skippers had difficulty performing under pressure and under these circumstances sometimes generated conflict themselves.

The higher-performing skippers were far more receptive to feedback which they actively encouraged. They were more able to handle criticism and learn from the feedback and less likely to become aggressive or defensive than the lower-performing skippers. The lower-performing skippers under pressure were inclined to withdraw from the crew.

Motivation

Striving to do things better encouraged the higher-performing skippers to facilitate constructive debate, seeing it as a way of exploring different options to a problem and then selecting the most appropriate. With a strong drive to achieve long-term goals, the higher-performing skippers also had a strong need to resolve conflict as they recognised it impeded performance.

In contrast, the lower-performing skippers were less focused on shared goals. Towards the end of the race there was only limited debate on issues and very little emphasis on reviewing to do things better. Conflict was avoided or allowed to fester; there was no drive to resolve issues.

Interpersonal sensitivity

The higher-performing skippers took the time to listen to others, sometimes on a one-to-one basis. They involved people in decision-making and as a result experienced less conflict. The higher-performing skippers also had processes in place which encouraged communication and brought out any potential or existing conflict, which they were able to deal with taking account of the needs of the crew. The lower-performing skippers were not so good at active listening and a couple developed leadership styles that discouraged any challenge or alternative views being offered.

Influence

Skippers had to be able to bring team members round to their point of view to help avoid conflict. Some of the skippers were seen to be good at taking the crew with them. This particularly applied when the skippers were making navigation decisions. The skippers performing less well experienced difficulties, especially later on in the race, when they had made decisions which had proved to be wrong under the prevailing circumstances. On one yacht a team was established to take navigational decisions because of the skipper's inability to influence his crew.

Conscientiousness

The higher-performing skippers were seen as fair, treating all people in an unbiased way. Upholding the agreed values on the yachts and modelling desirable behaviour helped avoid conflict.

The crews on one or two of the lower-performing yachts commented on a lack of fairness shown by their skippers.

SUMMARY

This chapter has drawn attention to the usual view of conflict being negative and to be avoided at all costs. To manage conflict well, leaders need to develop the mindset which sees the positive aspects of conflict. Leaders should recognise the importance of confrontation and active debate as a means of stimulating creativity and making the best decisions with buy-in from the team. Conflict has been described in terms of three categories, the 'what', conflict around goals and tasks, the 'how' conflict arising from processes, clarity and fairness, and the 'who' conflict concerned with the people involved and their relationships. The first two types can lead to positive outcomes, while the third is negative and should be resolved quickly.

There was a clear relationship between effective conflict management and overall performance in the BT Global Challenge race.

LESSONS FROM THE RACE

As a leader today you need to:

1. remember, effective conflict management makes the difference between high and lower performance
2. be aware that a degree of conflict is necessary
3. channel conflicting views constructively

4. resolve differences openly and sensitively

5. use clear and accepted processes for managing conflict

6. direct conflict away from people towards tasks and facts

7. make rules, processes and roles clear to avoid misunderstandings

8. believe conflict can be resolved and show a willingness to confront it

9. act fairly and consistently

10. use regular self-review against the relevant dimensions of emotional intelligence.

REFERENCES

Amason, A. C., Hochwarter, W. A., Thompson, K. R. and Harrison, A. W. (1995) 'Conflict: an important dimension in successful management teams', *Organizational Dynamics*, Autumn, Vol. 24, No. 2.

Crawley, J. (1996) 'What's the problem?' *Management Training*, January/February, pp. 46–47.

Eisenhardt, K. M., Kahwajy, J. L. and Bourgeois III, L. J. (1997) 'How management teams can have a good fight', *Harvard Business Review*, July–August, pp. 77–85.

Hultman, K. (1998) 'The 10 commandments of team leadership (Training 101: it's a team effort)', *Training and Development*, February, 52.

Jehn, Karen A. (1997) 'A quantitative analysis of conflict types and dimensions in organisations', *Administrative Science Quarterly*, September.

KNOWLEDGE MANAGEMENT AT WORK
BT

BT is facing increased levels of competition. The impact of the knowledge economy is such that the barriers to entry in its marketplace are fast disappearing. It was clear that in order for BT to compete effectively it needed to:

- become more efficient through better utilisation of the knowledge within its business
- retain and win customers through the delivery of an excellent customer experience and move 'up the value chain' to become strategic partners with its key customers.

Knowledge management is a solution that automates the sales and marketing processes of BT's major business unit. It enables BT to leverage the information that it acquires, to manage customer relationships proactively, create selling and marketing opportunities and deliver an excellent customer experience.

Knowledge management provides:

- a set of links to information resources that support a particular solution or sale, e.g. competitor intelligence, pricing information and access to sales collateral
- links to appropriate training
- the ability to generate a tailored customer presentation
- the ability to ask questions and request assistance from 'experts' across the organisation
- a personalised news feed on propositions and solutions, designed to allow the account teams to incorporate any new information during the course of the sales cycle.

A key objective of the system's implementation was to gain competitive advantage through the exploitation of knowledge assets and intellectual capital. This has resulted in an increase of 28 per cent in BT's major business 'win rate' and a significant increase in the number of prospects identified by the sales force.

The true benefits of the approach have been gained by implementing systems which are not solely reporting, command-and-control systems, but which are knowledge-sharing systems. The early adoption of Web-based technology has allowed BT to develop applications which proactively deliver the right information to the right person at the right time. This has supported the drive to win more business.

11

CREATING A KNOWLEDGE-SHARING CULTURE

**Contributions to this chapter were made
by the following Forum members:**
Colin Dunn and Julia Lloyd-Evans, BT
Suzanne Pollack, Henley Management College

INTRODUCTION

This chapter sets out to look at the subject of knowledge management and its importance for leaders. In the first instance, it will explore the definition of knowledge management and the difference between information and knowledge. It will then look at some of the reasons why knowledge management has become a business issue.

It will then review a model that looks at the key activities that a team or organisation needs to address to successfully harness collective energy and knowledge and utilise this to gain benefit. Taking this model, the chapter will look at the strategies used by the skippers and crews of the BT Global Challenge race in managing and sharing knowledge before and during the race and will draw on examples of good practice and the effect of these on performance. Reference will also be made to business examples.

A section will focus on the factors that affect the successful management and sharing of knowledge within teams and organisations. Reference will be made to the culture created by the higher-performing skippers.

The chapter will end with a review of the emotional intelligence behaviours required to create an environment for successful knowledge sharing and competitive advantage.

WHAT IS KNOWLEDGE MANAGEMENT?

Knowledge management is about getting the right knowledge and understanding to the right people at the right time.

Sir Peter Bonfield, former CEO, BT

There are many definitions of knowledge management and numerous interpretations of its meaning. Some organisations find the term too limiting and prefer to call it knowledge sharing or knowledge creation to encompass the real essence and value of the discipline.

Among the companies involved in the Inspirational Intelligence Research Forum, several definitions of knowledge management exist: 'Knowledge management is the evolving discipline that ensures more effective use of the knowledge, both explicit and tacit, that is available internally and externally to an organisation, takes into account people, business processes and technology, and is closely aligned with the objectives of the organisation' (Edward Truch, Henley Management College, 2001).

'Optimising the cultural and technical environment to ensure that people connect with whatever and whoever they need to help them do their job… regardless of the boundaries that exist' (Tom Boyle, BT, 2001).

Definitions vary according to the context. Cap Gemini Ernst & Young takes a client-focused perspective, defining knowledge as 'the professional "know-how" on which we capitalise in order to provide our clients with the greatest value', while The Document Company Xerox takes a cultural perspective, stating: 'Knowledge management is about creating a thriving work and learning environment that fosters the continuous creation, aggregation, use and re-use of organisational and personal knowledge.'

Whatever definition a company may choose to use, the underlying essence of knowledge management is capturing the expertise and experience of individuals in order to create knowledge and sharing it effectively throughout the organisation.

WHEN DOES INFORMATION BECOME KNOWLEDGE?

Information is not a synonym for knowledge and it is not true to say that knowledge management is about sharing information. According to Bonaventura (1997), information is the potential for knowledge. However, information is worthless unless it is understood, developed and applied. It may be helpful to view information as the raw material for knowledge and knowledge as something that is gained through interaction between people. Knowledge can be gained through personal experience, coaching from experts, feedback and learning. Unless there is an opportunity for interactivity in its acquisition, information cannot be turned to knowledge (see Figure 11.1).

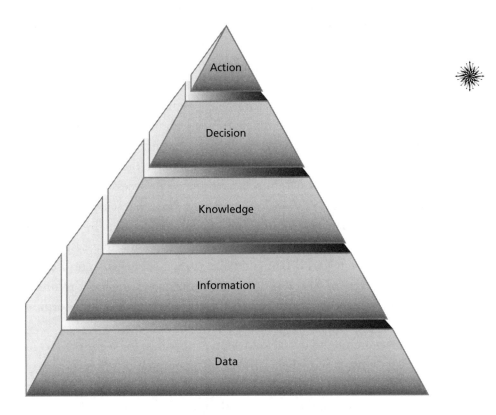

FIGURE 11.1 Processing hierarchy

(from *Managing Knowledge* (1996) by D. A. Wilson)

Nonaka and Takeuchi (1995) define two types of knowledge commonly referred to in the business context as 'explicit' and 'tacit' knowledge:

- Explicit knowledge can be articulated in formal language and transmitted through documents and written matter.
- Tacit knowledge is seen as personal knowledge, based on individual experience and values and therefore not easily transmitted.

WHY HAS KNOWLEDGE MANAGEMENT BECOME A KEY BUSINESS TOPIC?

The advances of technology and globalisation have driven the knowledge-based economy and for organisations operating in the global arena, knowledge management has become a business necessity. Creating and sharing knowledge has become an important element where competition is based more on what an organisation knows than on what it owns.

The reason for the rise of knowledge management can be reviewed in the context of several business trends seen in the past two decades. Ironically it was the advance in computer technology and the introduction of new IT systems in the 1980s that led to the loss of corporate 'know-how'. As information became more easily accessible and readily available through technologies, companies chose to restructure, cutting out layers of management to create a flatter organisation. By doing this they lost skills and talents of the people who knew how to use the information to create knowledge. Gradually companies began to realise that what they were missing was not explicit knowledge which was recorded but tacit knowledge which came from their employees, in the form of expertise and experience.

The realisation that tacit knowledge was critical for success led companies to reappraise the worth of their employees. They began to recognise the intangible value that knowledge added to the bottom line and put a value on their intellectual capital. They saw their employees as their competitive advantage and encouraged partnerships and collaborative working practices to deliver service and value to their customers.

Advances in technology and the emergence of the Internet and World Wide Web were seen to have major implications for traditional business methods. They were seen to create opportunities and provide more reasons to utilise knowledge and transform the shape of future business. As more and more technical tools become available, the opportunities for using knowledge and sharing best practice become greater. Technology has eroded the boundaries of corporate working and with web sites and Intranets giving access to chat rooms and online forums, employees can now share and debate ideas and opinions across time zones and countries.

With the pace of change, companies cannot afford to ignore their greatest assets. The need for continual learning and improvement is paramount. People need to be constantly developing and upgrading their skills in order to create knowledge and innovate further. Survival of many organisations depends on innovation and that in turn means risk. The challenge facing many organisations and leaders today is how to create an environment where knowledge sharing, learning and creativity are embedded and risk is accepted.

On average less than 30 per cent of the financial/market value ascribed to organisations relates to the organisations' 'book value' or tangible assets. Some 70 per cent resides within the 'heads' of the people who work there (Boulton *et al.*, 2000). Microsoft estimates that $100 invested in it would equate to roughly $1 worth of fixed assets. The other $99 worth of value will be found in the heads of the people who work for the company (Bonfield, 1999).

> *The most competitive and successful companies of the next decade will be those that know how to get the right knowledge and understanding to the right people at the right time, without formality and without delay.*

> Sir Peter Bonfield, former CEO, BT

KNOWLEDGE MANAGEMENT AND COMPETITIVE ADVANTAGE IN THE BT GLOBAL CHALLENGE RACE

Knowledge helps businesses gain competitive advantage and in today's turbulent environment where staying afloat is critical, leaders are always looking for whatever can give them that edge. The skippers and crew of the BT Global Challenge race were constantly looking for advantage. They were all too aware that this was a race where seconds could cost them a position. Many of the skippers implemented good strategies and processes for capturing information. They used their own and others' tacit knowledge to make seemingly minimal gains.

At the outset of the project, many of the skippers identified the elements that would provide them with a competitive advantage, such as team performance, yacht speed and tactical routing. As none of the skippers were experienced in all these fields, they identified and sourced the assistance of many experts, tapping into team development consultants, professional ocean racers, weather routing gurus, universities and meteorological bureaux.

Without big budgets, the skippers had to identify the critical elements of their project and allocate time and money accordingly. Some built up win-win alliances with these professionals. One team provided a weather researcher with detailed reports of weather conditions in return for advice. Another skipper managed to get assistance from six professionals without any budget at all. The professionals were able to share their expertise and provide practical assistance for the skipper and specific members of the team. They gave them advice, coaching and enhanced understanding of their resources to use while at sea. Weather information and tactical routing were critical for success. The sophisticated technology on board the yachts allowed access to some of the most up to date and valuable weather information available (see Chapter 9).

However, without the ability to translate this into knowledge, it remained useless. The skippers had to develop their own skills and expertise in these areas or identify others within the team who could take on this role. On the higher-performing yachts, skippers appointed

‘ It was competitor analysis – looking at what they were doing and doing it better. ’

one crew member to fulfil this role and they would spend all their time analysing and interpreting the constant stream of available data.

The importance of capturing information and converting this to knowledge was demonstrated clearly when one skipper spent three hours closely monitoring, through binoculars, a competitor yacht that was catching from behind. The skipper could not understand why this yacht seemed to be sailing faster. Comparing the set-up of the other yacht with his own, the skipper checked they had the same sized sails, tweaked the set of the sails and ensured the crew weight was positioned appropriately. Making these adjustments, the skipper was able to increase the yacht speed and within two days had gained 40 miles on the other yacht.

KNOWLEDGE MANAGEMENT AND PERFORMANCE IN THE BT GLOBAL CHALLENGE RACE

In reviewing the knowledge management strategies of the skippers, it was evident that there was correlation between those who managed knowledge well and the team performance in the overall race. Using a model known as the knowledge management helm, the next section will identify key factors for facilitating good knowledge management. Examples will be drawn from the race to highlight skipper and team activities.

Knowledge management helm

Knowledge management is the way in which the ‘intangible assets’ of an organisation are managed. In the model shown in Figure 11.2, knowledge management is placed at the centre of the wheel in recognition of its pivotal place within an organisation. It is intended to show that knowledge management is a key activity for any team whether on

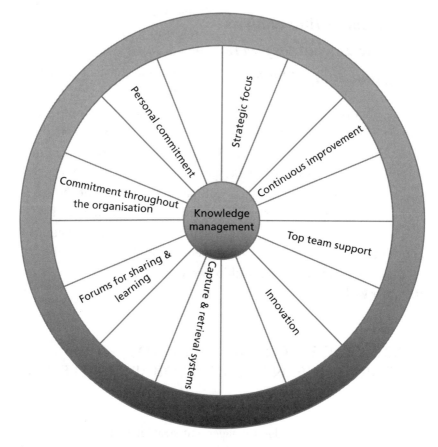

FIGURE 11.2 Knowledge management helm

(Reproduced with permission of Suzanne Pollack)

board a yacht or in business. Without strategies and processes in place, learning and knowledge will remain untapped, unharnessed or possibly will leak out of the organisation.

Effective knowledge management can be divided into two categories:

- creating and acquiring new knowledge
- sharing and transferring knowledge.

The knowledge management model has been designed to depict a helm. Each of the eight spokes represents a key element which steers the success of knowledge management whether on board a yacht or within an organisation. Combining some of the spokes, the model will be reviewed under the following headings and supported by activities demonstrated by the skippers and crews of the BT Global Challenge race:

- top team support and strategic focus
- enabling mechanisms
- innovation and continuous improvement
- commitment at an individual and an organisational level.

Top team support and strategic focus

Senior management need to believe that knowledge management is important and focus on it as an issue, devoting time and resources to ensure it happens. To manage knowledge effectively requires both a strategic understanding of what is important for the business and a genuine interest in making this happen.

The higher-performing skippers demonstrated their belief in the benefits of knowledge management at the outset of the project. In pre-race training, time was taken to ensure everyone got to know each other's personal objectives before agreeing a team goal.

One podium skipper shared explicit knowledge with his crew by writing a whole series of learning papers on various aspects of sail trim in order to transfer this in-depth technical knowledge to them. The skipper of BP

‘ You will win if you learn faster than anyone else in the race. ’

prepared a comprehensive team manual that covered every element of the project, from agreed goals and values, roles, clothing, sleeping arrangements, meal plan, cleaning rotas to sail plan, sail trim and important performance-related data. A copy of the manual was given to each crew member and legger before joining the yacht.

These higher-performing skippers delegated early on and during the race encouraged learning and took time out to coach the team. External professionals were used to support the team early and team development work also continued throughout the race in ports of call.

There was support for knowledge management in the middle-performing skippers. However, there was a lack of proactivity among some skippers in ensuring it was properly facilitated. One skipper created the right culture, encouraging openness and sharing, but did not put in place any formal mechanisms to support it. Another skipper started the race with a tendency to make unilateral decisions and not explain them. This skipper was also not receptive to upward feedback.

> ' *Accepting you are not perfect and knowing how to handle it is the most important factor.* '

The combined effect was a non-knowledge-sharing environment. However, by mid race the skipper had started to make some changes, having recognised the importance of feedback and the value of coaching and knowledge transfer within the team.

While other skippers espoused a positive knowledge management approach, the culture was not conducive to sharing. They adopted a directional style of leadership and had a hierarchical structure. They would 'instruct' rather than share. This stifled people's willingness to provide upward feedback and express views and ideas on how to do things better. One crew commented that they felt they were being held back by their skipper. These skippers didn't appear to change their approach during the race.

BT demonstrates commitment to strategic focus by supporting initiatives such as 'shared learning from the top'. Executive board members share their own learning, experience and tips for success with up-and-coming talent within the organisation.

Enabling mechanisms

Well-designed systems enable people to make sense of large volumes of data. Systems are also needed to collect softer types of information. This may be through reviews where individuals can exchange best practice or forums where learning can be captured.

Almost all of the skippers put formal mechanisms in place for sharing ideas and learning and for seeking ways to improve. The effectiveness of these and the extent to which the crew members contributed depended

' You have got to have a thirst for knowledge. If you stop asking questions then I will get worried. '

largely on the respective skipper's commitment to knowledge management, openness to questioning and feedback, and willingness to try new things and new ways of working.

Most of the higher-performing skippers held daily briefings not simply for sharing information. These were open forums where crew could discuss how things were going and what could be done to make things better. The teams conducted thorough watch handovers, briefing their respective number in detail. These skippers also held in-depth team reviews in ports of call and captured the ideas and knowledge of their departing leggers.

The higher-performing teams recognised the value of legger integration and made great efforts to get it right. To help them to integrate quickly, many teams assigned a core crew member as their mentor. The

' You often find there are assumptions made about how much people know. '

Compaq team had a comprehensive legger coaching and development plan. Leggers who had completed a leg would meet with leggers still to join the yacht. They would

share their experience, discuss how systems and procedures worked on the yacht and outline the role that the legger would be expected to undertake. The new leggers joined the yacht much better informed and prepared and were able to integrate more easily. The performance of this yacht team was consistent throughout the race.

Crew members on the more successful teams tended to have spe-

' Win by specialisation. '

cialised roles. These were dependent on individual ability and what was best for the performance of the yacht.

Some of the middle and lower-performing skippers held less frequent or unstructured briefings. They were sometimes slow to integrate their leggers and did not have a system or framework for doing this. One lower-performing skipper did not recognise the value of skills or experience that new leggers could bring to the yacht. A qualified yachtmaster joined the team but his skills and experience were never tapped.

When Anglian Water privatised in 1997 it knew that it had to capture the valuable lessons from staff who were retiring. The company organised masterclasses to capture that learning and published them over the Intranet. This led to a noticeable increase in performance.

BT has a large community of home-based workers. Conscious of the need to ensure these people don't feel isolated from the social element of being office-based and from the support infrastructure enjoyed by office-based people, the company established a community web site for home workers with links to various support functions and chat forums. The chat forums evolved into a mutual support network where, in addition to the social element, people share work-related ideas, issues and problems and benefit from the experience of others who have encountered and overcome similar problems. This has helped to increase the productivity of the home-based worker.

Innovation and continuous improvement

To keep ahead of the competition it is often necessary to push out the boundaries and experiment a little. Innovation inevitably involves an element of risk. The skippers were not prepared to jeopardise safety for competitive edge but many were keen to encourage their team to think outside the box.

During the second Southern Ocean leg, the skipper of TeamSpirIT identified a risky strategy that would take them way off course and add many miles to their passage but could potentially give them a huge gain on the fleet. Wanting to get crew buy-in he explained the two scenarios. If it worked they could gain a considerable

' *He would rather gamble and lose than be mediocre.* '

number of places in the fleet: if it didn't they could arrive in Cape Town several days behind the last yacht. With support from the crew he headed north, rounded the top of a huge high pressure area and sailed straight into Cape Town, moving up five places in the fleet.

> **'Even good sailors ask questions.'**

One middle-performing skipper clearly advocated a knowledge-sharing environment and gave regular briefings and reviews. However, this skipper was not open to creativity or innovation and stamped on new ideas. He insisted his own methods and practices were best and the crew quickly gave up proffering any ideas or opinions.

On yachts where a no-blame culture was endorsed, crew were openly seen to be more creative. On BP there was a problem with blocked toilets so the crew medic, a vet, was put to the test. Using his experience and skills from veterinary practice, this crew member unblocked the toilets and restored crew morale. The skipper of Logica couldn't understand why his yacht was sailing slowly. Using the creativity of the crew, they rigged up a video camera on the end of the boat hook. After dangling this beneath the yacht, the skipper was able to review the footage to ensure there was nothing wrapped around the keel.

Continuous improvement was seen to be critical to enhancing per-

> **'The race has been about reinforcing learning.'**

formance and was part of the culture of the higher-performing teams. These teams were continuously striving to do things better. Processes and procedures were reviewed and continuously updated and improved.

To continually improve requires an emphasis on learning new processes or procedures and personal development. Learning and development took place at different levels within the race as it would do within an organisation:

- At the individual level, crew members managed their own learning and development. Some had personal development plans that were shared with and supported by their skipper, as they might be with a boss in business.
- At watch level, some teams had systems in place to debrief at the end of each watch to exchange learning between themselves. They would also share this learning with the other watch. This would apply to different functions and departments within a business.

- At skipper level, some skippers had systems where the whole team, including sponsors' representatives and any other external supporters, got together at the end of each leg to review the leg and exchange learning. Businesses often learn from external sources such as their customers, suppliers or partners.
- At skipper level, some of the teams spent time in port trying to glean information about other campaigns from which they could learn. They also tapped into the resources of consultants or professionals. Many companies have departments that collate market intelligence and analyse competitor strategies.

' It is only with continual learning that you actually reach ultimate performance. '

Each level is ultimately crucial to the success of the organisation whatever its business and corporate goals.

The skipper of Olympic Group ran a rotating watch system where crew members moved across the two watches. This system allowed knowledge and skills to be transferred and best practice to be shared. Other yachts operated in two distinct watches with the two rarely meeting. They tended to work in isolation: knowledge and learning were not shared. Instead of creating a sharing environment, they competed with each other to the detriment of performance.

The BP skipper allowed only a technical sailing and trim book on

' Everyone should go on the yacht like a sponge. When time permits they should read about yacht performance. '

board for the short leg to Sydney. A crew member who was injured at the start of the leg and confined to his bunk read the book from cover to cover. He prepared a brief and on the next leg, when he was back on deck, he coached crew

members and shared what he had learned.

Nucor Corp has been the world's most innovative and fastest growing steel company for the past 30 years. It has achieved success by becoming and remaining the most efficient steel producer in the world, driven by developing a knowledge-creation and sharing environment. Employees were motivated to push the boundaries of manufacturing process know-how. High incentive bonuses were offered to every employee but these could be earned only through discovering new ways to boost productivity. The output had to meet quality standards and so employees were motivated to develop innovations that would help them to do things right the first time. As a consequence they expanded the frontiers of process know-how.

Commitment at an individual and an organisational level

If individuals are not committed to learning and helping others to learn, then knowledge management will be difficult. Leaders need to exhibit behaviour that is supportive of the activity. They need to implement processes and policies and ensure recognition or rewards are given that show commitment to knowledge management.

Many of the skippers were highly self-motivated and focused on the job in hand. They were passionate and committed to doing whatever was needed to achieve results. Reward for them was seeing the yacht perform at optimal speed, gaining miles and seeing their position rise among the fleet on the six-hourly fleet position schedules. Some of these skippers were able to inspire this passion into their teams.

> **' The crew has been infected by my desire to do well. '**

> **' I would give them the option but they always went for the extreme. '**

Coaching and support were encouraged among many crews. One skipper introduced a scheme where points were awarded for coaching other crew members. At the end of the leg the points were totalled and a prize awarded to the crew member with the highest score.

At General Electric, the then CEO Jack Welch introduced an upward coaching system where graduate recruits were assigned to a senior manager who would act as their mentor in return for coaching on new technology.

> **' Everything can be known if people want to know it. '**

OVERCOMING BARRIERS TO KNOWLEDGE MANAGEMENT

There are many technological issues that could be discussed as potential barriers to creating a knowledge-sharing environment, but this section focuses on two human issues that a leader will have to address:

- persuading people of the benefits of sharing knowledge
- creating an environment that fosters knowledge creation and diffusion.

Persuading people of the benefits

Traditionally, knowledge has been seen to give an individual power and in many companies employees are promoted and rewarded on the basis of the knowledge they have or the number of sales and ultimately revenue that they generate. Sharing one's personal knowledge for the corporate good is therefore not necessarily seen to be advantageous to the individual and may in fact be seen to dilute their competitive advantage within the organisation.

From an individual's perspective, sharing knowledge also takes time. Taking time out to join a working group, to regularly write and post a report to a web site, to contribute to an online forum debate or respond to a request for expertise all takes time. The cost of that time may be seen to be disproportionate to the value that it adds to an employee's particular business unit. It reduces the time that an employee has available to meet his project deadlines, achieve his already high targets or manage the ever-increasing demands of his workload.

A healthy knowledge management environment relies on the shared contributions of individuals. However, a knowledge-sharing environment is one that is open to all and not restricted to the contributors. It is possible therefore that there could be an imbalance in contributions. Some employees may uphold the corporate value of knowledge sharing and take the time to contribute their ideas and share their expertise regularly. Others may take the opportunity to enhance their own performance, capitalising on the knowledge they can glean and reaping the rewards without actually sharing or contributing at all.

Within the race environment, the issue of individuals protecting their own position or capitalising on the knowledge of others for personal gain was not so applicable. The ethos of the race centres around individuals working together to achieve performance. On yachts where the team was focused on agreed goals and the skipper created an environment of sharing and creativity, crews were keen to share their expertise, coach others and generate new ideas to enhance the speed and performance of their yacht. The result of their shared efforts was clearly evident at the end of each leg.

Leaders need to be fully aware of the 'what's in it for me?' factor that could hinder a knowledge-sharing environment. They need to ensure that measures are put in place to overcome these barriers and encourage knowledge sharing and creation. Rewarding people for their individual performance may need to be considered alongside team or business unit rewards. Jewson, the builders' merchant, identified a need for group incentives during a three-year knowledge-sharing programme. In addition to individuals' performance bonuses the company introduced a further incentive based on the financial performance of the whole group. This added incentive gave managers, who were already earning the maximum individual bonus, an extra incentive to share their knowledge and assist their colleagues.

Energy giant BP cultivated a scheme called the T-shaped manager to get employees to fully embrace the sharing culture. T-shaped management relies on sharing knowledge freely across the organisation (the horizontal part of the 'T') while remaining committed to the individual business unit (the vertical part of the 'T'). BP operates a number of knowledge-sharing initiatives, ensuring employees transfer knowledge across business units and create knowledge around the globe. One such initiative, called 'peer assists', involves collaborating in peer groups, giving advice to or taking advice from other business units. A further initiative involves connecting people from different parts of the company. Known as the 'human portal' this involves a particular type of manager who helps people identify third parties in the organisation who can provide needed information.

Any initiative needs clear incentives. Sharing knowledge has individual benefits as well. Working with colleagues and learning from them enhances an individual's knowledge and self-development and also enables individuals to accomplish tasks they could not otherwise achieve on their own. On yachts where a cultivation culture was evident, processes were put in place for personal development such as individuals wanting to learn more about navigation.

While managers at BP are judged on their ability to meet specific performance targets within their business units, they are also rewarded and promoted according to how effectively they and their team share knowledge with others outside their unit. Other systems used by companies include the balance score card system and annual performance reviews where recognition of an individual's contribution to company knowledge can be recorded and evaluated.

Creating the right culture

It is human nature to look after oneself and the factors affecting knowledge sharing and creation cannot be addressed in isolation. Any leader looking to create a true knowledge-sharing environment needs to look closely at the culture and ethos in which they operate and the behaviours and attributes of team members. What a leader wants to achieve is a culture where team members are continually asking, 'What do I know, how can I share it and how can we use this for our collective benefit?'

Observing the culture of the 12 teams of the BT Global Challenge race, there was seen to be a correlation between those skippers who embraced knowledge sharing and their overall performance in the race. These skippers were also seen to manage their resources and people well.

The higher-performing skippers created an environment characterised by:

- **openness** – where ideas, opinions and feelings are encouraged and welcomed; where individuals feel comfortable sharing their thoughts; where ideas are considered and good ones implemented; where positive recognition and reward is given

- **learning** – where everyone, including the leader, is encouraged to learn and develop; where there is top-down, bottom-up and cross-team learning; where no one is afraid to say they do not know; where sharing of ideas and best practice is central to the ethos of continual improvement and development
- **support and trust** – where team members give both physical and emotional support to one another; where responsibility for a job is shared by the team; where others will divert their attention and give time to assist a colleague in need; where trust is implicit
- **no blame** – where responsibility for mistakes and errors is not apportioned to an individual but where the team shares responsibility; where lessons are learned from mistakes and changes are made to ensure things are done differently or better in the future; where risk is valued as essential for creativity
- **team cohesiveness** – where the team are united; where there is a collective approach to working; where there is an alignment of individual and team goals; where proactivity is encouraged, accountability is shared and there is shared responsibility for success.

THE RELATIONSHIP BETWEEN KNOWLEDGE MANAGEMENT AND EMOTIONAL INTELLIGENCE

The emotional intelligence behaviours were rated high, medium and low based on judgements drawn from the data from the interviews. The following emotional intelligence behaviours were seen to be the most important for the skippers creating a knowledge-sharing environment.

Emotional resilience

The higher-performing skippers were able to retain their focus and were open to questions and challenges on all aspects of sailing, yacht performance and tactical decisions. They were confident to admit if they didn't know the answer or if they had made a mistake. They accepted questions positively and helped their crew to learn and develop. Several lower-performing skippers showed an inability to perform consistently when faced with questions from their crew.

Although the crew would ask questions about sail trim and systems in order to learn and develop their skills, these skippers perceived them as a personal challenge which cast doubt on their ability. One crew, whose skipper showed an inability to cope with questioning, sailed three-quarters of the way around the world without understanding how some of the basic systems on board the yacht worked.

Motivation

Skippers who were highly motivated to do well in the race were always striving to do things better and always looking for new ways of doing things. They encouraged continual learning and improvement through knowledge sharing and creativity. Skippers who were more directional in their style were less open to ideas. They often fostered a blame culture that did not engender learning. There was seen to be inter-watch rivalry on these yachts. One lower-performing skipper advocated a trial-and-error approach to learning but because there was a blame culture the crew were too scared to try anything new. The team would experiment when the skipper was asleep.

Interpersonal sensitivity

The higher-performing skippers were open to the ideas and inputs of crew members. They would listen and consider their suggestions, building on their own ideas to create a new or improved method. They actively sought out and involved individuals with specialist skills in problem solving and decision making. By involving their crew they gained their commitment which inspired them to want to do better.

Some skippers found difficulty in dealing with others and failed to tap into the resources and expertise they had on the yachts. They were unable to build up the support and trust that was needed for crew to want to offer their expertise and advice.

SUMMARY

Knowledge sharing is dependent on good team working and good team working is dependent on knowledge sharing. To lead a successful team, it is critical to create the right environment where team members are dependent on the sharing of knowledge. To facilitate sharing and encourage creativity it is necessary to have appropriate procedures in place. Individual contributions need to be valued and recognised and team-based incentives adopted. Team members need to support one another to achieve their agreed team goal. The culture must encourage learning and continuous improvement and recognise the risk associated with innovation.

LESSONS FROM THE RACE

As a leader today you need to:

1. recognise tacit knowledge as valuable and ensure you use the intellectual capital of your team members

2. create an open environment

3. lead by example and share your experience and expertise

4. recognise the contributions that others are making and reward these appropriately

5. encourage sharing of best practice, constant learning and continual improvement

6. set aside time for team members to be creative

7. accept risk as a necessity for innovation and avoid blame at all costs

8. give others responsibility and accountability and get them involved.

REFERENCES

Birkinshaw, J. (2001) 'Why is knowledge management so difficult?', *Business Strategy Review*, Vol. 12, Issue 1, pp. 11–18.

Bonaventura, M. (1997) 'The benefits of knowledge culture', *Aslib Proceedings*, April, Vol. 49, No. 4, pp. 82–89.

Bonfield, P. (1999) 'Knowledge management strategy at BT', *Managing Information*, Aslib, July/August, 6:6, pp. 26–29.

Boulton, E. S., Libert, B. D. and Samek, S. M. (2000) 'A business model for the new economy', *Journal of Business Strategy*, November/December, p. 29.

Cabrera, A. (2000) 'Making sharing good for all', *FT Mastering Management*, October.

Gupta, A. K. and Govindarajan, V. (2000) 'Knowledge management's social dimension: lessons from Nucor Steel', *Sloan Management Review*, Fall, pp. 71–80.

Hansen, T. M. and von Oetinger, B. (2001) 'Introducing T-shaped managers, knowledge management's next generation', *Harvard Business Review*, March, pp. 107–116.

Lucas, E. (2001) 'Creating a give & take culture', *Professional Manager*, May, pp. 11–13.

Manasco, B. (2001) 'Generating lasting value', *Knowledge Strategies*, July.

Nonaka, I. and Takeuchi, H. (1995) *The Knowledge-Creating Company*, Oxford University Press: Oxford.

Quintas, P. (2001) 'Guru interview', *ManagementFirst.com*, MCB University Press: Bradford.

Webb, S. P. (1998) *Knowledge Management: Linchpin of Change*, Aslib: London.

Wilson, D. A. (1996) *Managing Knowledge*, Butterworth-Heinemann: Oxford.

DIVERSITY AT WORK
Chaplaincy at The NEC Group

The NEC Group has offered a chaplaincy service dating back to the opening of the NEC in 1976. The chaplain, an ordained Christian minister, functions across the company's five venues in two separate geographic locations. The chaplaincy is wholly ecumenical in that it is supported by all Christian denominations, but the scope of the chaplain's work is not restricted by faith, commitment or cultural background. The NEC Group staff, with around 1000 full-time, permanent people and several thousand more in temporary and casual roles, is richly multi-ethnic and multi-faith.

Access to the service is available to all members of staff, organisers of events at the venues and visitors to those events. An essential element of the service is its availability irrespective of the faith community to which an individual belongs. Its multi-faith approach is illustrated well by the response to the attacks on the US in September 2001. On the European Day of Remembrance the chaplain led a short period of worship, observing three minutes' silence, attended by 300 staff and visitors from diverse faiths. The service was inclusive in its language and content so all could worship irrespective of faith, commitment or culture. On this and all public occasions, as well as in day-to-day practice of the role, the chaplaincy is committed to a style and content that engages all.

The current chaplain has been with the company since 1987 and is the fourth Christian minister to hold the post. In order to fulfil the role across two different geographic locations, the post is assisted by a lay chaplain.

The service is really appreciated by staff in the whole of the NEC. In a survey in September 2001, 79 per cent of both permanent and temporary staff agreed with the following statement. 'My colleagues respect individuals of other cultures and backgrounds.'

12

VALUING DIFFERENCE

Contributions to this chapter were made
by the following Forum members:
Sue Gover, Margaret Gordon and Erica Paterson,
Inspiring Performance

INTRODUCTION

Valuing difference is essentially about creating business benefit from
managing differences in race, sex, age and creed. It is about creating a
culture where difference is sought, respected and endorsed in order to
realise the full potential of the workforce. It is about creating a culture
of sustainability, a great place to be, where people want to work. This
means having the correct ethical standards, valuing difference and
developing each individual employee because of the value they bring.

> *Achieving diversity is about bringing together a rich mix of people,*
> *with differing perspectives and from different backgrounds, and cre-*
> *ating an environment in which their differences are valued. A*
> *vibrant, open and creative culture. A culture in which ideas flourish,*
> *where people thrive, grow and have fun. A culture where energy is*
> *unleashed. A winning culture for the 21st century.*

Schneider (2001)

One of the consequences of the emergence of global companies has
been the challenge of managing global workforces. Emirates Airlines in
Dubai employs 83 different nationalities; Jumeirah International has 53

in its hotel chain. So what are the major issues that have to be addressed to ensure that effective management of a diverse workforce can be a business advantage? They can be as disparate as age, personal and corporate background, education, lifestyle, religion, sexual preference, geographic origin and disability. In some organisations as many as 20 different issues are covered and chief diversity officers are being employed.

This chapter will help the leader understand why valuing difference is so important today and explore the nature and complexity of diversity. The areas of ethnicity, gender, ageism and religion will be looked at together with their relationship with performance. Lessons will be drawn from the race where applicable and causes and strategies will be supported by examples. The relationship with emotional intelligence will be addressed.

BACKGROUND

At the end of the Second World War, women, who had contributed to the war effort on both sides, returned to their domestic duties and the sense of sexual equality created by the wartime culture disappeared. Women were still given few responsible roles in helping to manage society.

The 1960s saw a change in the perception of the role of women in the Western world, with the rise of feminism, immigration into the first world from third world countries and the start of equal opportunities. Anti-discrimination legislation began to appear in Europe during the 1970s. In the US legislation was more a 'numbers' game. What mattered was how many women, how many people from ethnic minorities and how many people with disabilities were employed. Many organisations had not yet realised the benefits of a diverse workforce and instead focused on complying with legislation rather than dealing with the underlying issues.

Adherence to the concept of equal opportunity took on a momentum of its own. It brought an awareness of the inequality in the workplace and the need for radical change. The approach of 'treating everyone the same', often described as equal opportunities but in reality equal treatment, does not address or value difference and yet for many people is seen as all that is required. The problem is that it often brings men and women into direct competition with one another as they endeavour to be the same. This can be unsettling in both working relationships and marriages. Affirmative Action, introduced in the 1970s by the US government to ensure equal opportunities, supposed that the contribution of all was potentially the same and should be judged the same; any variation was deemed unfair discrimination.

Today chief executives appreciate that meritocracy has to be paramount if bottom-line performance is to be maximised, so valuing difference has become a business imperative. It requires having an understanding of increasingly international markets, a diversity in skills to meet the operational needs and a diversity in age and experience to bring different perspectives.

Nationwide Building Society, for example, believes that a diverse workforce better reflects its customer base, helps it to understand customer needs and helps to develop business solutions that meet market needs. The company is fully committed to equal opportunities for both its customers and employees: 'It demonstrates we value the contribution of all employees which in turn improves commitment, motivation, morale, productivity, reduces stress and absenteeism and improves customer satisfaction.'

BT believes that introducing flexibility of work location and attendance is hugely inclusive, opening opportunities to women, carers and people with disabilities that may otherwise be inaccessible to them. The company believes that by addressing work/life balance it is addressing diversity as well.

Globalisation has also increased the need for valuing difference in the workforce in order to respond to different markets. Global businesses must adapt their products and services to the needs of local markets that may differ greatly from each other. British American Tobacco (BAT) has as one of its principles 'strength from diversity'. It emphasises the fact that it is a global company operating in a global market and hence needs to employ different nationalities in order to meet the demands of its customers. BAT focuses on the positive aspects of diversity and encourages its employees to understand other cultures in order to generate a more global perspective. Unilever describes itself as a 'multilocal multinational', reflecting the requirement to respond to local differences.

Valuing difference is no longer about getting others to fit in; it is about encouraging everyone to stand back and take a look at themselves in order to find out what it is that is preventing inclusion. Is there an aspect of a person or country's culture that is inappropriately excluding others?

> *You learn to live with people and become more tolerant.*

New ideas and innovation come from people and when people come together with different perspectives, greater creativity results. The more employees are involved in the decision making, the greater the retention rate of those employees. Sustainability, one of the major boardroom issues today, follows. In 2000 the UK government requested several large employers to undertake an audit of their employment practices in relation to the issues of sustainability.

UNDERSTANDING DIFFERENCE

Before there can be competitive advantage from valuing difference, it is important for leaders to try to understand the differences that exist and their implication in the workplace.

Ethnicity

One of the many problems facing the CEO of a multinational organisation is how to cope with the ethnic pressure groups that can lie within the workforce. Ethnicity is adhering to a distinct culture with a long shared history. It arises when individuals of a particular ethnic and cultural background band together to promote their particular ethnic interests. Two examples are the Hispanic lobby in the US and the Asian lobby in the UK. In both cases these groups expect consideration for their particular cultural needs from the countries/organisations to which they belong. The problem arises when the needs of another ethnic, cultural or religious group from within the same country or organisation are diametrically opposed. A classic example is the expectation of Jewish or Muslim workers to be allowed to observe their religious holidays when working in an essentially Western/Christian organisation. Finding a solution is not easy.

Individualistic and collective cultures

Another difference that has to be addressed is the approach that different cultures take to decision making and communication. Individualism (Hofstede, 1980) is the extent to which individual decision making and action within a specific culture is accepted and encouraged. Some cultures view individualism positively and see it as the basis for creativity; others in a collective culture see it as disruptive to group harmony and co-operation. In individualistic cultures, such as the US, UK and Germany, communication tends to be in the transmitted message. The message is usually loud and clear and direct in its approach. The idea of encouraging dissent is healthy. Relationships are formed as a result of individuals doing business together. Business is not normally mixed with pleasure and the principle of 'don't take this personally' is acceptable. Business life and home life are separated.

In collective cultures, predominantly in the East, communication tends to be less direct and more based on inference. Only minimal direct information is transmitted; much is left to interpretation. Candour is more difficult than in individualistic cultures. Here, personal relationships have to be cemented before business can begin. Significantly, there is lower employee turnover in these cultures and greater corporate loyalty. Home life is very much part of work life and there is a strong affiliation between the two. People from individualistic cultures can find it very difficult to penetrate collective cultures.

Although the BT Global Challenge originates in Britain, it attracts crew volunteers from all over the world. Within various crews both individualistic and collective cultures existed. Those with an individualistic culture tended to have good inter-group relations with other yachts. Some yachts had a more collective culture, and one crew deliberately chose to nurture a very collective culture. Their aim was to be perceived that way and their behaviour endorsed it. They were more distant from the other crews and were less gregarious. It was hard for other crews to penetrate this culture.

Many of the leggers came from other countries. Joining their yachts for just one leg at different stages throughout the race was often not just about joining a well-formed team, but also about joining a culture that could be very different from their own. Where a strong collective culture was established, great attention was paid to the integration of leggers. Some teams relished the diversity that the leggers brought to the team and were able to utilise them fully. One legger, from a collective national culture, found the culture on the yacht very individualistic and very different from anything he had experienced previously. Other skippers were unable to capitalise on the diversity of their teams and leggers never felt either valued or part of the team. They were never asked for input, nor what expertise they had.

Language

Within different cultures the forms of expression vary greatly. Where there is neutral expression, feelings are controlled and seldom expressed. Where there is affective expression, emotions play a large part in the communication. Tone of voice varies, body language is different, the amount of personal space required varies, as does the amount of acceptable touching. Many Southern Europeans become very animated in their conversations and there is a lot of physical contact, whereas Northern Europeans tend to be more reserved in their approach, with less visible emotion or physical contact.

For some crew members English was not their first language and they found it difficult to understand the full meaning of what was being said, particularly if strong regional accents and vernacular were involved. They also had to learn the technical terms of sailing, which added to the language barrier. The use of slang exacerbated the problem and in such adverse conditions this sometimes led to real problems. The way in which the same swear words were used to describe events that were very good and very bad was particularly confusing.

The words spoken can also cause confusion through different understandings of the same word. It has been said that America and Britain are two countries divided by a common language. Words and gestures do not travel across the ocean and can cause misunderstandings and offence.

Humour was another area of difference. Humour is culture- and language-dependent and often includes a different understanding of the same word or phrase. One British watch leader played a practical joke on a crew volunteer. This was viewed by an American as an abuse of power and out of line. Some skippers had nicknames for their crew members which did not translate easily.

Language includes body language. Interpreting body language can be far more hazardous for foreigners than the spoken language. Gestures vary in meaning and can be offensive in some cultures. Physical contact was viewed by some crew members as inappropriate behaviour; others as reassuring and comforting. The acknowledged greeting and the accepted way of eating are all potential pitfalls for the unwary business traveller. To fail to understand the ritual of exchanging business cards before starting a business meeting in Japan implies getting off to a very bad start. To be offended by lip smacking at a Chinese meal denotes misunderstanding of the pleasure implied.

Although the crews had a predominance of British subjects, each yacht had a mix of cultures. Some yachts had as many as five or six nationalities. These ranged from North European, South European, North American, South American, Canadian, Australian, New Zealand, Chinese and Singaporean.

On BP one of the crew members was profoundly deaf. The skipper and the crew spent a great deal of time addressing the issue of communication. During training they spent time with ear plugs in their ears to try to understand the difficulties. Systems were set up to help integrate this crew member into the team.

For businesses to communicate effectively in local markets they must have employees who can speak the local languages.

Ethnocentrism and parochialism

Some cultures are based on the assumption of superiority over others.

This is caused by either:

- ethnocentrism or
- parochialism.

Ethnocentrism (Punnett, 1998) is the belief that 'our way' is better than 'their way' based on a historical perspective. There is a conscious evaluation of other societies and a consequent belief that the home country is superior. Parochialism (Adler, 2001) also assumes that the home culture is superior but for different reasons. It arises from an in-built suspicion and lack of knowledge of other cultures.

Some yachts became very parochial – 'we always do it this way.' They viewed themselves as best and were unable to look at other yachts and honestly compare them. National differences produced both ethnocentric and parochial tendencies over humour, behaviour and values. There is a natural tendency to put negative labels on those whose behaviour differs from our own. Some skippers were unable to understand cultural differences and consequently took the defensive stance that their culture had to be superior. One crew, by the start of the race, had so isolated themselves from the rest of the fleet by their apparent sense of superiority that they had lost the support and camaraderie that are an inherent part of the Challenge ethos. The skipper realised what was happening and the culture of this crew changed early on in the race and they became an integral part of the fleet.

It is important to understand what lies behind the culture being dealt with. Where different nationalities are meeting to work together, a deep understanding of their different cultures is almost a prerequisite. It is equally important to understand that some cultures have an inbred suspicion or historical feeling of superiority over other cultures. To this day the Chinese word for 'foreigner' also means 'foreign devil'.

Ascription and achievement

Another significant factor is how different cultures accord status. Ascription cultures (Trompenaars and Hampden-Turner, 1998) respect age and experience and background far more than achievement. Historically, ascription cultures have attributed status by birth, kinship, gender and age. Today, in these cultures, age and experience, education and professional qualifications are the important elements. Recognition in Japan is based more on experience than on merit. The belief is that you cannot get to the top unless you have spent a lifetime learning, maturing and proving yourself. It is culturally oriented rather than work design oriented. They have always held older people in great respect. In their culture older people command particular respect because of their implied wisdom; for a Western business to choose to send a young negotiator to deal with a Japanese executive 10 or 20 years his senior implies an ignorance of cultural difference. When the first Nissan plant was opened in Tyneside the British workforce was not used to Japanese management and work techniques and took a long time to adjust.

Achievement cultures feel that ascribing status for reasons other than achievement is archaic and inappropriate for business. Achievement is about results and not what you have done before or where you have come from. Setting up a Western company in South East Asia with a focus on output figures per employee will encounter problems with the local culture.

The BT Global Challenge was concerned with achievement, not ascription. Entry was open to everyone (provided they could raise the money); there were no barriers on the grounds of class or ability. The ethos was to allow everyone the opportunity to take part. Sir Chay Blyth was looking for crew volunteers with determination, commitment and enthusiasm. He was interested in what they could achieve, not what they had done, nor where they had come from. People went to enormous lengths to raise the money. They held auctions, fetes, sold home-made produce, sold their houses, their cars, etc.

Today there is no evidence to suggest that either ascription or achievement is more successful in business terms. Success is probably best attained by combining the two cultures. Ascribing status to people by way of their skills and qualifications and getting them to live up to it through achievement produces high performance.

Religious customs

One of the greatest areas of difference today comes from religious belief and customs. With global travel, global organisations and immigration, many people are living and working in countries whose founding beliefs are different from their own. Mosques and Buddhist temples are far more prevalent in the Western world than they were 20 years ago. The New World comprises nations of people who are historically from very different backgrounds and creeds. According to Trompenaars and Hampden-Turner (1998), there is a correlation between Protestant cultures and achievement orientation, and Catholic, Buddhist, Hindu and Jewish cultures and ascription. With many different historical cultures, living together in one country can have its problems. As a result many ethnic groups live together in townships within cities. There they live according to the customs of their culture rather than the culture of the host country (see 'Ethnicity', page 348). Many Western cities have a Chinatown and a little India where the shops and places of religion are those of the immigrant population.

There are many areas of difference in religious custom that must be understood and valued in order to avoid offence.

The working week

As mentioned in Chapter 8, work/life balance is being threatened by a seven-day week. The weekend is different around the world, based on the religious beliefs of different countries. Islamic countries observe Friday as a day of prayer; the Jewish Sabbath is Saturday; the Christian Sabbath is Sunday. Valuing these differences shows a respect for that religion. Failure to do so not only shows a disrespect but also encroaches on people's private lives.

Holidays and festivals

Holidays around the world also vary in their religious festivals. In cosmopolitan societies these must be added to the calendar, if not for observance then for awareness. These vary from Jewish festivals to US Thanksgiving, from Chinese New Year to Christmas. Some Christian countries in the West have ceased to talk about Christmas and Easter holidays in deference to other religions and many greetings cards around these festivals now say 'Happy Holidays'.

On most yachts Christmas, New Year and Easter were celebrated with special meals and gifts.

Prayer observance

Companies today are more aware of employees' requirements for daily prayer and are making provision for them.

On the yachts, there was little official religious observance except on Olympic. This crew observed a broadly Christian Sunday service, which accommodated other beliefs and included a prayer to the Greek god of wind when they were becalmed.

Religious food observance

There are many religious observances around food and the way it is prepared. Some foods are viewed as 'unclean' within certain religions; some animals must be killed in a certain way. There are some who eat no meat at all. This can make catering in multi-national organisations much more complex. Conferences, conventions and events must be carefully planned and co-ordinated to account for the many requirements. For example, when planning the dates and venues for leadership and teambuilding workshops for a year-long contract for a global organisation, Inspiring Performance had to take into account the different festivals and food requirements of many nationalities involved.

While the yachts did not need to provide specific food on religious grounds, vegetarians needed to be included in the provisioning.

Women in society

Religions view the place of women in society in different ways. Some are allowed to work, others not. Some have strict dress codes. When working with women of different cultures it is important to respect these differences.

In light of the terrible atrocities of September 11 2001, executed in the name of religion, it is the responsibility of everyone to seek to understand and value different religions, their customs and beliefs.

Ageism

For at least the past three decades age has not 'had its privilege' in the Western world. CEOs have got younger and younger and those with grey hairs have watched in awe as their younger colleagues have taken the top jobs. Generation battles have ensued and the middle-aged have learned to be acutely wary of those coming up behind them.

Nevertheless, people are beginning to respect age for several reasons. According to Matthew Gwyther (2001), one of the reasons for this is that in the Western world the age balance is changing. For example, in Britain by 2020 the number of working people under 50 will have dropped by 2 million and a quarter of workers will be over the age of 50. There is an ever-increasing population of over 65-year-olds and an ever-decreasing number of people to look after them. There is pressure to re-employ older people and to dissuade them from retiring early.

However, other reasons have also come to the fore in favour of the more mature. Physically people are staying active much longer and even within showbusiness glamour is no longer the privilege of the young. Those who have been in business longer have been tested and have learned from their mistakes. They have an understanding youth cannot have. The health and energy of many 50-year-olds is every bit as good as that of their younger colleagues. Another reason for the change of heart is that job movement is so great. The fact that an older person may want to work for only another five years is irrelevant. The average time in any one job today is around three years.

Different age ranges bring different abilities (Gwyther, 2001). Table 12.1 shows the advantages of each.

The BT Global Challenge was open to anyone from 21–60. The age range was roughly equal on all the yachts. The youngest watch leader was only 23 and the oldest was 58. One of the oldest members of the fleet was on the fore deck, usually associated with young, fit 'lads'. On the whole, this large age diversity provided great depth to the teams, with both young and old learning from each other. However, ageism occurred on some yachts. One skipper made derogatory remarks to an older member of the crew. One older crew member was not allowed to do fore deck work until an incident occurred where he was the only

TABLE 12.1   The abilities of different age groups

Age range	Different abilities
20–25	Have better short- and long-term memories and are probably fitter, but they are still short of life skills and can be seen as insensitive and arrogant
26–35	Are more prone to stress-related conditions as they have a tendency to have few commitments outside work and a demanding lifestyle
36–45	Staying power is as much about the state of mind as the state of body and this age is the perfect combination of mental and physical endurance
46–55	Have wisdom but slower learning
56 upwards	Reduced physical strength but greater ability to cope with the crises in life

person available. The skipper then saw how capable he was and added him to the fore deck crew.

Several yachts made full use of the diversity of age. Wisdom was sought both by the skippers and the younger crew volunteers. On one yacht one of the older crew volunteers was used as a sounding board for many of the skipper's concerns and provided experienced counsel when dealing with interpersonal problems. 'Mother figures' emerged, becoming pivotal for the team and their skippers. One older female crew member, who went on permanent motherwatch in the Southern Ocean, raised the morale of the team by her 'second effort' in all things. The best possible meals were provided, very often from a bare cupboard, and always on time. A cup of tea was always there when crew were woken for a watch.

What is needed today is a mixed workforce of all ages with the blend of energy and experiences that brings. It is a matter of balance. The podium skippers were best able to strike that balance which channelled the strengths of all ages into the appropriate jobs.

Gender

Although more women are 'breaking the glass ceiling' and moving into executive and leadership positions, the top echelon in most companies is still a man's world. According to Susan J. Wells (2001), in the US 43 per cent of the middle executive, administrative and managerial occupations are held by women but only 3–5 per cent of top executive positions are held by women. The Fortune 500 companies have doubled their number of female corporate officer titles, but that still only brings the proportion to 10 per cent. In many Latin American companies there is not a single woman on a corporate board. There are still countries where girls are not educated and female babies are left to die.

This lack of female promotion is hard to understand when many international surveys have indicated that many women possess a unique combination of interpersonal and work ethic traits that are ideally suited for today's environment. The many reasons for the problem range from 'glass ceiling' issues to interruptions in career to a high attrition rate as women leave to start up their own companies.

To succeed in business many women have 'mimicked a male role'. However, this strategy may have backfired on those adopting it. Talent wars, demanding stakeholders and other intangibles, ask for a different kind of leadership than was required even five years ago. Many companies are not looking for a top-down authority figure but want more collaborative, inclusive approaches to leadership – and the stereotyped macho leader may not meet the bill.

Tom Peters (2001) argues that women understand the primacy of massive investment in relationships. He believes that one of the premier untapped sources of leadership talent in the world today rests with women. In his article he asks the following questions:

- Who manages more things at once?
- Who usually takes care of the detail?
- Who finds it easier to meet new people?
- Who asks more questions in a conversation?
- Who encourages harmony and agreement?
- Who keeps in touch with others?

The answer to all the questions was women.

In the main, men and women choose to lead and follow in different ways and this can be ascribed to physical differences in the brain.

- In 1962 Roger Sperry won a Nobel Prize for identifying that the two hemispheres of the brain were home to different intellectual functions. This affects the way we perceive things.
- Carter (1998) shows the physical differences of the male and female brain. Not only are they physically different but they work in a different way. The female brain has a larger bridge connecting the left- and right-hand sides of the brain. This gives them the ability to use both sides of the brain at the same time. The male brain, with its smaller bridge, allows for concentrated working on one side or the other, not both. As a result, the genders' approach to the same situation is very often totally different.
- Women see things holistically and tend to want to talk through a situation both rationally and emotionally before reaching a decision. Men tend to shut down one or other side of their brain in order to concentrate fully on either the rational or the emotional side of the situation. Gray (1992) points out how difficult it can be for men and women to see things from the opposite perspective. Men tend to jump straight to solutions, women like to share emotions before arriving at solutions. Men want space, women want understanding. Men state what they want, women ask what others want.

Because of our differently formed brains we learn in a different way. In 2001 girls were still outperforming boys at GCSE level. Boys have a shorter attention span than girls but demonstrate aptitudes for detailed memory tasks. Girls develop verbal and written skills more rapidly and have better communication skills.

Men tend to lead from the top through action; they are highly competitive, task driven, focused and tend to take more risks. Women tend to lead from the middle through relationships. They like to talk, to make decisions through debate, to look at

‘ It was important to remember the left/right side of the brain and to allocate tasks accordingly. ’

issues from all angles. They concentrate more on alliances than competition (Cook and Rothwell, 2000).

On the yachts the way in which problems were addressed were seen to be different in men and women, as shown in Table 12.2.

In a complex and changing world, leadership has moved away from the command-and-control school of leadership, more suited to the male brain, to one of relationships and communication, more suited to the female brain.

Out of a total of 392 people participating in the BT Global Challenge race, the gender split was 27 per cent females, 73 per cent males. This ratio was the same for both core crew and leggers. However, an interesting difference emerges when considering positions of authority: at the outset only 8 per cent of watch leaders and 16 per cent of the skippers were

TABLE 12.2 The behaviours observed in problem solving by the different genders

Women	Men
Relationship focused	Action centred
Consensus seeking	Decision making
Active listening	Doing
Coaching	Directing
Analysing	Inventive
Interpersonally sensitive	Visualising
Intuitive	Risk taking
Detail focused	Factual
Team oriented	Looking at the big picture
Recognition oriented	Achievement oriented
Multi-tasking	Tunnel visioned
Interdependent	Independent
Transformational	Transactional

female. Out of the 186 skippers who applied for the race, there were only two female skippers. They were both selected on merit. These figures compare with industry in that the ratios are similar in the general workforce where males predominate in leadership and management roles.

The contribution of women to high performance

With each yacht having an equal number of females within the core crew, it is difficult to make hard links between performance and gender. Key themes that emerged during the race can be grouped into characteristics, behaviours and culture/environment.

Characteristics

It was recognised throughout the fleet that many females had great tenacity and resilience. They showed a greater attention to detail and a greater concentration span. They showed more intuitive and sensing behaviour and were mentally stronger, having the ability to dig deeper inside themselves when circumstances warranted.

Women were often better able to handle interpersonal issues and on several yachts the male skipper successfully passed this responsibility over to female crew. 'In times of adversity the guys would meet it by being macho and the women would just quietly deal with it and endure it.'

Behaviours

In the 'pressure cooker' environment of a 72ft steel racing yacht the ability to deal with interpersonal issues is vital. Crew members interviewed generally felt that women were more tactful at addressing issues, talking things through before confronting people, whereas the men generally went straight for confrontation or became introspective. Women tended to be more emotional and were less able to forgive and forget.

‘ The women seem to air and discuss issues, get more involved. The guys walk away. ’

Women brooded more than men who favoured aggression to release emotion. Men tended to focus on solving the problem or getting the task done, whereas women would be concerned about the relationships and how the task got done. Women tend to look through a wide-angled lens, the male through a telephoto lens (Cook and Rothwell, 2000).

Culture/environment

It was felt on many of the yachts that women brought a levelling element to the culture. Several women strengthened their position through their femininity. They approached difficult situations sensitively and encouraged sharing of feelings.

> **' I feel that I am as big and strong as any man on the boat. I never feel that I am in any way less of a person and I can hold my own. I have more experience and can do every role on the yacht. '**

One crew member, on a less successful yacht, commented that, while he was personally impressed with the ability of some of the women, his (male) skipper was less enthusiastic; a female crew member in his team commented: 'In decision-making sessions you are absolutely not heard … do I even exist? I've never been anywhere where I've been less encouraged to think.'

Relationships

Perhaps an obvious aspect to consider when looking at the impact of gender in the workplace is that of relationships within a team. At the outset of the race, most of the teams' 'ground rules' stipulated that there should be no personal relationships on board. On most yachts there was a feeling of being androgynous. However, during the race a number of relationships did develop, either within the same crew or between members of different crews. In the main, provided the relationship was not disruptive to the rest of the team, this was regarded with tolerance.

> **' They do behave appropriately and it isn't a problem. '**

Inspiring leadership

Organisations are looking for inspiring leadership as the rate of change in the environment requires quantum leaps rather than progressive transitions. The attributes can no longer be either male or female. The transformational models introduced by Alimo-Metcalfe and Alban-Metcalfe (2001) and Goffee and Jones (2000) set out behaviours required for leadership today that are both male and female (see Chapter 3). Although it is accepted that women tend to be more trans-formational in their leadership and men more transactional, the real requirement is an ability in both.

In today's competitive business world, where the workforce is split 50:50 men/women, we need a culture that encourages 100 per cent contribution from both genders. If women are trying to compete with men and if men are anxious about offending women or are ignoring them, there is a loss of effort, energy and talent.

Mutuality

Belbin (2001) believes that mutuality is needed today. People should build on gender differences rather than ignore them, promote team-building rather than assertiveness, encourage women to develop their own leadership style and believe that mixed gender groups offer a better balance. Some skippers recognised the differences in gender right from the start and by

' We use the best skills of each volunteer and if the cooking skills are with a female member of the crew, so be it. '

working on strengths built them into the infrastructure. Skippers who found out what each person brought to the team were able to use their skills and talents to best effect, while those who applied a stereotypical judgement to abilities lost opportunities.

A member of the fore deck crew on one of the yachts was the smallest and probably one of the lightest girls in the fleet. One of the strongest men in the fleet was used for his abilities to coach and motivate the team. One skipper, who acknowledged that attention to detail is generally a female attribute, gave all the details of required flags, documentation and deadline for submissions for ports of call to one of his female crew members. Another female crew member was given the job of PR. The winning skipper had a male and female watch leader. The combination of different attributes was complementary in his management team.

VALUING DIFFERENCE

Valuing difference effectively requires acknowledgement, recognition and value.

Acknowledgement

Valuing difference is about learning to acknowledge people for what they are, where they come from, what their preferences are and what their strengths are. It is about listening to others and having tolerance to others' ways even if they are very different. It is about recognising that the world is made up of many different cultures, that people have many varying reasons for their behaviour. It requires patience and takes time.

Recognition

In order to value difference, we must first understand it. In order to understand the difference between ourselves and others we must first understand ourselves.

Value

The business value of difference was best summed up by Meredith Belbin (1999) in his early research that proved conclusively that teams that were made up of very similar individuals fared worst whereas those that demonstrated the greatest range of differences, in all its richness already described, performed best.

THE RELATIONSHIP BETWEEN VALUING DIFFERENCE AND EMOTIONAL INTELLIGENCE

The emotional intelligence behaviours were rated high, medium and low based on judgements drawn from the data collected from the interviews.

The following emotional intelligence behaviours were seen to be the most important for skippers valuing difference.

Self-awareness

Fundamental to the skippers' ability to understand their crews was their ability to understand themselves, not least controlling their emotions in situations of great stress and danger.

> ' I learned more about myself on this race than I learned about my crew. '

A particular demand on the professional sailing skippers was to see beyond the initial flounderings of their amateur crew to the broader depths of talent that lay within them. This required tolerance, which for many skippers had to be learned. The higher-performing skippers showed a greater tolerance of others than some lower-performing skippers. There were times when perspectives on issues were very different. These were often caused by background and culture. There were times when disagreements as to what was right and wrong had to be resolved. The skipper of VERITAS had to make the right call as to whether or not to return to the Southern Ocean after the accident that seriously injured two crew members.

Interpersonal sensitivity

The skippers had to manage the needs and perceptions of their crew members all the time. It required sensitive handling. Getting buy-in to decisions could be a difficult task when dealing with people from varied cultures and backgrounds.

> ' He's aware in a people sense. '

Another demand was when dealing with leggers, who were joining the yacht in the middle of the race and coping with a culture that was often not their own. One of the podium skippers realised that he had not been sufficiently aware of the needs of his leggers in the early legs and made a huge effort to include them in decision making in the latter legs. The ability to utilise interpersonal sensitivity was essential in order to understand their needs and perceptions and to ensure that their strengths were both understood and utilised.

Influence

Bringing together the many and varied factions that emerged on different crews throughout the race required great influence on the part of the skippers. The BT Global Challenge race always has the inherent anomaly that crew members are both fee-paying clients and subject to the maritime authority of their skippers. The skipper's ability to exert influence as well as authority was the combination that produced results. The higher-performing skippers, who had built up a trust through their ability to value each individual for what they were and not for what they should be, found the ability to influence a much easier one.

' His whole being allows him to influence the crew into accepting his viewpoint. '

Conscientiousness

Dealing with crew members from such a varied background required patience and clear commitment on the part of the skippers. The key was to behave honestly and openly in a way that was sustainable, treating each crew member with dignity and endeavouring to build relationships with all crew members. It required tolerance and understanding when dealing with cultures that were different, when opinions were based on different value sets and when customs were not aligned. The ability to utilise conscientiousness enabled the skippers to behave in an ethical manner and to genuinely value the differences in their crews.

SUMMARY

Valuing difference is about bringing together the wealth of difference in people. It is about taking advantage of cultural differences, backgrounds

' The skipper recognises that people are different – he will always find the best in people. ' and preferences to produce a culture that is full of colour and strength. It means each person is treated as an individual and valued for their beliefs, values, training needs, roles and responsibilities. For sound historical reasons, cultures approach right and wrong, good and evil in a different way. Individuals need to discuss their differences and to respect the feelings and convictions of other people.

LESSONS FROM THE RACE

As a leader today you need to:

1. never take things for granted and expect that people understand what you have said. Probe for clarification

2. remember to use humour appropriately and be aware of your audience

3. manage gender appropriately and use the strengths of each to advantage

4. use joint gender decision making – it can be powerful

5. replace the age of discrimination against minority groups with a positive understanding of everyone's strengths

6. understand and tolerate cultural and religious differences

7. value all ages

8. understand that valuing is no longer purely a moral issue but a competitive advantage

9. use the emotional intelligence behaviours as an aid to valuing difference.

REFERENCES:

Adler, N. J. (2001) *Managing a World View,* Thomson Learning: London.

Alimo-Metcalfe, B. and Alban-Metcalfe, R. J. (2001) 'The development of a new transformational leadership questionnaire', *The Journal of Occupational & Organisational Psychology,* 74, in press.

Belbin, M. (1999) *Team Roles at Work,* Butterworth Heinemann: Oxford.

Belbin, M. (2001*) Managing without Power,* Butterworth Heinemann: Oxford.

Carter, R. (1998) *Mapping the Mind,* Weidenfeld & Nicholson: London.

Cook, L. and Rothwell, B. (2000) *The X and Y of Leadership,* The Industrial Society: London.

Goffee, R. and Jones, G. (2000) 'Why should anyone be led by you?', *Harvard Business Review, Sept–Oct,* pp. 63–70.

Gray, J. (1992*) Men are from Mars, Women are from Venus,* Thorsons: London.

Gwyther, M. (2001) 'Battle of the ages', *Management Today,* April.

Hofstede, G. (1980*) Culture's Consequences,* Sage: London.

Peters, T. (2001) 'Ladies and gentlemen, the captain has turned on the "fasten seat belt" sign', *Fast Company,* March, pp. 126–140.

Punnett, B. J. (1998) *Cross National Diversity: Does it Affect International Expansion Decisions?,* The Fraser Institute: Vancouver, Canada.

Schneider, R. (2001) 'Variety performance', *People Management,* 3 May, pp. 26–31.

Trompenaars, F. and Hampden-Turner, C. (1998) *Riding the Waves of Culture,* Nicholas Brealey Publishing: London.

Wells, S. J. (2001) 'A female executive is hard to find', *HR Magazine,* June.

IV

A GREAT PLACE TO BE

CULTURE AT WORK
Tenon Group

Tenon began life as a company in February 2000. The company's intention was to acquire high-quality accountancy and other business advisory groups in the UK in order to establish a broadly based professional services group. Since its formation, Tenon has acquired nine firms and three niche businesses and has established one new venture.

Because of this exceptional growth and the resulting need for teamwork of the highest order, the business has foreseen the need to grow a common culture that links all the people in Tenon.

One of the first steps was to develop the core values that link all the businesses. These values arose from extensive consultation among the group. Tenon's values begin with its commitment to its clients and people. It is a unique business that offers a *fresh* and innovative approach and is open *and* honest, showing the highest standards of professionalism and *integrity*. It works as one team across all its disciplines, and takes a commercial and practical approach to improve its clients' success. These values have started to be embedded into all the recruitment and induction processes as well as training programmes. They will become part of the measure of performance management and leadership evaluation.

Because of the rapidly changing business it has been essential to extensively communicate within the group. Each stage of change has involved consultation and feedback. A meritocracy principle has been established, ensuring that the right person is selected for the job and that there are opportunities for all. This has generated a wide range of new opportunities within the group.

These benefits and activities are not just internally focused as Tenon offers a number of business services to its clients. It acts as business adviser and mentor to new and growing companies. Professionalism in Tenon is encouraged through the organisational support for professional qualifications. More than 65 per cent of the workforce have achieved or are studying for professional examinations. This learning culture is orientated to achieving the best result for the company's clients.

The openness within Tenon is assisted through the use of technology, communication and teamwork. Everyone has access to everyone else via email. News is announced simultaneously. Teambuilding programmes and social events are open to all.

In 2002 an integration team will build common processes in all the businesses and the cultural challenge will continue.

13

CREATING A CULTURE

INTRODUCTION

This chapter sets out to look at the subject of culture and what it takes for a leader to create an environment where the team feel inspired, committed and driven to achieve results. The chapter will explore the elements needed to produce a culture of openness, collaborative working practices, continued learning and sustained performance.

Initially we will look at what constitutes a culture and the different types that may be seen within teams and organisations. Working with a model identified by William Schneider (2000) and focusing on the four core cultures of control, collaboration, competence and cultivation, the chapter will identify the cultural indicators of the teams in the BT Global Challenge race.

The chapter will then address the interrelation between goals, leadership and culture in the pursuit of performance and outline the need for cultural flexibility that was evidenced during the race.

Taking the two types of culture seen within the fleet – performance and inspiring – the chapter will identify the factors that contributed to the creation of these cultures. It will conclude with a look at the synergistic effect of bringing these two cultures together and the creation of 'A Great Place To Be'.

WHAT IS CULTURE?

Trompenaars *et al.* (1998) argues that a fish discovers its need for water only when it is no longer in it. Culture is like water to a fish. It sustains individuals. They live and breathe through it. Culture is the repeated behaviour of individuals handed from one generation to another. These behaviours come from a mutual interpretation of core beliefs and values based on inner assumptions. What one culture may regard as essential may not be so vital to other cultures.

Atkinson (Mullins, 1999) explains organisational culture as 'reflecting the underlying assumptions about the way that work is performed, what is 'acceptable and not acceptable' and what behaviour and actions are encouraged and discouraged'.

Trompenaars believes that these inner assumptions are based on individuals' differing needs for survival. Historically, civilisations have fought daily with nature, whether it be too much water, too little water, cold, heat, avalanches or swamps. The solutions to these problems become so obvious that they disappear from consciousness. They become part of our assumptions. It is only with a realisation that the basic assumption must change for survival purposes that the culture usually changes.

The explicit culture is what people see, the behaviours that result from the environment. This can be likened to the tip of an iceberg above the surface. These are the outward manifestations of deeper cultural levels. Beneath the surface is a level of norms and values. Norms are the agreed sense of what is right and wrong; values are what is good and bad. Norms give the feeling of how one should behave and values give the feeling of how one aspires to behave.

Cultures can be distinguished from each other by the differences in shared meanings they expect and attribute to their environment. It is not a thing, but the interaction of people. The difference in these interactions leads to different relationships within a group or organisation and determines the explicit culture.

Goffee (2000) argues that every business culture is unique and cannot be identified simply by using a checklist. He believes cultures are a result of the nature of social relationships and structures, not formal organisational structures. There are two measures of relationships:

- sociability
- solidarity.

Sociability is a measure of friendliness between people. It recognises relationships for their own sake. It is concerned with how individuals share ideas and values. The benefits of sociability are clear. It fosters teamwork and creativity and people enjoy the friendly atmosphere. The downside is that friendship can be an excuse for accepting poor performance and consensus can replace constructive conflict.

Solidarity is based on a keen awareness of common goals and shared interests whether or not people like each other. A threat to these interests will galvanise these organisations instantly. A clearly perceived external enemy could also bring solidarity. The benefits of solidarity are the focus on goals, the desire to win and the swift response to a threat. The downside is that unless the focus is correct they can self-destruct and it can break down into battles between different parts of the organisation.

People are more likely to be happy if they work for an organisation whose core values and beliefs are in line with their own. In an extract from *The Sunday Times* February 2001 Survey on '50 Best Employers', the culture of the organisation was seen as the main reason why people work for these companies. Building a culture that meets the business needs and the needs of individuals within it is likely to retain and attract quality people and so lead to the organisation achieving its goals. These organisations had all created a working environment that was 'A Great Place To Be'.

THE IMPORTANCE OF CREATING 'A GREAT PLACE TO BE'

Organisational culture is often shaped by the leader and in many companies this comes directly from the CEO. Examples of companies whose leader has shaped the culture are set out below.

GEC

Putting people before strategy, making business fun and aligning rewards with measurement was how Jack Welch, Chief Executive of GEC until 2000, created 'A Great Place To Be'. Being highly competitive, his vision from the outset was for GE businesses to be No 1 or 2. He focused on shareholder value and shed the bottom 10 per cent of his workforce if employees did not respond when identified as underperforming. With integrity at the core of every relationship, he created an atmosphere where anyone could express a view or an idea. In striving to find 'a better way every day', he nurtured his people and cultivated a learning organisation. Employee effort was recognised and successes celebrated. Recognising that employees spend most of their waking hours at work, he was keen to create an atmosphere of fun.

Go

Barbara Cassani, chief executive of low-cost airline Go, has achieved success in an overcrowded and competitive market. The company started in 1997 with two planes and 70 people. Today it has 15 aircraft and over 600 people. Through high productivity, simple design and outsourcing it has been able to focus on low costs with great service. Cassani believes that the basic reason for the airline's success is its people. The company's approach to its people, how they work with its customers and how they work with each other has created 'A Great Place To Be'. The workforce is committed to performance and punctuality to the extent that some of the captains unloaded baggage during an Italian baggage handlers' strike. They completed a buy-out in 2000 that made all the people part-owners.

Semco

Ricardo Semler, whose company, Semco, is described as the world's most unusual workplace in his book *Maverick*, has created 'A Great Place To Be' by empowering his workforce to the extent that most employees decide their own salary. Flexitime extends down to the factory workers, sabbaticals are encouraged every year or two to give people creative thinking time and there is reverse evaluation where managers are evaluated by the people they supervise. Semco is one of Latin America's fastest-growing manufacturing companies, acknowledged to be the best in Brazil to work for and has a waiting list of thousands of hopeful applicants.

Microsoft

Bill Gates has created 'A Great Place To Be' by recruiting only the best minds and then valuing that talent. The design of the headquarters at Redmond, Washington, US was specially created to suit bright young people because that is whom he employs. The campus has simple aesthetics, open communal areas and green spaces similar to a college atmosphere. There are numerous cafes and food suppliers at subsidised prices and dress is informal. There are no executive dining areas nor special office furniture. The ethos is thrift – all employees travel economy class, including Gates. Gates' voracious appetite for work translates into the Microsoft culture, best described as 'work hard, then work even harder'. Pizza is delivered to desks so that employees don't have to stop working to eat. Anything with caffeine in it is free.

The reason for Gates' success is that he shares his challenge with his staff. They feel involved because their leader is in the trenches with them. He gives clear goals and leaves them to get on with it. The reward is the option to buy shares at a fixed price. In Microsoft's class of 1989, 2200 developers were millionaires within two years. Gates believes that ownership is one of the main things that binds them together.

TYPES OF CULTURE

The 12 yachts in the BT Global Challenge race were regarded as 12 organisations and each developed its own culture. Nine months before the start, the crews came together as teams, identified their goals and

> **‘ The race has to run as a business. ’**

defined a set of standards by which they wanted to live and work together. The way the skipper and team behaved in relation to these goals and values created the culture of each yacht. As the race progressed, the culture of each yacht evolved around the goals and motivation.

The four core cultures of organisations identified by William Schneider (2000) were used as the basis for the assessment of the culture of each of the 12 yacht teams. The Schneider core cultures were defined as follows:

- control – based on a military system, with power as the primary motive
- collaboration – emerging from the family and/or athletic team system, in which the underlying motive is affiliation
- competence – derived from the university system, with the fundamental motive of achievement
- cultivation – growing from religious system(s) and motivated by growth or self-actualisation

Each of the four cultures was associated with a strong motivational driver, as shown in Table 13.1 (see Chapter 6).

TABLE 13.1 Four types of culture and primary motivators

Control culture	Collaboration culture
Motivator – power	Motivator – affiliation
Competence culture	Cultivation culture
Motivator – achievement	Motivator – self-actualisation

(Schneider 2000)

Control

This culture is about certainty and exists to ensure predictability, safety, accuracy and dependability. The basic issue was to preserve and grow and ensure the well-being and success of the team. At the outset of the race the technical sailing skills and abilities of the crew were limited which meant there was a high level of risk when undertaking any operation on board one of these powerful yachts. For the skippers it was important to create an environment where the safety and preservation of the crew and the equipment were paramount.

In the Southern Ocean, the skippers also needed to create a control culture. While the crew was much more experienced and capable by then, the conditions were unpredictable and dynamic. It was important to minimise the risks that the crew and yacht faced. Skippers exerted their authority to ensure procedures were followed and corners were not cut. Some skippers also chose to take a more conservative strategy in their routing from Sydney to Cape Town, staying further north rather than heading deep down south towards the dangers of Antarctica. The indicators of this type of culture seen in the race are:

- professionalism
- seriousness
- values
- respect
- pride
- self-regulation.

Competence

This culture is about distinction and exists to ensure the accomplishment of unparalleled performance, setting the team apart from the rest. Skippers who set out to achieve a good result within the overall race were highly focused throughout the race and evoked a competence culture. These skippers were continually striving for excellence among their team members and set standards by which the team would operate. The skippers were assertive and influential in getting the team members to adhere to these systems and procedures.

At critical times, such as near the end of a leg when yachts were racing in close contention, some skippers were able to persuade their team of the need for ultimate performance. Rather than go to their bunks at the end of their watch, these crews would stay up on deck to ensure that their body weight was positioned in the most favourable place for yacht speed. These crews would sit on the side of the yacht for hours, eating and sleeping there to ensure they were achieving optimum performance. The indicators of this type of culture seen in the race are:

- learning
- continual improvement
- passion
- trust
- 100 per cent effort
- performance focus
- belief.

Collaboration

This culture is about synergy. Within teams, this can be seen as unity, working in partnership and sharing experiences to achieve reality. Skippers were keen to evoke a collaborative culture at certain times, particularly when crews were being physically challenged for weeks on end. Exhausted, cold and wet, crew members needed support from team mates to get them through the perpetual watch system.

On two occasions where yacht teams suffered major setbacks, the skippers evoked a collaborative culture. They rallied their teams, drew out the positives and revised their goals. Being several thousand miles behind the fleet, these teams restarted the leg with a determination not to finish last in the leg. In both incidences, through working together, they achieved this goal. The indicators of this type of culture seen in the race are:

- openness
- no blame
- support
- humour and fun
- team cohesiveness
- shared leadership
- partnerships.

Cultivation

This culture is all about enrichment and exists to ensure the fullest growth of the team members. The fundamental premise is about the realisation of ideals, values and higher-order purposes. During the race it was important that the skippers evoked a culture of cultivation, helping develop the skills and abilities of the crew. Some skippers ran a yacht where crew members rotated through a number of key roles on the yacht, giving them a chance to develop their skills across a range of roles rather than focus on one particular task.

Realising the personal aspirations and growth of individuals was important. Some skippers identified specific weather conditions and legs of the race when coaching and job rotation was possible, without affecting the performance of the yacht. The light wind conditions on leg 6 towards La Rochelle was a time when many skippers encouraged crew members to develop new skills, e.g. navigation, helming. The indicators of this type of culture seen in the race are:

- purpose
- feedback
- work/life balance
- team identity
- development
- recognition.

DETERMINING CULTURE

Culture can be determined by a team's lifestyle – the habits and attitudes by which the team live. By identifying the habits and attitudes (cultural indicators) of each yacht team, it was possible to group these into the four core organisational cultures shown in Table 13.2 (adapted from Schneider, 2000).

TABLE 13.2 Cultural indicators of yacht teams grouped into four core cultures

Control – power	Collaboration – affiliation
Professionalism	Openness
Seriousness	No blame
Values	Support
Respect	Humour and fun
Pride	Team cohesiveness
Self-regulation	Shared leadership
	Partnerships

Competence – achievement	Cultivation – self-actualisation
Learning	Purpose
Continual improvement	Feedback
Passion	Work/life balance
Trust	Team identity
100 per cent effort	Development
Performance focus	Recognition
Belief	

(Adapted from Schneider 2000)

ALIGNING GOALS AND LEADERSHIP WITH CULTURE

It was clear that the goals set by the teams at the outset of the project were significant in the development of their culture. The goals were reflective of the motivational drivers of the skipper and team, seen in Chapter 6.

' If you get enough commitment to the goal, you get followership. '

However, the leadership of the skippers was critical in steering the team towards achieving these goals. The skippers influenced the way in which the team operated, their attitudes and habits. This in turn created the culture (see Figure 13.1).

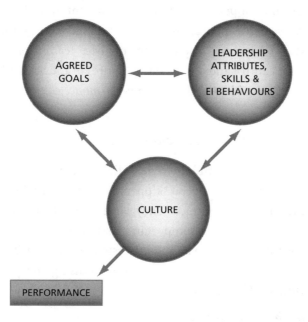

FIGURE 13.1 Alignment of goals, leadership abilities and culture to achieve performance

Performance culture within the BT Global Challenge

The goals of the podium teams were clearly performance-focused. There was an emphasis on winning through maximum team effort and a strong element of control and continuous improvement. The goals of the three podium skippers were:

- win through doing our best and continuously improving
- win, but with same crew we started the race
- win through maximum effort.

To achieve the performance-related and measurable goals, these skippers created an environment where the accent was on competence and each crew member had a specialist role. The team were driven towards achievement, a strong work ethic was evident and crew members were continually learning and improving the methods and procedures by which they sailed the yacht.

The podium skippers created this environment by leading in a manner that drove performance. They all showed high levels of the X Factor identified in Chapter 5. The cultures of these teams appeared to be linked to the control and competence cultures of the Schneider model. The research team identified this as a *performance culture*.

Creating a performance culture

The leadership abilities and the style of the skipper were seen to shape the culture of the yacht. Several skippers developed a performance culture at the outset of the race. They were focused on winning. The relationship side was far less important. Getting on with each other did not matter provided the goals and interests were aligned. The skippers were utilising the performance drivers (X Factor):

' We spend all our time working hard to perform as well as we can as a team. We try not to mess around when it is a serious time. '

- self-motivation
- performance focus
- discipline
- control management
- conflict management
- resource management.

The skippers shaped their culture through the following:

Goals

The goals of these teams were task focused and were usually specific and measurable.

' Goals need to be clear, understood and agreed if they are to be achieved. '

- To be in the top 3 in every leg.
- To be in the top 5 overall.
- Not just to win but to be respected winners.

The skippers secured buy-in to their long-term and short-term goals. At the initial teambuilds they spent time ensuring that they were setting goals that were stretching and were agreed. One sponsor believed that the key to the success of its yacht had been team development before the race started and the focus on a common goal. The culture was one of committed performance focus. The team bought into the winning strategy and were fully committed to that goal.

Values

The values that were set with these crews were aligned to performance:

- commitment, guts and unity
- honesty, trust, openness and integrity.

' Values were just there – they were part of the culture. '

In the teambuilding before the start of the race the teams spent time ensuring that their values were right and would enable performance. Many yachts had their values pinned up somewhere and for some they became an integral part of everyday life.

Discipline

These skippers realised that respect came from a team who knew where they were going and how they should get there. They were not there necessarily to be liked and were not afraid to reprimand and be strict when required. Little issues were dealt with before they were allowed to grow. There was a disciplined approach that led to a professionalism and seriousness that became part of the culture.

Control management

These skippers ensured that there were control measures in place to track their performance. A culture of continuous improvement was achieved by the relentless focus on performance. Sail changes were timed, sail trim and helming accuracy were tracked. Spreadsheets were designed to track performance. There was a culture of continuous improvement and 100 per cent effort.

Conflict management

These yachts had systems in place to deal with conflict in a positive way. Humour was used in a number of situations to defuse conflict. The culture became one of performance focus rather than problem focus.

> **' Getting the issues on the table is essential for winning. '**

Resource management

Every resource was used to its full potential. The attributes and skills of the crew members were carefully analysed in order to achieve 100 per cent effort in the right direction.

Leadership

The skippers in these performance cultures did not have the same charismatic attributes as the skippers who evolved an inspiring culture. They built the culture around the achievement of goals and the standards and values that had been agreed. They were able to direct and coach to the point where the team could function without the leader being present.

> **' He's a normal manager – he is not inspiring. '**

Inspiring culture within the BT Global Challenge

Some teams agreed less performance-focused goals and placed an emphasis on creating an environment of enjoyment and personal fulfilment.

- To inspire others by what we do.
- To achieve our maximum and enjoy our challenge.

These teams also developed a culture that was reflective of their goal. They worked well together, supported one another, had fun and developed personally. The skippers and teams wanted to do well and were seen to be able to perform to a high level at specific times. However, the critical element of performance drive was not in their culture and when it was really needed to hold a leading position the focus was not always there.

These skippers created this environment by leading in a manner that inspired performance. They showed high levels of the Y Factor identified in Chapter 5 and put less emphasis on the drivers of performance – the X Factor. The cultures of these teams appeared to be linked to the collaboration and cultivation cultures of the Schneider model. The research team identified this as an *inspiring culture.*

Creating an inspiring culture

The leadership abilities and the style of the skipper were seen to play a large part in shaping this inspiring culture. They were less focused on performance and the teams were focused on relationship building. The skippers were utilising the performance enablers (Y Factor):

> **' The concept of the race was for happiness, passion and maximisation. You put in and get out as much as you can. '**

- purpose
- recognition
- belief
- shared leadership
- integrity

- self-belief
- self-control
- sensing
- openness
- vulnerability.

The skippers shaped their culture through the following:

Goals

Their goals were focused around people, development and deeper purpose. On one yacht the aim was 'to inspire other people by doing the race'. The crew were both sociable and displayed solidarity for most of the time. They had an excellent relationship with the sponsor and the families and involved them in activities in every port of call. Everywhere

❛ The goal is to get round the world by growing people, all as friends and leaving as individuals. ❜

they went people wanted to become their supporters. They had pictures of their loved ones up round the yacht.

On another yacht the goal was to continuously build, develop and support each other as a team, to achieve the maximum and enjoy the challenge. This crew spent a lot of time maximising their personal development and felt that the whole race was about something far larger than winning. Even on the legs where they came well down the fleet their demeanour was such that they may have won. There was a huge camaraderie between team members on this yacht and with others in the fleet.

Values

The values that were set by these crews were aligned to team dynamics:

- Team support for each other.
- Respect for each other.
- Friendship.
- Keep in touch.
- Be comfortable with the values, even the skipper.

The initial teambuilding sessions were built around these values to ensure that the team functioned well together. The aim was to have a greater understanding of each other. These crews supported one another and formed very cohesive teams early on in the race.

Belief

The culture was one of belief in the people. Every effort was made to integrate everyone into the team. The crew recognised each other's efforts and were prepared to give each other feedback. They made time for each other, developed the team dynamic, had fun and built a lasting commitment to each other.

Leadership

The skippers who shaped these inspiring cultures gave a great deal of themselves to their teams. The teams were energised by them and emulated the behaviour of their skipper. On several of these yachts the skippers inspired their crews with motivational speeches, prose and poetry.

' We have a very open culture which is sharing and has no cliques. '

When food was running out on VERITAS, the skipper gave each crew member a small 'sausage' necklace made out of leather. When they were really hungry they sucked on the leather to stave off their hunger pangs, a trick learned from Shackleton.

For these teams, crew identity was important. Crew kit was carefully thought out and even where money was tight they unified with T-shirts or 'party' shirts. They enjoyed being together.

Table 13.3 shows the combination of indicators for a performance culture and for an inspiring culture.

SUMMARY

The skippers who evoked a performance culture, with its relentless pressure, found it an effective culture in the short term. Several skippers realised the dangers of driving the team relentlessly and changed their cultures to take into account the teams' needs. They introduced elements of an inspiring culture.

The skippers who evoked an inspiring culture, with its relationship focus, created an environment that was fun and creative. It was a culture that was essential when team morale was low. However, without a disciplined and controlled environment there was less focus on outcome and less drive for performance.

' The strength of the team is in the motivation and unity of the crew. '

TABLE 13.3 Combined cultures, cultural indicators and primary motivators

Performance culture (Control/competence)	Inspiring culture (Collaboration/cultivation)
Cultural indicators	**Cultural indicators**
Professionalism	Openness
Seriousness	No blame
Values	Support
Respect	Humour and fun
Pride	Team spirit
Self-regulation	Shared leadership
Learning	Partnerships
Continual improvement	Purpose
Passion	Feedback
Trust	Work/life balance
100 per cent effort	Team identity
Performance focus	Development
Belief	Recognition
Motivators	**Motivators**
Power	Affiliation
Achievement	Self-actualisation

The culture of the podium yacht teams was derived from a combination of both the performance and inspiring cultures. The podium skippers achieved success through knowing when it was appropriate to evoke which culture.

A summary of the leadership components that shape culture is given in Table 13.4.

TABLE 13.4 Leadership components that shape culture

Culture	Cultural indicators	Essential attributes and skills of leader	Emotional intelligence behaviours	Leadership style
PERFORMANCE	Professionalism	Self-motivation	Self-awareness	Directing
	Seriousness	Performance focus	Emotional resilience	Coaching
	Values	Discipline	Motivation	Supporting
	Respect	Control management	Interpersonal sensitivity	Delegating
	Pride	Resource management	Influence	
	Self-regulation	Conflict management	Intuitiveness	
	Learning	(X Factor)	Conscientiousness	
	Continual improvement			
	Passion			
	Trust			
	100 per cent effort			
	Performance focus			
	Belief		*continued overleaf*	

TABLE 13.4 *continued*

Culture	Cultural indicators	Essential attributes and skills of leader	Emotional intelligence behaviours	Leadership style
INSPIRING	Openness	Purpose	Self-awareness	Directing
	No blame	Recognition	Emotional resilience	Coaching
	Support	Belief	Motivation	Supporting
	Humour and fun	Shared leadership	Interpersonal sensitivity	Delegating
	Team cohesiveness	Integrity	Influence	
	Shared leadership	Self-belief	Intuitiveness	
	Partnerships	Vulnerability	Conscientiousness	
	Purpose	Self-control		
	Feedback	Sensing		
	Work/life balance	Openness		
	Team identity	(Y Factor)		
	Development			
	Recognition			

A GREAT PLACE TO BE

' There is a synchronicity about the team – everyone is flying together. '

By the end of the race, the podium skippers had created 'A Great Place To Be'. This was characterised by a combination of the majority of cultural indicators seen in both the performance and inspiring cultures. Throughout the race, the focus of these three winning yachts was clearly on performance. However, each of the skippers realised the importance of balancing the performance drive with the needs of the team in order to sustain the crew through the length of the race.

' I realised that the race was not all a performance driver but a people issue. '

The predominant cultural indicators seen across all three teams were:

- performance focus
- values
- learning
- continual improvement
- openness
- no blame
- humour
- shared leadership.

Achieving the right balance

The podium skippers all started the race with a culture more akin to the performance culture. They were professional, highly focused on the goal, very intense, competitive, results orientated and set high standards that they expected their crew to meet. While the crews had bought into the goal of winning, the intensity was overwhelming and there was a real need for this to be balanced with some light relief.

These skippers had the ability to sense the environment and early on in the race they openly addressed the issue of an inappropriate balance. This helped to avoid a complete breakdown of the team cohesiveness.

> ❛ *Being relaxed is the best way of winning.* ❜

The skipper of LG FLATRON introduced an above and below-deck culture. This meant that crew maintained total performance focus while on watch, but once down below they could, quite literally, let their hair down. Theme parties and raves with strobe lights were characteristic of the team spirit, humour and work/life balance that was brought to this yacht.

The team of BP had agreed team values of safe, happy, fast. Their skipper had to be reminded to bring these back into alignment. Having

> ❛ *I started the race by being very hard on the crew, now I am putting the team needs in place.* ❜

had a successful early leg, the competitive spirit took over and by the time they reached the next port, the humour and team spirit had evaporated and the 'happy' had dropped from their value set. By reintroducing the fun element, the skipper rebalanced the culture and performance was greatly enhanced.

Shaping the culture

As the race progressed the culture of each of these yachts evolved. The skippers were seen to develop their skills and attributes and utilise their emotional intelligence behaviours in ways that brought out the best in the team. While the podium skippers shared a considerable number of competencies (see Table 5.1, page 106), including the five indicators of the X Factor and most of the indicators of the Y Factor, they all took differing approaches to create a similar culture. There was clearly more than one recipe for creating 'A Great Place To Be'.

LG FLATRON

The skipper of LG FLATRON appointed a second in command, a young and energetic crew member with complementary attributes. While one had the courage to take risks, the other provided the conscience and was more reserved. Together they worked extremely well, sharing the responsibility of the navigational role. This allowed the skipper the time to regulate his sleep and stress and stand back to reflect. There was also a great deal of distributed leadership with other members of the team, especially the watch leaders. The team's strength came from finding the right level of balance in leading the team.

Compaq

The Compaq skipper demonstrated a more managerial approach. He was seen to be serious, controlled, analytical and non-confrontational. Detailed planning and clear procedures and the use of visualisation techniques ensured that the crew were well prepared for any eventuality; when faced with a difficult situation they could respond without the need for detailed direction. The cool, calm and professional approach taken by this skipper was an inspiration to his team.

' *He's like a serial killer, dreams every step with meticulous detail and with a lot of forethought.* '

BP Explorer

The BP skipper developed throughout the race and showed the ability to balance both management and leadership. With clear procedures and processes in place this skipper was quick to monitor and refine. At the same time he was sensitive to the needs of his crew, showed an ability to inspire others and led a highly motivated and extremely cohesive team that was completely behind him and demonstrated a great team spirit.

' *How he deals with people is tremendous.* '

In their own way, using their own style, all three podium skippers showed extremely high levels of energy and drive. They were professional about what they were doing and used humour to rally their crews. The podium skippers were passionate individuals who agreed highly motivated and focused goals with their crew at the outset of the project.

' *He doesn't do second best.* '

These goals emphasised the need for maximum team effort and the skippers demonstrated a high work ethic on each of these yachts. With a strong racing ethos, the skippers were in pursuit of continual improvement and pushed their crew to trim the sails constantly and maintain accurate direction when helming.

How the podium skippers achieved 'A Great Place To Be'

The podium skippers were all *self-motivated* and *performance focused*. These skippers:

Maintained discipline

There was a high level of discipline on board these yachts. Team members were expected to take minimum kit, be punctual for watch, sit and sleep on the high side of the yacht to ensure optimum weight distribution and give 100 per cent to any task they undertook. On these yachts, jobs were never left undone and rotas were established to ensure the tedious jobs such as pumping the bilges and completing the logbook were always completed. Sail changes were undertaken as soon as the conditions dictated. The fact that there was only ten minutes until the end of a tough six-hour watch was no excuse for the change not to be undertaken. This was despite the fact that a major sail change could take the watch the best part of an hour. There was a pride in every job that was undertaken.

Focused on tactics

These skippers were focused on tactics and weather routing and spent considerable amounts of time gathering and analysing weather information to ensure the yacht was positioned in the most favourable weather systems. The crew was expected to sail the yacht fast while the skipper was expected to put the yacht in the right place in the ocean. This achieved the performance focus that was necessary.

Managed resources

Resources were managed carefully and Internet time was monitored in minutes to ensure there was enough time for retrieving the latest weather information. At the outset of the project, the skipper of LG FLATRON undertook a comprehensive weighted factor analysis to identify where their limited financial resource should be focused. The skipper identified the elements of the project that would impact on their goal of winning the race. There were four key areas:

- crew performance
- crisis management
- strategy
- weight.

From these four areas they identified 160 items to be factored. By giving a percentage to each item they were able to work out the priority. It also gave the crew an understanding that attention to all 160 items would make the difference to performance. The bilges were sponged every hour. On many occasions as little as a teaspoon of water was sponged up, but it was this attention to detail that made the difference. There was also a balance to be struck between the morale of the crew and weight, for example there was no point in having food so limited that it became unhealthy or so uninteresting that people would not eat it.

Clothing was considered critical for performance. The skipper had noticed in training that crew members were being hesitant for a second on the bow when going up to make a sail change. He realised that this was time spent pulling up collars and zips. He realised that having smocked tops rather than zipped jackets would make a difference. Although the budget from the sponsor was limited and immovable, each crew member agreed to fund the purchase of a smock jacket.

Used the best person for the job

Each of the podium yachts adopted the policy of 'best person for the job' and crew members took up specialist roles. Helming was restricted to a core few and controls were put in place to ensure that target speed was achieved and the yacht was always sailing on the right course at its optimum speed. The skipper of LG FLATRON had a core of specialist crew members on each watch and swapped the rest around to stimulate variety. The culture of learning and continual improvement was deeply embedded. There was an openness that allowed feedback to be given in a blame-free environment.

Protected the team

The attitude of these skippers clearly demonstrated their commitment to the goal and a desire to win the overall race. However, they were conscious of safety and the need to preserve their people, yacht, sails and equipment. A delicate balance had to be struck between short-term performance in each leg and achieving the longer-term overall race goal. There was respect for each other and a respect for the equipment.

Utilised motivation

All three skippers showed high levels of the emotional intelligence behaviour of motivation. They were highly self-motivated, focused on results and committed to long-term success. They had the ability to balance the short- and long-term goals and found the fortitude to pursue their goal in the face of setbacks. They

> **' This is not a sprint but a marathon. '**

remained optimistic in adversity, raising crew morale by highlighting their achievements. These skippers were striving for continual improvement and were always looking for new and better ways of performing any task.

The podium skippers gained respect from their teams by showing *integrity* and *setting high standards* that they lived and breathed. Like their goals, values were agreed with the team at the outset and these skippers were quick to ensure that the standards set were maintained by all. As the race went on, these teams became self-policing. These teams showed a deep sense of pride and a high level of solidarity. The skippers created an environment where the yacht would function to the same standard regardless of whether the skipper was on board. These skippers:

Strove for improvement

'Striving for constant improvement' was common to them all. Information and knowledge was shared at watch handovers and tasks

> **'** *Accent is on being competence-based and self-driven.* **'**

were debriefed so lessons could be learned. Crews coached one another in the skills of their specialism, allowing cross-over of roles when the occasion required. LG FLATRON's skipper set up focus groups to concentrate on specifics such as boat speed. The appointed group members would spend time considering and identifying best practice. BP had a safety value and held daily safety briefings where one crew member would be responsible for presenting on a specified topic.

Retained a focus on the job

Performance focus was at the heart of these three teams. Compaq adhered to a policy of the trimmers and helm focusing on the job and only talking about performance issues. The rest of the watch sat on the

> **'** *It happens, understand why it happened.* **'**

side of the yacht as ballast to assist performance and they were allowed to talk freely so long as it did not disrupt the

trimmers and the helm. Retaining the focus on the job in hand ensured that mistakes were minimised and performance was maintained continually. If mistakes were made, a no-blame culture existed and rather than a witch hunt, the team would focus on recovering the situation and eliminating the possibility of it happening again.

Never stepped over a job

'Never step over a job' was a phrase that was adopted from the previous race and referred to the fact that jobs could not be ignored. The podium teams were serious about their performance. They were proactive in looking for things to do and they lived by this phrase. If a sail tore, it would be taken below and worked on immediately. Crew members responsible for specific jobs showed intricate levels of care. The sailmaker on BP drew complex diagrams of each sail, pinpointing any small nicks or damage which could help predict and prevent the possibility of more. Again there was a constant endeavour to improve performance.

Utilised conscientiousness

These skippers showed high levels of the emotional intelligence behaviour conscientiousness. They showed clear commitment to the race and a high level of consistency between what they said and the actions they took. They set high standards for their teams and encouraged them to live up to these. They dictated the tone for the culture of the yacht.

> ' Cut him through the middle and he is like Blackpool rock. '

The podium skippers realised there was a need to *share information* in order to *identify best practice* and *new ways of doing things*. These skippers:

Managed communication

Although the podium skippers did not all start the race with a commitment to communication, they quickly realised its importance. One skipper realised early on that there was a need for review and feedback and introduced a midday briefing by day 5 of leg 1. It was a driving factor in bringing them back from tenth position to second by the end of the leg. All three were holding briefings and sharing information on weather and tactics with the crew quite early on in the race.

Gave clear briefings

The podium skippers saw the need to share information in order to identify best practice and new ways of doing things. They insisted on clear briefings at watch handovers and were keen to ensure sailing manoeuvres were briefed and debriefed regardless of how smoothly the task had actually gone. Learning through knowledge transfer and continual improvement was paramount to performance. 'Eliminate mistakes/maintain the pressure' (EM/MTP) was the motto of the Compaq team and in an environment of no blame, this was possible.

Got buy-in

As the race progressed, these skippers realised the importance of getting team buy-in. When decisions needed to be made they ensured that the team understood the whole picture, why something had happened, what they wanted from the situation and how they were going to achieve this together. Having the discussion ahead of making the decision engendered a sense of shared responsibility and leadership.

Built trust

These skippers learned the need for openness and honesty. They built the trust and support of their crew by discussing issues together. When conditions ahead looked bad, it was better to be frank and honest with the crew. LG FLATRON and BP skippers talked about the wind and sea state that the team might face rounding Cape Horn and suggested ways in which they would handle the situation. The Compaq skipper used visualisation techniques to help his crew visualise what lay ahead in the turbulent conditions of the Southern Ocean.

Handled conflict

None of the skippers relished conflict and found it one of the most difficult things to handle. Using reasoning and foresight they often averted an issue and this was a favoured approach taken by these skippers. While none of them avoided it, they couldn't always deal with it. As part of an ongoing team development programme, the Compaq team took time out in Wellington to address on-board issues.

Learned through reviews

Briefing and debriefing were an important factor in the campaigns run by the three podium skippers. Learning and continual improvement was part of the culture and at the end of each leg the entire team, including leggers, would take time out for a thorough review. No stone was left unturned and each individual was given the opportunity to air their views and concerns. Lessons were extracted from these reviews and taken forward into the next leg of the race.

Utilised interpersonal sensitivity

As crew members developed skills and learned from their experience, these skippers began to utilise the emotional intelligence behaviour of interpersonal sensitivity more. They showed more willingness to accept input from the crew and were seen to be more prepared to listen. Retaining their authority and responsibility for tactical decision making, they were open to discuss their thinking and showed a willingness to change their minds if appropriate. Acknowledging the different specialisations among the crew, skippers sought input from the appropriate members and would bounce around ideas related to their area of expertise.

> ' *Seeking the views and opinions of the crew – this was simply the culture of the team.* '

Self-control and *consistency of behaviour* were paramount to the success of these podium skippers. They needed to be approachable to gain the confidence of their team and crews needed to know that their skipper would react in the same manner whatever the situation. Being highly driven and competitive skippers it was all too easy to let frustration take over and to vent this on some unassuming crew member. Compaq skipper put a process in place for he and the crew to manage their stress, which was known as 'the squeeze'. As part of the build-up to each leg the crew would gather in a group huddle on the front of the yacht for some words from the skipper and a last minute 'rev up'. The squeeze was also employed a number of times at sea when it was apparent that tensions were building up on board due to the pressure of the racing and the conditions. On these occasions the crew gathered together at the back of the boat and expunged the bad feelings by shouting loudly. Many crew members expressed deep satisfaction at the benefits of this. The skippers:

Were self-regulated

Regulating their sleep and managing their stress were imperative in controlling their behaviour. These skippers learned just how much time they needed to recharge and revitalise themselves. Some put systems in place at the start to ensure that they had sufficient sleep. Others, when bad weather was forecast which ultimately meant they would be needed on deck, would take to their bunks, get some sleep and be ready and rejuvenated to face the conditions.

Allayed fears

In challenging conditions these skippers needed their teams to be able to perform but knew that fear could easily cause crew members to freeze. The podium skippers were controlled and calm in a crisis, taking charge of the situation yet not undermining the watch leader. They would be available up on deck and their presence alone could engender a positive and calming effect on the crew. They gave support and built up trust within the team.

The podium skippers had high levels of *self-belief* and by showing *appropriate leadership* they were able to instil confidence in their team. When setbacks occurred or situations turned unfavourable, these skippers were able to draw out the positives and use these to raise crew morale. All three appreciated that keeping the crew motivated was critical. Although they were not all good at sensing if something was wrong with a crew member, they did identify others who could operate as their eyes and ears. These skippers:

> **❛ Remember, you can't always be in the lead. ❜**

Used humour

With a constant focus on performance the atmosphere became a little tense. Humour was used extensively to lighten the atmosphere or diffuse an otherwise potentially destructive situation. At the 10.00 daily meetings on Compaq the skipper would sometimes try to lighten the competitive atmosphere. He did this by either telling a story about past experiences or reading passages from various books including Shackleton, and Coleridge's *Rhyme of the Ancient Mariner*. Sometimes he would have a word of the day, where one person chose a word from the dictionary that the rest of the crew would have to guess. The crew also enjoyed the mock trials that took place when a 'crime' occurred on board. At the same time these skippers kept a sense of authority. Rather than join in a 'mickey taking' session it was sometimes more appropriate to retain a slight distance.

Showed vulnerability

Admitting mistakes and showing vulnerability were not highly visible among these three skippers. The skippers identified a fine line between maintaining the confidence of the crew and showing them they were not infallible. However, the

> *' Dig deep – work together, work it through and we will succeed. '*

skipper of BP was quick to admit his tactical mistakes. He knew it was his responsibility to put the yacht in the right place in the ocean and when he didn't, he turned to the crew for help. Admitting his mistake, he then asked for their support in sailing the yacht as fast as possible in the new direction.

Were prepared

All three podium skippers were well organised with meticulous planning and preparation before and during the race. They delegated roles early and gave individuals the power to make decisions. During the race they coached their crews to fine-tune their skills. These skippers led by example. They were prepared to 'muck in' and turn their hand to more mundane tasks. They all fostered a sense of shared leadership as they felt it was important that the crew won the race. This, in turn, built up a tremendous pride in what they were doing and created a strong team spirit.

Were in control

While they needed to have a level of control, none of the three skippers was seen to be overly controlling. By the end of the race, they had also developed the ability to stand back. They would take themselves away for a quiet time out or sit and reflect at the chart table. It allowed them to take another look at their purpose and their goals.

Were flexible

These skippers also showed flexibility and were quick to adapt to the ever-changing conditions. If they tried one course of action without result, they were quick to try something else that would possibly pay off.

Gave recognition

With high personal standards and a strong work ethic, none of the three skippers was quick to give recognition or praise. The crews really needed to know they were doing a good job. Their work rate was high and they wanted to know this was appreciated. It was too easy for these skippers to assume that the achievement of good results was enough. Deep down these crew members needed this implicit reward.

Were passionate

All three skippers were driven by passion and this was explicit in two of the three. The skipper of BP wore his 'heart on his sleeve' and it was obvious to his crew that he cared immensely about the race. Being fired up himself served to inspire his crew. LG FLATRON skipper would work himself up to give a passionate speech at the start of each leg. The skipper of Compaq contained his feelings to the point that he had to actually tell the crew how he was feeling. However, after a powerful teambuild in Cape Town, he returned to the race course completely fired up and showed his emotions in a way he had never done before.

‘ He is too well disciplined to show his emotions. ’

SUMMARY

From the goals of these podium skippers, evidenced at the beginning of this chapter, it was clear these three skippers were highly focused on performance. What they managed to achieve as the race progressed was a combination of the performance and inspiring cultures. As their attributes and skills developed and they utilised their emotional intelligence behaviours more, they knew when to put more focus on which of the cultures. These podium skippers clearly showed the factors of inspiring leadership and ultimately created 'A Great Place To Be'.

LESSONS FROM THE RACE

As a leader today you need to:

1. align your goals to leadership and culture

2. adapt the culture to the needs of the team or the situation

3. achieve success by knowing when to evoke a particular culture

4. use the X Factor when creating a performance culture

5. use the Y Factor when creating an inspiring culture

6. create a 'A Great Place To Be' by evoking both cultures at the right time and in the right situation

7. achieve 'A Great Place To Be' by:

   - being highly motivated and performance focused

   - showing integrity and setting high standards

   - sharing information for best practice and innovation

   - showing self-control and consistency

   - showing self-belief and instilling confidence.

REFERENCES

Goffee, R. (2000) 'Innovation and creativity in business', *RSA Journal*, 1/4, pp. 113–119.

Handy, C. (1991) *Gods of Management*, Arrow Books: Reading.

Mullins, L. J. (1999) *Management and Organisational Behaviour*, Financial Times Pitman Publishing 5th Edition: London.

Schneider, W. E. (2000) 'Why good management ideas fail', *Strategy and Leadership*, Vol. 28 Issue 1, pp. 24–29, MCB UP Ltd.

Trompenaars, F. and Hampden-Turner, C. (1998) *Riding the Waves of Culture*, Nicholas Brealey Publishing: London.

V
SUMMARY

14

INSPIRING LEADERSHIP – STAYING AFLOAT IN TURBULENT TIMES

KEY LESSONS FROM THE RESEARCH FINDINGS

The research team set out to identify the factors that contributed to sustained performance during the race. They also hoped to identify the factors needed to retain cohesiveness and loyalty within a team.

The questions originally posed were:

- What skills are required for management?
- What attributes are required for leadership?
- How important is personal performance?
- Are there other factors yet undefined?
- What is the impact of emotional intelligence behaviours on performance?
- How does a leader create 'A Great Place To Be'?

Through this comprehensive study and the in-depth profiling of each of the race skippers the answers to the questions were revealed. The podium skippers sustained performance and at the same time retained the cohesiveness and loyalty of their team. They were seen to have used a number of skills and attributes that were enabled by the utilisation of emotional intelligence behaviours. They are considered to have shown inspiring leadership.

The following pages summarise the important factors that you as a leader require to manage and lead yourself and others effectively.

Inspiring leadership is not determined by any single formula but comes from a combination of certain skills, attributes and behaviours. It takes effort and requires enthusiasm and determination. By combining the elements summarised below, we hope that you will be able to inspire and lead a high-performing team.

Management skills

The essence of good management is planning and preparation. Being able to manage your team and project efficiently and effectively is important. Team members need to understand and agree the goals they are striving to achieve. They need to have clear parameters within which to work and clear procedures for the way things are done. As a leader you should ensure that your management procedures are regularly reviewed and refined to ensure the goal is achievable.

LESSON I

1. Ensure there is collaborative agreement to your team and project goals.
2. Be thorough in your preparation and planning and stay ahead of your team and the competition.
3. Establish management procedures that are understood and effective.
4. Enhance performance through continuous review and improvement.

Leadership attributes

The single most important factor that you require to inspire and lead others is respect. Respect can be earned and retained if you show integrity and consistency of behaviour. Ensure your team know where they are going and are working together in a manner that is accepted and respected by all.

> ## LESSON 2
>
> 1. Share your vision with your team to help them see where you are leading them.
> 2. Inspire your team to live by the values agreed.
> 3. Create an environment where support is ingrained and trust is implicit.
> 4. Inject appropriate humour into the team and inspire a fun-loving culture.

Personal attributes

Personal attributes are critical. If you are not anchored in yourself, your ability to lead others will be severely impaired. Self-belief is the vital ingredient and an awareness of your feelings and ability to manage your emotions is essential for ensuring a consistent level of personal performance.

> ## LESSON 3
>
> 1. Be driven by your inner purpose and show passion for your personal mission.
> 2. Stand back from what is happening around you and give yourself time to review and reflect.
> 3. Be consistent in the way you behave and show yourself to be dependable.
> 4. Retain a respectable distance from your team.

Technical skills

Having the knowledge, experience and professional know-how to do your job is critical not only for the success of the project but for you to remain in control of yourself, manage your emotions and retain your self-belief. Ensure your skills and expertise are right for the role you are about to undertake.

> ### LESSON 4
>
> 1. Make sure you are adequately skilled for the job you are doing.
> 2. Ensure your team members have the skills and abilities to do what you ask and expect from them.

X Factor – driver of performance

> ### LESSON 5
>
> The X Factor was identified as a group of competencies seen to be instrumental in driving performance. As a leader focused on achieving results and driving performance within your team, the following attributes and skills are essential:
>
> - self-motivation
> - performance focus
> - discipline
> - control management
> - resource management
> - conflict management.

Y Factor – enabler of performance

> ### LESSON 6
>
> The Y Factor was identified as a group of competencies seen to be instrumental in inspiring individuals. As a leader who wishes to inspire team members and gain support and commitment, the following attributes and skills are essential:
>
> - integrity
> - self-belief
> - self-control
> - sensing
> - openness
> - vulnerability
> - purpose
> - recognition
> - belief
> - shared leadership.

Emotional intelligence

Emotional intelligence behaviours will assist you in achieving an appropriate balance between hard decisions and being sensitive to the needs of your team. You need to understand your feelings and emotions and use these in a manner that inspires others and drives performance within your team.

LESSON 7

1. Utilise self-awareness to understand your feelings and manage and control your emotions. Understand how your behaviour impacts on others around you.
2. Use emotional resilience to manage your emotions and perform consistently when under pressure or facing setbacks.
3. Your motivation is your drive and energy to achieve results and to pursue demanding goals in the face of rejection or challenge.
4. Involve your team in decision making and use your interpersonal sensitivity to take into account their needs and perceptions.
5. Listen to your team members, understand their perspective and use influence to persuade them to your point of view.
6. Use your intuitiveness to help you make decisions when faced with incomplete or ambiguous information.
7. Show your conscientiousness by establishing a code of conduct by which you live and live up to these standards.

Leadership style

One of the greatest strengths in a team is its ability to grow and develop. This can be achieved only if you create a learning culture and an environment of encouragement. One of the greatest leadership strengths is to understand the different leadership styles and to use them appropriately.

> **LESSON 8**
>
> 1. Being flexible is the key to being able to use all styles.
> 2. Know your people and their needs in order to give them the leadership they require.
> 3. Beware of inappropriate directing when under stress.

Team development

The power of the team is far greater than the sum of the individuals within the team. In order to realise the potential of a team, you must understand the dynamics involved and work through the different stages of team development.

> **LESSON 9**
>
> 1. Align your personal goals with the team goals at the outset of any project.
> 2. Improve performance through teambuilding.
> 3. Understand the emotions of the team as you guide them through the stages of development.

KEY LESSONS FROM THE BUSINESS ISSUES

Motivation – staying ahead of the competition

With the right approach to leadership you can motivate your team to stay ahead of the competition. You will need the right blend of focus on performance and visionary leadership to inspire your team. Winning hearts by inspiring passion, involvement and a belief in success helps sustain performance over a longer timeframe.

LESSON 10

1. If you focus on achievable shared goals, the confidence from achievement will help people survive the tough times.
2. People who are intrinsically motivated are inspired to do their best, both enjoying their work and experiencing a feeling of pride and involvement.
3. Show people how their role fits into the bigger picture and explain why they are doing things.
4. Adopt a positive attitude towards your people and they will be more likely to achieve results.

Stress management as an enabler of high performance

Stress can become an enabler of performance. You will feel in control of yourself and enjoy a sense of well-being if you are technically competent and have self-belief. Recognise the signs of excessive stress early and use appropriate coping strategies to ensure performance is sustained in turbulent times.

LESSON 11

1. Optimal stress is more likely to be achieved when you have competence, self-belief and commitment.
2. Maintain stress at optimum levels and you will be energised, flexible, in control of yourself and able to access your emotional intelligence.
3. You and your team can keep stress at optimal levels through self-regulation, thorough preparation and planning and becoming practised at operating in pressurised situations.

Work/life balance – the war for time

One dimensional lives are the most damaging to both work and life. Without a healthy approach to all areas, life becomes distorted and stress can be the outcome. Neither side of life benefits. It requires discipline and self-regulation to bring back the balance.

> ### LESSON 12
>
> 1. Get all the areas of your life in balance.
> 2. Value output not attendance in the workplace.
> 3. Build in flexibility.
> 4. Involve families within the organisation.

Managing and inspiring team communications

Communicating is an essential part of good leadership. It is not just a matter of having processes in place for regularly sharing information. The essence of good communications comes from your behaviour. It is important to appreciate the messages you communicate through your words, style and tone and the impact these have on others.

> ### LESSON 13
>
> 1. Consider the feelings of your team members and the way in which they may interpret your message or actions.
> 2. Keep your team informed, involve them and give them responsibility.
> 3. Show you genuinely value their contributions and praise and recognise their efforts.
> 4. Inspire your team through leading by example, show you are focused, be consistent and approachable.

Effective conflict management

As a leader you should recognise the positive aspects of conflict and the mindset changes needed for effective conflict management. An important first step towards effective decision making and gaining buy-in from the team is ensuring you create the right opportunities and have processes in place to discuss issues. Deal with interpersonal conflict quickly before it has time to fester.

LESSON 14

1. Appreciate that a degree of conflict is necessary to increase awareness of others, air differences and develop a cohesive team.
2. Believe that conflict can be resolved and be prepared to confront it.
3. Understand that effective conflict management increases creativity, minimises defensiveness and leads to higher performance.
4. Implement clear and accepted processes for managing conflict and deal with it openly and fairly before it escalates or causes damage.

Creating a knowledge-sharing culture

Leaders must recognise the expertise and experience of their team members and create an environment in which this can be shared and valued. Sharing knowledge leads to the creation of new knowledge and enhances competitive advantage. In creating a sharing environment, the leader must encourage learning and continuous improvement and recognise the risk associated with innovation.

LESSON 15

1. Value the expertise and experience of your team members.
2. Lead by example and share your knowledge.
3. Encourage sharing of best practice, constant learning and continual improvement.
4. Recognise the contributions that others are making and reward these appropriately.

Valuing difference

Life is full of colour and dimension. It is full of misrepresentation and suspicion. It is full of inequality and unfulfilled potential. Everyone has a responsibility to look for the positive contribution of individuals, to assess their potential, no matter the colour or the creed, and to value difference as a way of realising potential in every situation.

LESSON 16

1. Endeavour to see the positive differences in others, not the negative.
2. Value the differences in everyone.
3. Use both genders, where possible, in decision making.

Creating a culture

As a leader you need to create an environment that is appropriate for the situation. At times there may be a need for a performance drive when the utilisation of the X Factor will evoke the right culture. At other times you may need to build the morale of the team and the utilisation of the Y Factor will evoke this culture.

LESSON 17

1. Know when to evoke the right culture to achieve your goals.
2. Sustain your team performance by balancing cultures.
3. Be aware that your management skills and leadership attributes will shape your culture.

APPENDIX I

Performance table

Overall position	Yacht name	Skipper	Leg positions	Overall points
1	LG FLATRON	Conrad Humphreys	3, 1, 1, 2, 1, 8, 1	95
2	Compaq	Will Oxley	4, 4, 3, 4, 5, 1, 5	86
3	BP Explorer	Mark Denton	2, 7, 11, 1, 4, 3, 6	78
4	Logica	Jeremy Troughton	9, 3, 8, 3, 8, 2, 8	71
5	TeamSpirIT	John Read	10, 10, 4, 5, 6, 7, 2	68
6	Spirit of Hong Kong	Stephen Wilkins	8, 2, 10, 7, 9, 5, 9	62
6=	Quadstone	Richard Chenery	1, 6, 5, 12, 3, 10, 10	64
7	Norwich Union	Neil Murray	11, 11, 7, 10, 2, 8, 3	60
8	Isle of Man	Lin Parker	6, 9, 6, 8, 7, 6, 12	58
9	VERITAS	Will Carnegie	5, 8, 9, 6, 10, 11, 7	56
9=	Olympic Group	Manley Hopkinson	12, 5, 2, 9, 11, 12, 4	56
10	Save the Children**	Nick Fenton	9, 12, 12, 11, N/A, 9, 11	37

Overall position
= Denotes that Quadstone and Olympic Group did not complete all the legs which was necessary for each to achieve a sole position in the overall ranking. They are shown in equivalent positions corresponding to the points which they gained in the overall event. Both yachts started all of the legs. Quadstone retired in Wellington after

beginning leg 4 when she accepted full responsibility for a collision with Save the Children. Olympic Group retired from leg 6 in the Bay of Biscay when becalmed close to the end of the leg from Cape Town after racing some 6000 miles.

**Save the Children as innocent party was seriously damaged at Wellington in the collision with Quadstone and was awarded by the International Race Jury average points for legs 4 and 5 and the status of having completed all the legs.

APPENDIX 2 – CREW LISTINGS

BP Explorer – total number of crew 35

Lynda Attrill, Glyn Baker, Erik Billings, Tony Botterill, Stephen Breen, Christopher Brown, Maureen Clark, Helen Couling, Paul Dockrill, Juan Douin, Nancy Doyle, Paula Dutson, Jeremy Francis, Lauren Ginn, Christopher Heffron, June James, Daren Jarisch, Richard King, Charlotte New, Katherine O'Connell, Richard Olver, Kelvin Pemberton, Andres Penate, Seb Pepper, Carol Redgrave, Alexandra Salicath, Bill Singleton, Paul Smith, Juan Theodorou, Angela Van Amberg, Vince Van Oostenbrugge, Graham Watts, Stuart Whyte, Giles Wilson, David Wright.

CGNU – total number of crew 33

John Aries-Tyler, Claire Batson, Bob Bradford, Andrew Buddell, Jon Desborough, John Ellicock, John Fairley, Michelle Ferrier, Steve Kitt, Chris Laufale, Beverley Lufkin, Neville Maggs, Belinda Marklew, John Mason, Glen Matthews, Will McLorn, Jeremy Message, Keith Moore, Toby Mortleman, Annabel Pearson, Brendan Rens, Blue Robinson, Marc Shaw, Richard Simon, Heather Sinclair, James Slaughter, Alan Standford, Michelle Stephenson, Tim Thomas, Dan Thorne, Ross White, Georgia Williams, Susan Willmer.

Compaq – total number of crew 30

Hans-Georg Brokmann, Ned Caswell JR, Toby Clayton, Paul Ellison, Alan Evans, Christopher Fay, Sanny Gibson, Philip Glenn,

Allison Gordon, James Greenman, Nick Hannah, Mark Harbord,
Michael Hedges, Vincent Jordan, Jo Langford, Emily Little,
Fiona Madine, Darrell Matthews, Robin McCandless, James Mitchell,
Clare Newton-Smith, David Nuttall, Glenda Porter, Chris Serle,
Stuart Smith, Peter Stewart, Pam Taylor, Andy Turnbull,
Caroline Watson, Lee Wilson.

Isle of Man – total number of crew 29

Bill Ashton, Alan Bell, Gill Bowyer, Christopher Campbell,
Ashley Carpenter, Michael Cook, Mat Desforges, Hank Donaldson,
Jan Giffen, Diana Hunt, Philip Johnson, Derek Kalinski, Peter Knight,
Fiona Leech, Rebecca Legg, Nick Lipscomb, Gavin Macfadyen,
Karen Marti, Juanita McLaren-Brown, Rob Peake, William Revels,
Lisa Rogers, Eddie Shallcross, Robert Tobin, Patrick Towle,
Juan Walters, Ralph Weisener, Martin White, James Wilkins Jr.

LG FLATRON – total number of crew 29

Timothy Ballantyne, Bob Bell, John Campbell, Archie Carr,
Tim Farnell, Elizabeth Hurst, Jeremy Irons, Tim Jeffery,
Kester Keighley, Richard Kidd, Jared Kreiss, Scott Lajoie,
Andrew McGrath, Ginger Mackenzie, Cian McCarthy,
Amanda Millichope, Ian Morfett, Marie-Jo Moro,
Christopher Morton, Peder Nielsen, Katherine O'Connell,
Laura Parish, Anne Pugh, Dickon Purvis, Andy Reid, Gillian Ritchie,
Bob Schmidt, Clifford Scott, Anne Weir.

Logica – total number of crew 29

Helen Armour, Johan Atting, Robert Bell, Glyn Billinghurst,
Bill Cleland, Martin Conder, John Davie, Jeremy Douglass, Ali Fraser,
Emma Gage, Jasmine Georgiou, Andrew Given, Robert Graveley,
Tony Haile, Cathal Horan, Matthew Lamey, Sarah Lindsley,
Andrew Lomas, Paul Martin, Genevieve Maton, Sam Molan,
Claire Nicholson, Robert Powell, Larry Quinn, Geoff Terry,
Adam Tuffnell, Claudia Van Gils, Mike Villis, Doug Webb.

Olympic Group – total number of crew 28

Robert Abraham, Murray Bridge, Asbjorn Damhus, Michael Dick,
Neil Dunnet, Roy Essam, Alex Finos, Matthew Fleming, Lee Gallacher,
Crispin Hill, Deon Hubner, Matthew Hunt, Richard Keeling,
Roger Leitch, Andrew Lippman, Deborah Lloyd, Justine Maddock,
Annee de Mamiel, Ed Martin, Donna Newman, Richard Price,
Alan Sandbrook, Ian Sheeran, Susie Smith, Matt Stafford,
Pamela Vaughan, Mark Ward, Ray Wassel.

Quadstone – total number of crew 34

Richard Ashford, John Bailes, Don Baker, Kate Bosomworth,
Lizzie Brown, Simon Chapple, Paul Covell, Caspar Craven,
Jonathan Cutts, Sharon Dickie, Sam Dunnet, Malcolm Girling,
Anders Hellstrom, Alan Hulbert, Ali Husain, Julian Johnson,
Simon Jury, Frank Karbe, Alex Lewis, Philip Marshall,
Daniel Moorcroft-Towers, Chris Morley, Andrew Norrie,
Phil Robinson, Liz Rowen, Freddie Shanks, Ian Sinclair,
Alison Stephens, Lesley Stewart, Philip Strong, Suzi Telford,
Robin Thorogood, Grant Tullo, Georgia Williams.

Save the Children – total number of crew 32

Klaus Allisat, Garry Beverley, Christian Bowerman, Derek Brennan,
Chris Calkins, Rona Cant, Elaine Chua, Heather Clancy,
Andrew Clark, Alec Crawford, Johanna Curtis, Nye Davies,
Ben Dobson, Ed Elgar, Miville Gauthier, Chris Girling, Neil Gray,
Peter Haycocks, Hayley Higgins, Richard Kirby, Rory MacIntosh,
Jacky Pampling, John Quigley, Anne Serle, James Smith,
Deborah Stevenson, Cathy Sullivan, David Taylor, John Thompson,
David Wicks, Graham Wills, Robert Woodall.

Spirit of Hong Kong – total number of crew 32

Katherine Armitage, Adrienne Barnett, Bjorn Berger, Hilary Bowden,
Holly Day, Christine Denchfield, David Gay, Vincent Gayme,

Barry Hacker, Mike Hale, Peter Halliwell, Bart Hallmark, Rupert Harris, Mike Hewson, Brian Hutchinson, Jennie Jackson, Andrew Jones, Ingrid Kane, Peter Kastner, Alice Liu, Richard Loughlin, Paul Lynch, Andrew Mahon, Mario Parent, David Pinkney, Zoe Savage, Sophie Streatfield, Charles Taylor, David Thomson, Richard Thorpe, Stephen Strong, Mark Willard.

TeamSpirIT – total number of crew 33

Mark Bailey, Edwina Bates, David Beckett, Anne Bennett, Col Betts, Bob Bradley, Chris Broadway, Clare Canning, Stuart Clarke, Christophe Faraud, Iain Fenna, Angus Fuller, Keith Gibson, Andy Heads, Ian Henderson, Dennis Hobday, Jonathan Howes, Charlie Johnson-Ferguson, Sameer Kothari, Greg McCray, Chris McLaren, Jeff Overfield, Vincent Piguet, Spencer Pilbrow, Ian Roberts, Helen Scares, David Scotland, Valeria Sesto, Paul Sherry, Mark Taft, Tina Williamson, Rob Willing, Carla Wytmar.

VERITAS – total number of crew 31

Paula Balch, Charles Bottrell, Will Brammer, Robert Brooke, Zinzan Brooke, Peter Clift, Arthur Duran, Geraldine Egan, Tom Fagan, Stephen Fillery, Lee Floyd, Wes Garcia, Fiji Goss, Colin Gruar, Deborah Hadwen, Sieraj Jacobs, Guillermo Jofre, Emily Lodge, Ian Luddington, Malcolm MacVean, Mike Morgan, Babs Powell, Kevin Sinnott, Charles Smith, Tina Smith, Alistair Taylor, Ian Teague, Malcolm Thornley, Hilary Thwaites, Mark Wilson, Kurt Wobken.

APPENDIX 3 – CHALLENGE YACHT SPECIFICATIONS

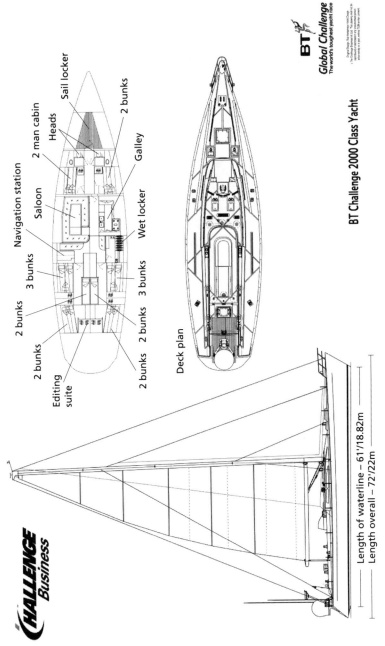

Sail locker

2 man cabin

Heads

2 bunks

Navigation station

Galley

Saloon

3 bunks

Wet locker

2 bunks

2 bunks

3 bunks

2 bunks

2 bunks

Editing suite

Deck plan

BT Challenge 2000 Class Yacht

Length of waterline – 61'/18.82m

Length overall – 72'/22m

GLOSSARY

NAUTICAL TERMS AND EXPRESSIONS

Aft	Towards the back of a yacht
Ballast	Weight placed to stabilise a yacht
Bilges	Bottom of the ship's hull where all the dirty water, diesel and oil collects
Boom	Spar that runs along the bottom of the mainsail, fixed to the mast at one end
Bow	Front of a yacht
Buoy	A marker used for navigation, mooring or racing around
Chat shows	Twice-daily radio link-up between the yachts to convey yacht position and exchange news
Cockpit	Aft working area of a yacht
Core crew member	Individual who has signed up and paid to undertake the entire race (seven legs) from Southampton to Southampton
Crew member	Generic term used to describe both core crew members and leggers
Doldrums	Also known as Inter-Tropical Convergence Zone (ITCZ). Area between the weather systems of the Northern and Southern hemispheres characterised by frustratingly light winds, major shifts in wind direction and sudden violent squalls

Equator	Line of latitude at 0 degrees – equal distance from both poles
Forestay	Wire rigging that joins top of mast to the bow of the yacht
Galley	Kitchen on a yacht
GPS	Global Positioning System. Satellite navigation which gives yacht's exact latitude and longtitude position
Guardrail	A safety rail along the side of the yacht
Guy	A rope used to adjust the position of a spinnaker pole
Gybe	To alter a yacht's direction by steering until the stern swings through the wind
Halyard	Rope for hoisting a sail or flag
Heads	Toilet/basin/shower on a yacht
Headsails	Sails flown between the mast and the bow of a yacht
Helmsman/Helm	Person steering the yacht
Hot bunking	The practice of sleeping in a bunk on the side of the yacht where the individual's weight is most advantageous for the yacht's performance
Inmarsat B	A digital satellite communications service providing video conferencing, email, Internet access, telephone and data transfer from ship to shore
Inmarsat C	A store-and-forward messaging and data communications system for sending and receiving short messages
Latitude	Angular distance north or south of the Equator, measured from 0–90 degrees north or south
Lee	Sheltered from the winds, possibly by an island or land mass
Legger	Individual who takes part in one or more legs of the race

Leg	A stage of the overall race; there were seven stages to the BTGC
Longtitude	Angular distance east or west of the Greenwich Meridian, measured from 0–120 degrees east or west
Mainsail/Main	Largest sail on a yacht which is secured to the mast and the boom
Mast	Made of aluminium extrusion and supported by the rigging, the mast is used to hoist the sails
Mate	Person second in command, after the skipper
Mobiq Marine	A ship-borne variant of the low-cost satellite phone
Motherwatch	The 'housekeeping' watch on board a yacht. Crew on motherwatch cook and clean
Neptune's Feast	Traditional mariners' ritual carried out when a person crosses the Equator for the first time. Usually fermented slops are poured over the individual to absolve them of their sins
Podium position	First, second and third position overall in the race
Port	Left-hand side of a yacht
Position	The exact point on the earth's surface at which a yacht is located. This is determined by the geographical co-ordinates of latitude and longtitude
Reefing	Reduces the area of the main sail by furling up the bottom of the sail
Rig/rigging	Wires or ropes which support the mast
Roaring Forties	Area between 40 degrees and 50 degrees latitude noted for strong wind and huge seas
Saloon	Sitting/dining area
Sheet	A rope
Side rail/sitting on the rail	Crew members sitting on the edge of the deck, facing out, acting as ballast

(Snake) Pit	Area of the boat from which sails are controlled
Spinnaker/kite	Large, full-bellied sail that is flown out in front of the yacht, usually when the wind is right behind the yacht
Squall	Sudden and frequent gusts of very strong wind, usually accompanied by rain
SSB radio	Provides long-range services – communication to shore and receipt of weather faxes
Stanchion	Pole supporting the safety wire running around the side of a yacht
Starboard	Right-hand side of the yacht
Stay	Rigging wire
Staysail	A small sail flown between the mast and the inner forestay
Stern	Back of a yacht
Tack	A manoeuvre to alter the direction of a yacht by steering until the bow swings across the wind. The sails also swing across the yacht until the wind fills them on the opposite side
Trim	To alter the set of the sails
Under motor	To proceed using the engine
Watches	Teams within which the crew operate, taking it in turns to work, sleep and eat
Waypoint	Set of co-ordinates identifying a position
Winch	A drum around which the sheets are turned to tension and ease out the sails
Wind shadow	A windless area or patch caused by the position of another yacht or landmass
Windward	Upwind side of yacht

INDEX